Christian-Buddhist Conversations:
Foundations for Dialogue

Christian-Buddhist Conversations:
Foundations for Dialogue

A.W. Barber *&* Timothy Harvie

Vogelstein Press
Calgary, Alberta

Published by:
Vogelstein Press
Calgary, Alberta, Canada
Cover and interior layout: Trish Kotow
Book ISBN – paperback – 978-1-7752615-0-6
eBook ISBN – 978-1-7752615-1-3
All Rights Reserved

Library of Congress Cataloging-in-Publication Data
Barber, A.W. 1952–   and   Harvie, Timothy 1976–
Christian–Buddhist Conversations: *Foundations for Dialogue*
A.W. Barber and Timothy Harvie
Includes: endnotes at end of each chapter, bibliographical references,
      index

  1. Buddhism, Christianity
  2. Religion, dialogue

ISBN 978-1-7752615-0-6

Cover art:

Left: "Christ" Assumption of the Virgin Mary Cathedral, Palermo, Sicily; © A.W. Barber
Right: "The Great Buddha" (Jp. Daibutsu) Todai-ji Temple, Nara, Japan; © A.W. Barber

This book is dedicated to William, Paul and Michael.

Table of Contents

Acknowledgments   *i*

Conventions Used   *iii*

Introduction   1

Chapter 1: Christ and Buddha   17

Chapter 2: Religious Authority   47

Chapter 3: Sacred Texts   75

Chapter 4: Sin and Karma   107

Chapter 5: Salvation and Liberation   137

Chapter 6: Love and Compassion   167

Chapter 7: Monasticism   193

Chapter 8: The Place of the Human Being in the World and Cosmos   217

Chapter 9: Public and Political Participation   243

Bibliography   *273*

Index   *289*

Acknowledgements

This book is the fruit of a long process—over several years—of dialoguing together with my co-author, A.W. Barber. It has seen many life changes and challenging health issues which prolonged the work as well as personal shifts in views on my part. Without his dedication to this project it would not have seen completion. I am grateful for his tireless work and support throughout. I am also grateful for those who have provided formal academic training to me in the historical and theological disciplines germane to Christianity. My contributions to this work reflect their influence. I would also like to thank my wife and partner, Brianna Harvie, for her unwavering support of my interests, academic and otherwise. She is a strength and has expanded my horizons. Finally, I would like to thank my former colleague, Dr. Michael Duggan, for his friendship and for embodying open, inter-religious dialogue for me in a profound and life-giving way. I dedicate my contributions in this book to him.

Timothy Harvie

I too am thankful to Tim Harvie for accepting the challenges and staying dedicated to this project even in the face of multiple trials scholarly and personal. I am also thankful to William and Paul who were the initial inspiration for this project and thanks to my wife who is always there. My appreciation extends to all those working in conjunction with Vogelstein Press and the help they all offered.

A.W. Barber

Conventions Used

The Latin and ancient Greek used in the sections on Christian tradition are in standard forms within English usage. Asian language words that have been standardized in English follow those standardized forms. Other Asian language words are presented in a popular spelling minus any diacritical marks or tone indicators.

Introduction

Christianity

Writing in the second half of the twentieth century, Catholic theologian Hans Küng notes that the global situation of religion has changed. He writes, "For the first time in world history, it is impossible today for any one religion to exist in splendid isolation and ignore others."[1] While Küng notes that Christianity has a long history of interacting with other religions, it has rarely done so in the spirit of dialogue and mutuality. The Second Vatican Council offers new insights into how Christianity, and Catholicism in particular, might proceed in such dialogues. In the declaration on religious liberty, the council teaches that the integral dignity of the human person entails that each person ought to be free from coercion in religious practice.[2] While the concept of the dignity of the person is most often applied in terms of bioethics,[3] the council sees here its importance in terms of religious freedom. This human dignity is central to how the council articulates the relationship of Catholic Christianity to other religions.

The Second Vatican Council teaches that because of a shared human dignity, "there is no basis…for any discrimination between individual and individual, or between people and people" including discrimination based upon various religious beliefs and practices.[4] Indeed, the Catholic Church teaches that there is much that is "true and holy" in other religions from which one might learn.[5] Such a dialogical engagement reflects the historical development of Christianity, and what the blessed John Henry Cardinal Newman described in the nineteenth century as the development of doctrine. While even a cursory history of Christianity is beyond the scope of this short introduction, it is important to highlight some of the key historical moments in the development of Christian thought and practice in order to better understand the type of dialogue taking place in this book.

Christianity has its historical roots in Palestinian Judaism in the first century of the Common Era, when the Roman Empire was at its zenith. The followers of Jesus of Nazareth were Galilean Jews (Galilee was a northern, backwoods region of Palestine) and for some time Christianity was indistinguishable from the other Jewish subgroups also present at the time.[6] The historical relationship between Christianity and Judaism is so essential and formative to both Christian self-understanding and the understanding of dialogue between religious traditions for Christianity, that it may be viewed as paradigmatic in the dialogue Christians have with other members of other religions as well.[7] Central to the historical connection between Christianity and Judaism was an apocalyptic understanding of Jesus and God's kingdom. The early Christians maintained the Jewish understanding of Jesus as Messiah and that this would entail an end to history and the current world within a generation in favor of the manifestation of God's eternal kingdom. Once this expectation was not fulfilled, Christians had to accommodate other views of the relationship between history and Jesus. While the apocalyptic view of judgment and recreation never vanished, it was now reconceived as Christianity spread throughout the Roman Empire and encountered Greek thought.[8]

The dialogue with and adoption of Greek metaphysics and modes of thought would transform Christianity's self-understanding and the development of its religious categories. Christ as the *logos* was no longer understood solely in terms of Jewish wisdom categories but was now conceptualized in Greek categories of metaphysics and eternity. This is reflected in the Christological debates surrounding the Council of Nicaea (325 CE). St. Athanasius argued for what would become the orthodox understanding of Jesus Christ as having two natures, fully human and fully divine, and yet being one person. This was largely in disputes with Arius, a priest and presbyter who maintained that Christ was subordinate to the Father and was not fully divine as was the Father of the Trinity. The first ecumenical council decided in favor of Athanasius's *homoousion* formulation that Christ is "one in being" with the Father and therefore fully equal to the Father. These categories were drawn almost entirely from Greek metaphysics and so it was in dialogue with the central concepts in contemporary intellectual thought that Christianity came to articulate its own self-understanding and core doctrines.

As Christianity gained social and political prominence under Constantine (313 CE) and Theodosius (380 CE) the mode by which Christianity engaged other cultures, views, and religions moved from dialogue to conquest. This led to the first great division in Christianity in 1054 CE, where the disputes over the role of the Holy Spirit within the Trinity[9] were central alongside the more secular concerns over the political roles of Rome and Constantinople respectively. The confluence of imperial political concerns with religious ideas played out in the relationship between Christianity and other religions for centuries. Most famously, this was seen in the violent conflicts of the Crusades. The reasons for the crusades were both economic and spiritual. Economically, the development of farming techniques led to increases in food production, which enabled population growth and the need for geographic expansion. The geographic expansion was understood to necessitate political expansion through military conquest. Spiritually, reforms in the eleventh century fostered a religious zeal among medieval Christianity's adherents and these people regarded the land of biblical literature in particular esteem. This reverence led to the conclusion that the geographic region of historical Palestine must come under the political control of Christianity. The first crusade (1096–1099 CE) attempted to reunite Eastern and Western Christianity to no avail. The final three crusades, occurring between 1147 and 1204 CE were mostly deemed unsuccessful endeavors and did nothing to enable unity within Christianity or a dialogue between Christianity and other faiths and cultures.

After the medieval era, conquest continued as the primary mode of Christianity's engagement with others and was brought together with Europe's colonial ambitions in what would become the American continents. Merging with colonial ambition for wealth and conquest, Christianity was often a willing participant in the forced conversion, and often the slaughter, of indigenous populations in North and South America.[10] The colonial and violent approaches between European Christianity with cultures and religions external to it mirrored the dialogical tensions internal to Europe and which resulted in the Protestant Reformation in the sixteenth century. When an Augustinian monk named Martin Luther first nailed the famed 95 theses to the church door in Wittenberg, Germany, he intended to spur conversation within Catholicism. The theses were written in Latin and, therefore, were intended for academic debate rather than public consumption. However, in the vitriolic responses both from Catholicism and from Luther, the Protestant Reformation was born.

From the Reformation's emphasis on the individual subject, choice, and freedom came the eventual development of the European Enlightenment. This intellectual and cultural movement emphasized individual rationality and the importance of the moral subject. The philosophical luminary of the Enlightenment, Immanuel Kant, argued that enlightenment was coming out from underneath the self-imposed tutelage of allowing traditions and authorities to shape one's mind apart from the individual responsibility to grow in reason, knowledge, and moral obligation to one's fellow human. The response to the Enlightenment—also called modernity—from the Catholic Church was initially one of animosity. Pope Pius IX published "The Syllabus of Errors" in the nineteenth century, condemning theses he thought to be modernizing. This response of condemnation was short lived and other Popes, such as Pope Leo XIII sought to engage the realities of the modern world, especially that of the worker and those in economic and social need. This approach of dialogue with others would come to typify some of the central motifs of the Second Vatican Council and exemplifies the dialogue of the early Church with its intellectual and cultural surroundings.

When Pope Saint John XXIII convened the Second Vatican Council, he famously stated that it was time to open the windows of the Church and let in fresh air. In doing so, the Church opened up a meaningful dialogue with the modern world and sought to emphasize the unity of humanity in a spirit of understanding and charity. This is based upon the classical Christian understanding of the dignity of the human person. This book carries out this dialogue between a Catholic Christian scholar and a Buddhist scholar in the same spirit of respect, charity, and desire to learn from one another to enhance our understanding of each other and ourselves. Christianity has dialogued with Buddhism throughout the post-conciliar era. Thomas Merton learned much from Buddhist practice, and in particular Zen practice, in his own monastic life.[11] Protestant theologians have also been impacted by the study of Buddhism. Paul Knitter engages in a dialogue with Buddhist thought in a comparative effort that mirrors some of the themes addressed in this book.[12] However, each of these is the work of an individual author approaching the questions from a singular perspective: that of the Christian.

This book is unique in that it is a genuine dialogue. In bringing both a Buddhist scholar and a Catholic Christian scholar together in a comparative approach to questions central to each religion, we are able to learn from one another and also note the points of connection and those instances where each tradition offers something unique and different from the conversation partner. The work is written in a style intended to be approachable for a non-specialist audience. You do not need to be an expert to read this book. Each chapter revolves around common points of comparison between the two traditions, and while sometimes these comparisons are questioned, they are intended to introduce the reader to both. When writing, we had primarily a Christian audience in mind, with the hopes of introducing Christians living in the Western world to Buddhist thought and practice via different entrance points from their own tradition. However, in this the book actually has a twofold aim. It introduces Christians to the history, thought, and spiritual practice of Buddhism, but it also functions to reacquaint Christians with their own tradition through descriptions that are historical, systematic, and instructive of Christian thought and practice. This book is aimed at a genuine dialogue between traditions from scholars within each of those traditions. We invite you, the reader, to join us in this conversation.

Buddhism

DNA evidence informs us that the subcontinent of South Asia was inhabited by two races of people; the Australoid and a branch of the Indo-Europeans. Although the migrant central Asian peoples developed advanced civilization along the Indus River, we know very little about their religious beliefs as their writing has not been deciphered and their civilization was eclipsed. The Indo-Europeans who called themselves "Aryans" being the cousins of the ancient Greeks, Italic tribes and other peoples of Europe shared not only a source language but gods, cosmology, and theological underpinnings. For example, Jupiter (Gr. Zeus-patar) in India is called Dyaus-pitri and Mt. Olympus is called Mt. Meru. The religion of the Aryans called "Vedic," is preserved in

Introduction

some of the oldest religious books and some of the rituals, more than 4,000 years old, are still performed. Indo-European religious elements are also preserved in Buddhism.[13]

The world along the Gangetic plane was rapidly changing in the half millennium before the Current Era. The ancient Vedic religion of the early Aryans had been undergoing significant changes producing both a shift in orientation which can be identified as "Brahmanism" and the incorporation of new ideas clearly not Vedic in origin. In addition, iron technology was slowly spreading and advancing from the North-west across the land. Into this world was born Siddhartha Gautama Shakya the man who would later become the Buddha. The area where he lived was considered to be on the outskirts of civilization as it did not accept Brahmanism in full yet.[14] The advances in iron technology started to allow for the rapid clearing of the thick Gangetic jungle producing surpluses in agricultural goods and more advance weaponry. These in turn radically changed society. The world Siddhartha was born into had a declining old order and the rising new world. Various social, economic, and religious factors created an environment for considerable religious speculation producing a host of non-Vedic religions and philosophies. Most of these groups we know only from accounts given in ancient works. Sharing the yogic tradition of wandering seekers, only two of these groups survived. Buddhism is one of these two and the other is Jainism.

The Shakya clan claimed decent from the Sun god and occupied the land in the area now the border region between India and South-west Nepal. Their kingdom was a democratic republic similar to Athens or Rome. Siddhartha's father was Shuddhodana, his mother was Mahamaya and he was born into an illustrious family during the sixth or fifth century BCE. His cremated ashes were found by the British when they ruled India, but scholars debate the exact dates of his life. Although enjoying the protected life and all the benefits that a noble family can provide, Siddhartha left home when he was 29 years old. He was moved by the full impact of the suffering of humanity which was unbeknownst to him in his protected world. For six years he practiced various yogic disciplines and intense asceticism. Arriving at awakening while sitting under a pipal tree his new status as a Fully Awakened One, i.e., Buddha, was acknowledge by the gods and people. He taught, assisted people out of compassion, and passed into final Nirvana at the age of eighty.

Gautama Buddha did not seem to think he was establishing a new religion but believed that his teachings were universal and timeless and that he was only reintroducing them to mankind. In addition to providing teachings, he established a four-fold assembly of followers consisting of monks, nuns, laymen and laywomen. The inclusion of nuns was controversial in his day. His teachings are called the Middle Way (between asceticism and sensual overindulgence) and consists of texts on doctrine/practice, analysis and monastic culture. If internal sources are accurate, thousands of people became his followers. This, however, did not exclude them from still being Hindus. His teaching called Buddha Dharma continued to develop and spread over the following centuries. Probably the first development after his death was the editing of the teachings on monastic culture. This was followed by the organization of the teachings and philosophical developments. These arrangements facilitated memorization of the multitude of teachings.

A major shift occurred when the Emperor Ashoka (304–232 BCE) became a Buddhist. Much of India was united under one ruler in reactions to Alexander the Great's conquests in the far North-west of the Subcontinent. One large powerful kingdom along the eastern coast resisted Ashoka's unification. It finally succumbed to the might of the Mauryan Dynasty wherein accounts of the war dead range from 100,000 to 200,000. The sight of this much human tragedy turned the Emperor's mind towards religion and Buddhism garnered imperial support. Buddhism had already divided into at least two sects which would eventually develop into more than eighteen sects. Ashoka not only supported his local Buddhist establishment, but he also exported the teachings. His own son and daughter brought it to Sri Lanka after becoming a monk and nun respectively. Buddhism was spread to all parts of the empire as is documented in accounts and in rock edicts found at different locals. It is also held that some monks were sent as far as Alexandria.

The Buddhist community continued to fracture during this time with many new sects being established. Yet, there were also attempts at reuniting the various communities with the holding of several councils. These attempts failed in part because of the isolation of communities due to large tracks of land still being wild and shifts in priorities. For example, with the shift in India from scattered republics to true monarchies, authority patterns in Buddhism also changed with some sects holding on to the older patterns longer. In addition to differences in monastic culture there were significant philosophical differences that also developed. For example, one class of awakened individuals is called a Worthy (Sk. Arhat). Some sects held that Worthies and Buddhas were the same but others disagreed. Also gradually there developed a major chasm between those who took the period of Gautama Buddha's life from his leaving home until his awakening as the model of how to practice Buddhism and those who took the period of Buddha's life from the awakening to his death as the model. That is those who held that renunciation was the major emphasis (the Auditors' tradition with the eighteen sects) and those who held that compassion for others was an emphasis (the Great Vehicle with two philosophical schools, one philosophical movement and two major styles of practice).

Philosophical debate, being a competitive sport in ancient India, led to lofty developments and subtle distinctions in Buddhism that could easily be compared to the ancient Greek philosophical developments. The Buddhists were major contributors to the development of logic, linguistics, psychology, metaphysics, art, literature and more in classical times. Three examples may suffice. In logic they advanced syllogistic theory, in mathematics they developed the concept of zero which was unknown to the Romans and in art they blended Greco and Indian Buddhist currents. However, doctrinal developments were not the major driving force in sect affiliation. Instead, it was monastic culture that became the foundation for distinctions. Later Chinese travelers to India inform us that monasteries often had inhabitants who advocated different Buddhist philosophies living therein but all inhabitants followed the same one of five monastic cultures.

Sri Lanka received some of the various Auditors' sects and Great Vehicle teachings. However, over time only one of the sects survived. That sect is called Theravada or "followers of the elders." This sect thrived on the island and continued its development. It was also exported to South-East Asia in due course. This is still the dominant religious group on the island today and the only surviving sect from the Auditors branch.

In addition to Sri Lanka receiving Buddhism at the time of Ashoka, Buddhism also was being transmitted to other kingdoms in South-East Asia in the last centuries BCE and the first centuries CE. During this time India was trading with Rome via the Arabian Sea, Red Sea through Egypt and then the Mediterranean Sea. Not only were Indian goods moving along this sea route, but India acted as a transshipping point for South-East Asian and limited Chinese goods. This created the situation that Indian culture became a significant influence in South-East Asia. Buddhism was a major component of this mix. Both the Auditors' and the Great Vehicle traditions spread to this region initially during the early centuries of the first millennium, but later mainland South-East Asia retained the Auditors' tradition and Indonesia maintained the Great Vehicle.

At the time of Ashoka, the Greeks in the wake of Alexander's conquests had a number of kingdoms in Asia and one of these was Bactria. In the second century BCE its king was Menander I. It is recorded that he became a Buddhist documenting that Buddhism had spread to Central Asia by this time. The Greeks were replaced by the Kushana an Indo-European people who created an empire that at its height spanned from its border with Sogdiana in the north to central India in the south and from Parthia to China west to east. Emperor Kanishka (second century CE) was also a promoter of Buddhism and controlling the Silk Route, spread it as far as China. However, by this time Buddhism was already known in China and found strong support in the palace with the Emperor's brother and to a lesser extent with the Emperor a century before. Both the Auditors' and the Great Vehicle traditions were found in Central Asia.

Central Asian culture was greatly influenced by India in the last centuries BCE and the first centuries CE and although Central Asian Buddhism can be distinguished from Indian Buddhism in some concerns, it considerably reflected its origins. This is not the case in China. Chinese spiritual dialogue was radically different from that found in India. Over a period of about five hundred years the Chinese translated, committed upon and ultimately sinicized Buddhism creating new schools that were clearly Chinese, but which respected their Indic origins.[15] These sinicized forms of Buddhism along with the monastic heritage and the Chinese translation of the Buddhist canon were exported to Korea, Vietnam, and Japan, and partially to Central Asia and Tibet. The height of Chinese creative efforts regarding Buddhism took place during the period spanning the fifth century to the tenth century. Consolidation of these creative development happened during the eleventh to the fourteenth centuries. Encyclopedic scholasticism continued from the fourteenth century to the modern period. Although the Auditors' tradition was transmitted to China, it did not spark the Chinese imagination like the Great Vehicle tradition did and only the Great Vehicle tradition was retained.

Vietnam in ancient times received Buddhism directly from India primarily in the Great Vehicle form. However, when the sea route was cut off and because of the proximity to China, later Chinese Great Vehicle schools were transmitted and developed in Vietnam. Vietnam became a strong base for Buddhism through the centuries. In the early modern period, the Auditors' tradition began to migrate into Vietnam from border countries to the west.

Korean Buddhism was hardly distinguishable from Chinese Buddhism from its inception in the fourth century CE. In fact, some Korean monks seem to have been significant contributors to Chinese Buddhism at times. However, the Koreans were struck by the divisions in Chinese Buddhism and began striving to create a more consistent holistic version. Buddhism was state religion from the tenth century to the fourteenth century but faced repression from the fourteenth century to the modern period due to the prejudice of the neo-Confucians. However, it maintained its popularity during this period with the people.

Buddhism entered Japan from Korea and China by the sixth century CE. From the beginning it was connected with Japan's unique political structure and sectarian popularity rose and fell along with the fortunes of various clans. The regent Prince Shotoku (572–622) based Japan's first constitution on Buddhist and Confucian principles and wrote commentaries to Buddhist works. In time, all the major Chinese forms of Buddhism were transmitted to Japan and began their independent development in that country influenced by Japanese cultural. Japan produced one

Introduction

new school of its own but also expanded and enhanced its inherited traditions in unique ways.

Tibet was near impenetrable from the South with the frontal range of the Himalayas acting as a barrier. Passes were found first by going to the extreme west and then down into Kashmir and later leading into Nepal. Buddhism arrived along these routes in the seventh century. It also arrived through the northern border with Central Asia/China. Tibet had internally united and began expanding into Central Asia gaining control of parts of the Silk Route and raiding into China at this time. It also raided into Nepal and parts of India. The Tibetan emperor in the seventh century, built Buddhist temples. His successors built monasteries and supported translation projects just like the Chinese emperors supported translation projects. Eventually, the Indian forms of Buddhism became the most influential and the imported Chinese forms died off. The empire lasted from the seventh to the ninth centuries with the last emperor being assassinated for persecuting Buddhism. Tibet fell back into regionalism, but Buddhism continued to grow. The Mongolians were greatly influenced by Tibetan Buddhism and after invading Tibet in the thirteenth century made an important monk their viceroy in Tibet. With this beginning, Tibet became a theocratic state with rule eventually passing to the Dalai Lama. The office of the Dalai Lama has maintained power until the Communist Chinese invaded the country in the 1950s.

Although Mongolia received different currents of Central Asian Buddhism it was Tibetan Buddhism that became the most influential beginning in the twelfth century. Mongolian monks were sent to Tibet for their education and this form of Buddhism became the dominant force in Mongolian culture. From Mongolia Buddhism spread westward in Russia but was clearly a minority religion. Be this as it may, Russia hosted the only Buddhist population of note in Europe (in Kalmykia) in the seventeeth century.

At its most expansive Buddhism was a major religion from within the eastern boundary of the Persian Empire in the west, to Japan in the east and from Mongolia in the north to Sri Lanka in the south. Further, according to European estimates, Buddhism was the most popular religion in the world at the beginning of the nineteenth century. It came to be known in Europe and slightly later in North America because of the colonies and imperial holding of the European powers. The first recorded encounters between Buddhist and Europeans was with the Portuguese and the Spanish as they ventured into Asian waters. Adventurers, colonials and missionaries studied Buddhism and sent back texts, reports, and artifacts of Buddhist to their native countries in Europe. Buddhist travelled to Europe and Europeans returning from Asia who had converted to Buddhism also began spreading the teachings in the west.

There are legends yet unproved of Buddhist contact with North America dating as far back as 500 CE, but most experts are highly skeptical. The earliest of these was a Chinese expedition but other stories tell of Japanese travelling to the west coast of North America. Provable accounts are later in dating. Japanese Buddhists already inhabited Hawaii before it became a state. The Chinese built a system of temples from Victoria to San Diego in the mid eighteen-hundreds. These temples were often not purely Buddhist, but Buddhism was a major component. At the same time, East Coast Americans and Canadians were becoming interested in Buddhism because of the various activities in Europe. Ralph Waldo Emerson and Henry David Thoreau were influenced by Buddhist ideas. The Civil War colonel Henry Steel Olcott became the most public convert in the nineteenth century.

Buddhist temples, monasteries, and centers are now found in every major city in the west. There are representatives of every form of Asian Buddhism living in North America and cities like New York, Toronto, Vancouver, Los Angeles and others have very dynamic Buddhist scenes. In addition, indigenous produced groups that are led by Americans or Canadians and are not affiliated with a particular Asian tradition is a growing current. The same situation prevails in Europe where Buddhism in all of its varieties forms a growing community. The largest Buddhist temple in Europe is only a short distance from the Vatican.

Buddhism from its initial expression by Shakyamuni and throughout its development has been in dialogue with other religions. This volume brings together information from Christianity and Buddhism in a manner not before seen, as noted above. The reader is asked to join in this discussion by thinking critically about the different points presented not to necessarily reach agreement but to achieve understanding of insights and expressions that avoid unjustified overlays. It is hoped that readers will find the beauty of difference, the inspiration from uniqueness, and the openness of the human spirit to reach fuller and deeper meaning in what makes us spiritual.

---

[1] Hans Küng, *On Being a Christian* trans. Edward Quinn (New York: Doubleday Books, 1976), 89.
[2] Second Vatican Council, *Dignitatis Humanae*, nos. 1–8.
[3] See Andrew Kim, *An Introduction to Catholic Ethics Since Vatican II* (Cambridge: Cambridge University Press, 2015), 145–154.
[4] Second Vatican Council, *Nostra Aetate*, no. 5.
[5] Second Vatican Council, *Nostra Aetate*, no. 2.
[6] See Martin Goodman, "The Emergence of Christianity" *A World History of Christianity* Adrian Hastings ed. (Grand Rapids: Wm. B. Eerdmans, 1999), 7–16.
[7] Jacques Dupuis, S.J., *Toward a Christian Theology of Religious Pluralism* (Maryknoll: Orbis Books, 2001), 8.
[8] Jaroslav Pelikan, *The Christian Tradition Volume 1: The Emergence of the Catholic Tradition (100–600)* (Chicago: The University of Chicago Press, 1971), 123–171.
[9] This was the famous, and ongoing, dispute over the Latin West's later insertion of the Filioque phrase into the the Niceno–Constantinopolitan Creed of 381.

[10] See Bartolomé de Las Casas, *A Short Account of the Destruction of the Indies* trans. Nigel Griffin (London: Penguin Books, 1992); Bartolomé de Las Casas, *In Defense of the Indians* trans. Stafford Poole, C. M. (DeKalb: Northern Illinois University Press, 1992). See also, Gustavo Gutiérrez, *Las Casas: In Search of the Poor of Jesus Christ* (Maryknoll: Orbis Books, 1995).

[11] Thomas Merton, *Mystics and Zen Masters* (New York: Farrar, Straus, and Giroux, 1967).

[12] Paul F. Knitter, *Without Buddha I Could Not Be A Christian* (London: Oneworld Academic, 2009). See also Malcolm David Eckel, "Perspectives on the Buddhist-Christian Dialogue," *The Christ and the Bodhisattva* Donald S. Lopez, Jr. and Steven C. Rockefeller eds., (New York: SUNY Press, 1987), 43–64.

[13] A.L. Basham, *The Wonder that was India*. (Calcutta: Rupa and Company,1991), 234 *ff.*

[14] Hermann Kulke and Dietmar Rothermund, *A History of India* 6th ed. (London: Routledge, 2016), 27 *ff.*

[15] A.W. Barber, *Sinicizing Buddhism Studies in Doctrine, Practice, Fine Arts, Performing Arts* (Calgary: Vogelstein Press, 2019).

Chapter 1
Christ and Buddha

The Christ

It may be obvious that the central figure in Christianity is Jesus Christ. However, the questions of who Jesus of Nazareth was and what is his relationship to the religion that bears witness to him are live ones. Who is Jesus Christ for Christians? Many people, including many Christians, assume that the word Christ is simply a part of Jesus's name due to its historical association with this one person. Christ is not a name, but rather a title. The Greek word translated into English as Christ (Χριστός) is the word the early, Greek speaking Christian communities used to translate the Hebrew word, Messiah (מָשִׁיחַ). These words mean "anointed." To be anointed is to be chosen and blessed by God's presence. In the ancient Israelite tradition unique people experienced anointing and at times this was accompanied by symbolic ritual. The local tribal leaders in the pre-monarchial era of ancient Israel, called Judges, were said to experience an anointing by God's spirit to accomplish a victory in the field of battle (Samson) or to govern and lead wisely (Deborah).[1] The priestly class were "anointed" to perform their specific cultic duties in the religious observance of the people. This was accompanied with the ritualistic pouring of oil which was used to indicate divine presence in the ceremony. In addition to these, in the monarchial era of Israel's history, the king was also said to be anointed. The kings were anointed with oil. The oil was poured on the king's head to signify divine blessing and presence.

The ancient view of Israel's king being God's unique, anointed leader provides the origins for the ascription "Son of God." In the familiar Psalm for the king, the psalmist declares, "The kings of the earth set themselves, and the rulers take counsel together, against the LORD and his anointed" (Psalm 2:2). The king who follows in the Davidic line is described as experiencing the blessing and presence of Yahweh's anointing. The psalmist proceeds to expand the discourse to include the divine voice itself, and declare, "I will tell of the decree of the LORD: He said to me, 'You are my son; today I have begotten you'" (Psalm 2:7). From the standpoint of history, the declarations of the psalmist must have seemed odd to any contemporary listener. To assert that a local monarch with limited land, resources, military, or political capabilities, who was continuously ravaged by the truly dominant regional empires, would exert global influence must have seemed something of a cruel irony to the original audiences. The coronation ritual expressed in this psalm is clearly at odds with the historical circumstances of ancient Israel. Hence, this coronation psalm became an expression of hope in God's election of Israel for some salvific purpose. The term "Son of God," when taken up by the early Christian communities in the New Testament, is not an expression of the Hellenistic idea of a divine man, but rather the expression that God has elected and anointed this person for divine purposes.[2]

This understanding is aptly expressed in the first of two key Christologies found in the New Testament gospels. The two Christologies are: 1) Spirit-christology and, 2) Word-christology. It is true that Christians came to understand Jesus Christ as divine. This is best encapsulated in Word-christology. Christianity needed both approaches of Christology in order to comprehensively understand this person. However, prior to a discussion of the theological development of these two ideas, Jesus of Nazareth must be understood in his own historical context as a Jewish rabbi within the first century of the Common Era, in Palestine and under Roman rule.

The first century Jewish-Roman historian, Flavius Josephus, describes the three primary groups operating in Palestine at the time of Jesus. These were the Pharisees, the Sadducees, and the Essenes.[3] The Sadducees emerged from the Maccabean revolt against the Seleucids in the Greek era from 175 BCE until the Roman intervention of 63 BCE. Tracing their heritage from the Zadokite Temple priesthood, they increasingly became associated with a Hellenized (that is, connected with Greek culture) aristocracy.[4] Their belief system emphasized the written text of the Torah and eschewed beliefs which developed in the Persian era, such as the existence of angels, the resurrection of the body and the authority of the Hebrew scriptures outside the Torah. The Pharisees were not a priestly group, though their name suggests they emphasized separation from cultures and religions outside of Judaism. In addition to adherence to Torah, the Pharisees also viewed the other texts of the Hebrew scriptures as authoritative and developed a second, oral law, which they viewed as important as the written traditions of Moses in Torah. Unlike the Sadducees, Pharisees attested to belief in angels and a resurrection after death. The Essenes were an apocalyptic group best known from the series of scrolls found in the Qumran caves known as the Dead Sea Scrolls. The Essenes were critical of cosmopolitan Judaism and the priesthood in Jerusalem as being corrupt morally and theologically. They exalted a 'righteous teacher' who would be instrumental in bringing about the salvific messianic era. They separated themselves from society in a quasi-monastic type of existence after the social and doctrinal developments that occurred in the Herodian Temple after 152 BCE.[5] The Essenes enjoyed a community life of separateness where the preservation of texts, pious living, and apocalyptic expectation were paramount.

In the canonical gospels, some of Jesus's most fierce disputes are portrayed as happening with the Pharisees. However, Jesus of Nazareth's beliefs that are displayed in those early Church writings show similarities in views such as the belief in angels, eschatological expectations, and a rather liberal approach to scriptural interpretation. Most likely, the intensity of the exchanges portrayed in the New Testament can be understood as disputes among those who share resemblances in beliefs and thus making the debates that much more severe in tone. Such exchanges were frequent between Pharisaical groups who differed in the severity of their approach. Some scholars have discerned in the gospel's portrayal of Jesus elements of a more lenient tradition after the Rabbi Hillel, whose school often engaged in bitter debates with the more strict school of Shammai.[6] However, there are also elements in Jesus's life and teaching that illustrate some commonalities with the Essenes. Along with the community of Qumran, Jesus was known for his personal piety, his disdain for worldly goods, and in some of his teaching of an imminent eschatological era exemplified in the image of the kingdom of God.

However, these were not the only groups that can be discerned in first century Judaism. There were also those known as the Zealots. Zealots were political revolutionaries engaged in guerilla warfare and local skirmishes in acts of organized resistance to the conquering Imperial forces of Rome. It is possible that Jesus was understood by some of his contemporaries to support such groups. Indeed, the New Testament includes an individual known as "Simon the Zealot" among Jesus's closest comrades and disciples (Luke 6:15; Acts 1:13). It is also possible that Judas Iscariot—now infamously regarded as the one who betrayed Jesus to be crucified—was also a zealot. Iscariot is potentially a variant spelling of *sicarii*, which means "dagger" and could indicate connections with revolutionaries and possibly explain Judas's desire to force Jesus into armed resistance.[7] Such speculative reconstructions are historically plausible but cannot be verified. The groups of zealots, along with the three primary religious groups above do not reflect the majority of the population in the first century CE. The majority of people living in Palestine at the time of Jesus would be known as the common people. These were the poor, the marginalized, and those just attempting to live their lives under Roman rule. They would participate infrequently in synagogue life and would pilgrimage to Jerusalem for annual festivals. However, these would have been people of modest means, many illiterate, but some who were merchants. They would have spoken Aramaic and, for those who were able, Koine Greek would be the language of commerce.

All of these distinct groups within Palestinian Judaism in the first century shared the common experience of living under the oppressive rule of the Roman Empire. The Romans conquered violently and called the imperial subjugation of people the *pax Romana* (the peace of Rome). For the people living in Palestine in the time of Jesus, two key events would have been immediately impacting: Cassius's enslavement of 30,000 people around the area of Magdala on the Sea of Galilee in 53–52 BCE and the burning of the city of Sepphoris and the enslavement of the people in the surrounding area. Sepphoris was just a few miles from Nazareth where the gospels report Jesus to have been raised.[8] The Roman Empire would have dominated life in the first century and its influence can be seen in the gospel accounts of Jesus of Nazareth. For example, the Lukan birth narrative recounts angels proclaiming peace on Earth at the birth of a lowly peasant child which would have been understood as a strong repudiation of the *pax Romana* (Luke 2:14). Jesus was executed under Roman authority by crucifixion, which was reserved for those accused of being enemies of the Empire and of Caesar.

The central question remaining pertains to the nature of the relationship of Jesus of Nazareth to the Judaism of his day. While some scholars have sought to minimize the uniqueness of Jesus by arguing that there is nothing to distinguish Jesus from his surrounding culture (for example Geza Vermes) others have sought to minimize his Jewishness and offered universal, existential and demythologized readings of Jesus (for example, Protestant theologian Rudolph Bultmann). More likely a middle ground position offers the most historically accurate picture, such as that put forward by the Anglican scholar N.T. Wright.[9] It is impossible historically to separate Jesus from his Jewishness. He was deeply entrenched in the traditions, teachings, and worldviews of first century, Palestinian Judaism and his teaching bears affinities to the Pharisees in spirituality, but he was critical of the political realities, as were the traditions of Jewish prophets contained within the Hebrew scriptures. As such, it is reasonable to surmise that Jesus was a Jewish rabbi who located himself in the critical traditions of the Hebrew prophets and viewed his message for the kingdom of God as forming a climactic moment in Israel's history. In each case, Jesus of Nazareth cannot be separated from his Jewish background, but neither does he simply blend into the background so as to lose distinctiveness. As the Church developed, encountered Hellenistic Jewish communities, and eventually incorporated Greek philosophy into its own theological formulations, its understanding of Jesus as the Christ also developed and became articulated in varying vocabularies. Central among these were the biblical categories of Spirit christology and Word-christology.

Spirit-christology[10] can be seen in the Synoptic gospels of the Christian New Testament and is emphasized by the Protestant theologian, Jürgen Moltmann. These are the gospels according to Matthew, Mark, and Luke. Spirit-christology recognizes the role of the Spirit of God in the life of the rabbi Jesus. The Gospel that is generally considered the earliest is the Gospel of Mark. After a brief introduction of John the Baptizer, the narrative quickly portrays Jesus as having the Spirit descend on him at his baptism. The baptism account echoes the narratives of commissioning and calling for Israel's prophets. The scene sets the stage for Jesus's ministry as one that is infused with the divine presence as illustrated in the Spirit that descends on Jesus and remains on him throughout his public life. Building upon this christological tradition, the Matthean and Lukan narratives trace the Spirit's influence on Jesus back to his childhood and even his conception. It illustrates that the early Christian traditions of Jesus saw God's guidance and presence with Jesus from the beginning.

Word-christology[11] can be seen most clearly in the prologue of the Gospel according to John. Borrowing from Israel's wisdom tradition, where wisdom is personified and portrayed as being present and active with God at the beginning in the work of creation (Proverbs 8:22–31), the author of the Johannine gospel portrays the Word (λόγος) as present and active prior to the origins of creation. Word-christology provides the basis for the affirmation of the divinity of Jesus Christ as the incarnation of the second person of the Trinity. When debates about the nature and status of Jesus Christ became active in Christianity, the understanding of the passage, "the Word was with God and the Word was God" and that this "Word became flesh" (John 1:1, 14) became particularly prominent in the Christian understanding of Jesus Christ. It was not until the Council of Nicaea (325 CE), whose most prominent theologian was St. Athanasius, that Word-christology, expressed in the affirmation that Jesus Christ is both fully human and fully divine, received conciliar and definitive formulation. This understanding would be reaffirmed and deepened at the Council of Chalcedon (451 CE).

Both Spirit and Word christologies are formulated in connection to God's redeeming work in the world. The former expresses this in the relationships portrayed in the narratives of Jesus of Nazareth through his words and deeds to bring forward the dominant concept of the kingdom of God. The latter focuses particularly on the event of crucifixion and resurrection, which together form the fulcrum of history and salvation in the Christian life. Spirit-christology draws attention to the life of Jesus, empowered by the Spirit at the origins of his life and commissioned at his baptism, and the ministry which would lead to his execution. The metaphor of the kingdom of God is intended to convey the in-breaking and merciful reign of God to heal, restore, and fulfill humanity and the earth with us. For the Christian, this kingdom is inextricably connected with the person of Jesus. In Jesus's loving acts of healing sickness, nurturing friendships with marginalized persons, and sharing a meal with the poor and elite alike, the kingdom is manifest among us. Moreover, in Jesus's teaching on God as a loving father, an ethic of peacemaking and love, in the critique of religious and political power, the nature of the kingdom is explicated for the hearer. Because each of these acts is empowered through the Spirit's unique presence in the life of Jesus, the kingdom itself becomes present in these very words and deeds of Christ. The life of Jesus is a unity. His merciful acts and instructive words cannot be separated from his person.

For the Christian, the life of Jesus culminates in his death and reported resurrection. Word-christology highlights the particular efficacy of the sacrifice of Jesus and the divine confirmation of his life and creative power in the resurrection. For much of Christian history the incarnation, death, and resurrection have been understood as the divine solution to human wrongdoing, frailty, and sin. St. Athanasius says the following:

> You may be wondering why we are discussing the origin of [humanity] when we set out to talk about the Word's becoming Man. The former subject is

> relevant to the latter for this reason: it was our sorry case that caused the Word to come down, our transgression that called out his love for us, so that he made haste to help us and to appear among us.[12]

Athanasius has in mind the ancient Hebrew myth of the sin of the first human beings, Adam and Eve. For the patristic theologian, talk of the incarnation of God in Jesus Christ began with an understanding that this was the divine solution to what St. Augustine would later call "original sin." Similarly, writing at the end of the eleventh century, St. Anselm of Canterbury's book on the incarnation (*Cur Deus Homo*) framed the question of the human and divine natures of Jesus as the divine response to human sin. Anselm's theory became prominent in the history of Western Christianity. With sin, humanity incurred a debt that it could not pay. Humanity was both unwilling (through continued violence and wrongdoing) and unable (finitude cannot repay a wrong done to an infinite being) to repay this debt. Nonetheless, it must be humanity that repays. Therefore, the divine Word, the second person of the Trinity, became a human and paid the debt humanity could not and created a new possibility for life in the resurrection.

This way of viewing the relationship between sin and its solution in the death and resurrection of Christ has been called into question in recent scholarship. For example, if the early Christians understood the death of Christ in terms of the Jewish Day of Atonement, then therapeutic themes of purification, rather than substitutionary themes may be more appropriate. This can also be seen in St. Anselm's work insofar as the death and resurrection of Christ rectify a cosmic imbalance so that harmony and unity may be restored. The primary point to be made here is that christology has traditionally been closely associated with another central Christian doctrine: soteriology. Because of the unity of

Christ's proclamation and actions with his person, Christians have developed their understanding of who Jesus Christ is in connection with the salvific work accomplished on behalf of humanity. Stated differently, the Christian understanding of who Jesus is has been inextricably connected with a community which expresses faith in this person.

This opens a problem for the modern Christian which has occupied more than a century and a half of scholarship. How does one explore who Jesus of Nazareth was given that our information about him has been coloured by religious and ecclesial affirmations of his salvific role? This is framed as the classic question which attempts to discern between the Christ of faith and the historical Jesus and is expressed in the many "quests" for the historical Jesus. The presupposition operating in these quests is that the obfuscating husk of faith must be stripped away so that the historical kernel of who Jesus of Nazareth actually was may come to the fore. In other words, the "historical Jesus" is the Jesus who is reconstructed by historical research. However, from the outset one cannot extricate Jesus from the impact he made on his initial followers. This impact, which can be noted from the following which accrued to Jesus in the largely rural regions of Galilee in the first century of the Common Era, was already a type of faith, although not yet the faith of Christian communities after reports of the resurrection event began to surface.[13] The impact Jesus made on people highlights the relational and communal nature of Jesus which changed lives. This would come to be later expressed in Spirit-christology. That Christians would come to understand this impact as an interaction with the very divinity of God would come to be expressed in Word-christology.

Chapter 1

Buddha

In ancient India there were many individuals who were teachers and spiritual followers. Wandering yogis, seers, ascetics, Vedic priests, sages, philosophers, cynics, a few secularists, but all trying to answer the most fundamental of human questions. Of these, a Buddha was seen as unique. In the West, it is common for people to use the term "the Buddha." The implication is that there is only one in the history of humankind. True as this is, according to modern historical standards, this is not how Buddhists view it. The word "Buddha" was mistranslated (probably on purpose) when the modern Europeans became aware of this tradition during the colonial period. There are some indications that the ancient Greeks and probably Romans and Egyptians may have had some limited knowledge of Buddhism in the Mediterranean area. Some Buddhist teachers were supposed to have visited Alexandria. The Greeks ruling in the Near-East in the wake of Alexander the Great's conquests certainly did know about Buddhism. There is a Buddhist work reporting a discussion between one of the Greek kings (Menander I / second century BCE) and a Buddhist monk.[14] There are also coins with Greek writing and images of the Buddha. Another source supporting this historical encounter is the significant amount of Greco-Buddhist artwork demonstrating Buddhist themes with considerable Greek stylistic influences and techniques from these early centuries. Intriguingly, a statue of the Buddha was found in Helgö, Sweden (not far from Stockholm) that dates to the sixth century CE.[15]

In order to understand the unique status of a Buddha, we first have to understand the general nature of the gods within the Indian context. As mentioned above, one of the two groups that settled in the subcontinent were the Indo-Europeans known as Aryans. Like their cousins the ancient Greeks and the Latin tribes significant in the formation of Rome,[16] they believed in many of the same gods, goddesses, and theological ideas. Divinities such as Cupid/Eros, Mars/Ares, Minerva/ Athena and so many more are known in early Indian religion as Kama, Karthikeya and Sarasvati respectively. Like the Greeks and Romans, the Indians believed that the gods came amongst us and interacted, required sacrifices, and lived on the *Axis mundi*. These gods/goddesses were joined by various lesser "divinities" such as demigods.[17] Under various influences other gods that are transcendent to the world, some of which gain in prominence over time, are mentioned. There also are heavens that are connected with meditational states and much more. By the time of the historic Buddha, the "religious" world view of the Indians was complex. Be this as it may, all of these gods, goddesses and various heavens were seen by Buddhists as being inside the realm of rebirth. That is the beings in all realms from the lowest hell to the highest heaven must undergo rebirth.

A Buddha is one who no longer undergoes rebirth. He is not a god or divinity of any sort nor was he a semi-divine hero. He was born fully human but spiritually highly developed due to his training in many previous lifetimes. The word "Buddha" should be translated as the "Awakened One" meaning one who has woken up from the dream like nature of mortal existence. The term is not of Buddhist origin and we find it used by others in the mid-century of the first millennium BCE. Over time it comes to be more associated with the Buddhist movement. There is a distinction made between a Complete Perfect Buddha and an Individual Buddha. The historic figure whose name was Siddhartha Gautama Shakya was not known as a Buddha upon birth, but tradition refers to him as a Bodhisattva (a being who is focused on awakening), that is, a Buddha in training.

Buddhist literature has over one hundred titles or epithets of one who becomes a Buddha. These epithets are a guide to the development of the concept of "Buddha." Some of these epithets are: Arhat (Worthy One), Dispeller of darkness, Exalted One, Foremost Charioteer, Guide, Healer, Lord of the Teachings, Lion of the Shakyas, Lord of Sages, Physician, the Perfect One, Radiant One, Sage of the Shakyas, Teacher of the World, Unvanquished, Victor, Well Gone One, Thus Come One, and Supreme Among the Released. Some of these epithets were ascribed to other religious leaders in the same time period.[18] Some were also used for the most advanced followers of Shakyamuni. The most common is Arhat. According to tradition those who gained awakening under the teachings of Shakyamuni were also called Arhats. The term Bodhisattva was also used for all those who are training to become Buddhas. Although there were some disputes among various Buddhist schools as to the exact meanings of these terms.

The man born Siddhartha Gautama Shakya, that is Shakyamuni the Buddha, was a historic figure. The British, while ruling India, under a monument located at Piprahwa in Uttar Pradesh, India, discovered a cask with cremated human remains with an engraving stating they were Shakyamuni's in 1897.[19] Although scholars are still arguing the exact dates of Shakyamuni's life, most of these arguments are within one hundred years of each other. Legend tells us that he had twelve great acts or central events in his life: 1) he promised to be reborn a human, 2) his mother had a prophetic dream upon his conception, 3) he was born, 4) he mastered the schooling of his day, 5) as a prince he enjoyed worldly pleasures, 6) he had four encounters (a man bent by age, a dead person, a sick person and an ascetic) which turned him to the spiritual path, 7) he renounced the world, 8) he practiced austerities for six years, 9) he "defeated" the god of the realm of rebirth, 10) he became awakened, 11) he taught, 12) he entered *parinirvana*.[20] Some accounts even claim that all Buddhas have the same twelve events. The actual facts of his life are more problematic.

His father was probably not a true monarch as the realm he was from was a democracy. Thus, he was not a true prince in what that word currently implies. He was most likely from the most illustrious family of the realm and his father sat in the Senate. That is his family was probably closer to one of the illustrious families in Athens or early Rome than to the rulers of England. We can assume that he was schooled in the arts and sciences befitting a warrior of his day because he belonged to the warrior caste. How well he did as a student is unknown though claims are, he was excellent in all subjects. The four encounters assume that he was protected from the sight of people aging, being sick and dying which was highly unlikely as he lived into his twenties before his renunciation. Items 10 through 12 are reasonable given what we know.

Item 9 requires a special note. The god Mara is the god of the realm of rebirth and thus is above the other gods as the gods are born and die as well although their lives are very long by human standards. In order to become a god, one has to amass a vast collection of good merit. It is this karma that propels one into birth in the heavenly realms possibly as the god Mara himself. That is, although there is always an Indra (Jupiter) the individual who is Indra changes and so too with all the gods and goddesses. Mara's function is to keep the realm of rebirth ever turning and he does not like people leaving his realm. Freedom of movement is assumed in the modern world but in ancient times people could not just leave their realm of birth. Speaking metaphorically, as Shakyamuni approached awakening, he was also approaching the boundary of the realm of rebirth. Passing this marker, he would no longer be subject to rebirth. In order to prevent him from leaving, Mara sent his seductive daughters to entice him and a terrible army to frighten him. This strategy did not work. Appearing in person, Mara asked Shakyamuni who would bear witness that he had done all that is needed to leave his realm. At this point in the narrative, Shakyamuni reaches down and touches the Earth calling on the Earth goddesses to bear witness which she did. Many Buddha statues memorialize this moment in the awakening sequence. The Buddhist language materials make it clear that this was a question of freedom of movement however, in some English material the story has been recast in imitation of Christ's temptation by Satan. Christ's encounter with Satan does not have as its central theme freedom of movement. This is just another example of distorting the Buddhist tradition in western sources.

Whatever historical truth there may be in any of the twelve events it can no longer be proven. The earliest information we have on Shakyamuni's life in the scriptures is partial and does not provide a complete narrative. The focus is more on his life from his renunciation of the world and his spiritual training up to his death. Any events of his early life may have passed down the generations of followers in an oral form, but the texts are more often quiet. Only after several centuries following his death do we find full accounts of his life. This in no way detracts from the historicity of the man but only means our information from the earliest period of his life is incomplete. Early Buddhist scriptures offer a negative critique with regard to the stories of great men and events. This may account for the lack of interest in a fully developed narrative of the Buddha Shakyamuni's life close to his time.

Shakyamuni Buddha was sometimes referred to as an Arhat and a *shramana* (lit. striver/a wondering ascetic) he was far more than what these two terms signify. He was a *"muni"* or sage. "Sage" was a term originally limited in application to those of the highest wisdom. Both the Complete Perfect Buddha and the Individual Buddha were also given the epithet *muni,* but this term could be applied to those of the Brahmanical tradition as well. Both men and women could be called *muni.* As time passed the term took on mythic elements and the seven stars of Ursa Major became associated with different *munis* within Hinduism. Ichno-graphically, a Buddha is distinguished from the Arhats and other *shramanas* by the fact that he has hair and they have shaved heads. In some depictions his hair appears almost snail shell like.

Many of the epithets distinguish a Buddha as a teacher-extraordinaire. He is self-confident and fearless in teaching. He has brilliance, is sympathetic, and understanding. He has a fluency in his speech and is lucid. He was persevering, knew the inclinations of students, was tolerant with critics, strict to the lax, and had an even temperament. Above all he was wise and knew all that could be known about awakening. He turned none away who had a question even those who came to challenge him or who represented different religious perspectives.[21] When he taught it was called a "lion's roar" and this was memorialized by the Emperor Ashoka (fourth century BCE) as a capital with four lions facing the cardinal directions which now is the emblem of India.

A fairly strong argument can be made that Shakyamuni Buddha did not see himself as the founder of a religion. Generally, Shakyamuni's teachings are understood as a unique expression of universal truths that were propagated by others before him and by others who will follow. One of the key Buddhist text preserved in Sri Lanka provides an account of Shakaymuni's life but also informs the reader about twenty-eight Buddhas preceding him.[22] This list probably grew from earlier ones with less previous Buddhas listed. Therefore, the truths expressed in the words of any Buddha although individualized to time and place are separate from the person because of being eternal and universal. These teachings are known as *Dharma* or "supports." This term's connotations have various and multiple translations and to distinguish Shakyamuni's teachings (*Dharma*) from other instructions it is known as *Buddha Dharma*. The support system is understood as universal, timeless and cosmic in the sense that it is found everywhere in the vast universe. However, the particular support

Chapter 1

system expression pronounced by Shakyamuni is unique to our world system including its heavens, hells and all in between.

According to Buddhist understanding, the *Dharma* of any particular Buddha is limited in duration and the understanding of that expression will eventually change and fade. When the teachings of one Buddha have disappeared, another person will become a Buddha and reintroduce the teachings but with his own unique expression. However, not all of the *Dharma* of previous Buddhas is lost as a present Buddha trained under previous Buddhas can remember and explain some of their teachings. This is one of the characteristics of a Buddha. There is only one Complete Perfect Buddha at a time and this type of Buddha's primary responsibilities are to dispense instructions, establish a path leading to nirvana, and create a community of followers. In addition, a Buddha rediscovers the teachings without a teacher in his last life wherein he becomes a Buddha. Since Arhats and Bodhisattvas train under a Buddha this is a distinguishing characteristic.

In fact, remembering his past lives while under meditation is what helped Shakyamuni gain his awakening. According to legend, he remembered a few hundred of his past lives. This clearly demonstrated to him that rebirth was a fact. It also allowed him to see that suffering is the common denominator to all existence from heaven to hell. Further, by viewing multiple lives, he could vividly see how karma worked. These insights became the corner stones of his teachings. In addition, in a number of canonical episodes Shakyamuni tells one or another of his disciples that in a past life he was such a person or creature and because he did whatever action that karma manifested in the present life in a particular way.

A distinction is made in Buddhism between describing the world as dream-like and the world as a dream. In some Hindu teachings they say the world is a dream of the god. Buddhism says it is dream-like. What is meant is that the relationship between our experience of a deep dream and our normal awake state is similar to the relationship between our awake state and the Awakened State of a Buddha. This difference is that in all our normal states of mind self is central. The Buddha has eliminated the false notion of a self. The Sanskrit word for self (*atman*) is also translated "soul" and "ego." The Indian understanding of soul is slightly different from the Christian understanding. The doctrine of no-self is a key teaching and will be explained elsewhere. Within the realm of self, the driving force is karma. Karma is a universal law of cause and effect on a moral plane. Lost in the dream of self, we see everything from our self-centered perspective and act in our self-interest. A Buddha having eliminated self and awoken from this dream, sees things as they are and acts only out of compassion. Awakening does not have a statehood threshold as such but is scaled with individuals being partially awakened and those who are completely perfectly awakened.

We can distinguish between the manifestations of karma physically and mentally. However, the source of both is oneself. This may have been in a previous life or may have been some action we undertook in this life but once the cause is created the effect will follow although the effect will be influenced by circumstances. More on this concept will be found in the following chapters. When Siddhartha Gautama Shakya the Bodhisattva sat beneath the Bodhi Tree (the tree he sat under the night of his awakening) although spiritually advanced, he still had both physical and mental karma. After becoming a Buddha, he still had karma and so his awakening is called Nirvana with Remainder. Upon his death which is called *parinirvana* or complete nirvana, all karma was extinguished. The idea here is that the karma he made in the past still could and did manifest. For example, he still had physical karma and therefore still had to maintain and treat his body. He however, did not produce new karma that would drive him into a future rebirth.

Chapter 1

The active state of being a Buddha is ineffable. Hence, Shakyamuni refused to answer a number of questions about Buddhahood. Does the Buddha exist or not, both exist and does not exist or neither exist or does not exist after death remained uncommented upon. The questions remained unanswered not because of his inability to respond but because of the impossibility of our language to express it and our minds to comprehend. These were important topics in the religious milieu of India in the mid centuries of the first millennium BCE. Shakyamuni Buddha proclaimed that he was free of dogma and would not be drawn into these dogmatic questions fed on speculations. Although the completeness of Buddhahood may be beyond our capacities to understand certain aspects are known.

Being free from the cycle of rebirth which is achieving the supreme achievement, he is the teacher of gods and men and thus in a sense superior to them as a teacher is superior to a student. His mind constantly focusing on the principle of the unconditioned or absolute, he is beyond the petty concerns that trouble most people. He knows all supports, lacks any impurity, all his teachings are true, he never tires of awakening others, he constantly manifests compassion, his mind is always in meditation, and having ceased separating himself from the absolute, he is the absolute in relatable form. Many other characteristics are attributed to him over time and by different groups sometimes making him superhuman or god like. This trend seems to take centuries to fully develop. Throughout, his human side is never negated.[23]

Certainly, the amalgamation of the Aryan[24] myth of the Universal Emperor with the idea of a Buddha aided in the development of viewing the Buddha as more than a man. A Universal Emperor is someone who by virtue of the vast collection of merit conquers the world. Being so meritorious people want to be ruled by him and thus he has little need for an army. There appears in the sky a Wheel of Merit which turns and goes with him everywhere. Over time gradations in Universal Emperors was developed with the lowest only ruling part of a continent and on occasion needing an army. But a rather long list of thirty-two major physical characteristics and eighty minor characteristics is ascribed to such an individual. Some of these seem common to any hero such as thighs like a stag, golden hued body, lion like chest, some are signs of beauty in India such as eyelashes like a bull's, but many are unique. According to a legend, when Shakyamuni was born a Seer (old Vedic sage) came from the mountains and told his father that there were only two possible fates for the child. He would either become a Universal Emperor or a Buddha. This prediction was based on the Seer noticing all the characteristics. At what point this myth became associated with the idea of a Buddha is not known but it certainly happened within the first few centuries of Buddhism's development. From that time until now, the educated Buddhist masters and the common Buddhist followers have had to negotiate between the two trends of a fully human Buddha who did something extraordinary and an aggrandized image of an individual which often reflected something far more than commonly human.

In addition, stories of the Buddha Shakyamuni's miracle powers are also found in literature and depicted in various art forms. For a westerner it may be tempting to view such stories as identifying Shakyamuni as unique and somehow comparable to Christ. However, most of the supernatural powers associated with Shakyamuni were also powers believed to be held by other great yogis, at least in their generic themes. Shakyamuni had greater power but for the most part shared in the general Indian mythos of the yogic tradition. Further, we can point to other stories that will clearly distinguish the parameters that Shakyamuni worked within as contrasted by those that Christ worked within. For example, The Gospel of John relates the story of the resurrection of Lazarus wherein Jesus brings Lazarus back from the dead. This miracle is performed to demonstrate the glory of God's son and certainly acted to enhance and initiate faith in others. Kisa Gotami the wife of a wealthy man was driven mad by the loss of her only son. A kind old man advised her to speak with Shakyamuni. She pleaded with the Buddha to bring her child back from the dead. He said he would but first she must bring him a white mustard seed from a household that had never experienced death. Of course, she could never find such a household. Returning to the Buddha after failing her mission, the Buddha taught her, and she gained awakening becoming an Arhat.

Shakyamuni was keenly aware of the social context of his day. Because in the yogic tradition it was understood that donating food, clothing and other necessities to wandering yogis was meritorious, Shakyamuni advised his disciples to accept all that was offered for the good of the people offering. In addition, from the perspective of the disciple they should not discriminate between the people. So high caste or low caste, rich or poor, proper or improper, all were to be treated equally. It is taught that the compasssion of a Buddha and hence his disciples' compassion ought to be like the sun shining on all. One time when Shakyamuni returned to his home kingdom after becoming a Buddha, many of his country men and women wanted to become monks and nuns under his tutelage. Knowing the pride of the men in their lofty birth, Shakyamuni ordained a barber before any of the princes and nobles. In India a barber is a very low caste occupation and in the monastic order status is simply determined by seniority thus making the barber more respectable that the nobility.

As referred to above, there are Complete Perfect Buddhas and Individual Buddhas. The Individual Buddhas also do not have teachers in their last life and discover these universal truths on their own. The real difference between these two types of Buddhas is that the Individual Buddha does not fulfill all three functions of dispensing instructions, establish a path leading to nirvana, and create a community of followers. Since all three of these functions are associated with a Complete Perfect Buddha's compassionate teaching, the focus of the Individual Buddha is more limited and thus individualized. These Individual Buddhas were also mentioned in non-Buddhist texts and so here we are probably dealing with a very ancient tradition.

Finally, in this regard, Bodhisattvas training to become a Buddha can be partially awakened or their awakening can come very close to a Buddha's awakening. There are a number of well-known Great Bodhisattvas that have independent spiritual activities associated with them. However, these Great Bodhisattvas who are still active in the world did not begin as historic figures by modern standards and in many ways are manifestations of powerful principles. According to one branch of Buddhism, the Arhats enjoy the same awakening as a Buddha while other Buddhist traditions consider an Arhat's awakening to be lesser than a Buddha. However, in either case, their awakening is superior to the average person's normal states of mind.

Another theory which originated in India but became very popular in East Asia is the idea of the Buddha within. This theory has two generally different forms. The basic idea is that since there is no difference between an average person and a Buddha then what is necessary for awakening is something inherent in humans. This is called the Buddha within. In some schools of Buddhism this Buddha within or better Buddha Nature, is only covered over with adventitious defilements and once a person realizes his or her true nature, he or she will wake up to the Buddhahood that always was there. The other way of viewing this is that each of us has the potential to become a Buddha. This doctrine touches on several important points. First, theoretically everyone is capable of awakening. Awakening is not dependent on karma and it is not even directly connected with monastic practices like meditation. There are stories of people gaining awakening from unusual circumstances although meditation and similar practices are very helpful. Second, the idea that Buddhahood is inherently human, harkens back to the human Buddha and not a transcendent Buddha. Third, since it is something within, engaging in various activities trying to gain the necessary equipment or "manufacture" Buddhahood is unnecessary. Fourth, since the absolute is often called the non-dual then the dichotomy between average person and Buddha must be false. If the Buddha is within, this dichotomy is dissolved. However, most schools of Buddhism do not adhere to this philosophy.

In a very technical way, there is no notion of soteriology in Buddhism. A Buddha is not a savior, nirvana is not a heaven or heaven substitute and "salvation" is not a topic of concern. Part of the understanding of the concept nirvana is that one is liberated from rebirth not saved to heaven. So, the "science of salvation" is not an issue. Although in many western books on Buddhism they use the word soteriology. A Buddha is only a teacher who is very compassionate. He will do all that he can to help each person find awakening, but that process can only be accomplished by each individual. No one can grant awakening, nor can anyone lead someone to awakening simply because they have faith. Each person has to awaken for themselves but the Buddhas, Bodhisattvas, Arhats and masters are helpers on the way. A Buddha is the most able to help one because of his vast store of merit, wisdom, and compassion.

As mentioned, there were Buddhas before Shakyamuni and there will be others who follow him. The next one to be born on earth is called Maitreya. Most readers are familiar with one of the images of this future Buddha as he is the fat happy Buddha found in many Chinese restaurants. Technically, he is a Bodhisattva now and we have no clear idea when he will become a Buddha, but it will be after Shakyamuni's teachings are no long efficacious. Beliefs in the coming of Maitreye lead to a number of millennial movements in countries such as China. As with other such movements they arise in difficult times and as the difficulties are passed by the society, the movements lose their appeal and fade away.

Yet other Buddhas are known and we have the names of over a thousand. None of these are considered historic by scholars and many are not claimed to have walked on earth. Most are considered Buddhas in other realms throughout the universe and primarily accessible through advance states of meditation. The most popular of these Buddhas particularly in East Asia is Amitabha Buddha. There are a number of texts dedicated to this Buddha and his special realm. Amitabha is presently supposed to be teaching and along with him are two popular Bodhisattvas. His realm, often called a "Pure Land," is like a paradise in its beauty and because of the fact that anything an inhabitant wishes for appears before him or her (this is similar to Indian concepts of heaven). Most importantly, everywhere in the realm are the teachings of the Buddha. Thus, it is a perfect place to practice and gain awakening. In some understandings of these Great Vehicle teachings, by meditating on Amitabha Buddha and his realm one can gain awakening. However, the most popular understanding of this teaching is that by developing karmic connections through meditation or more commonly by reciting the name of the Buddha, one can be reborn in that realm and gain awakening in one's next lifetime.

The teachings on Amitabha and his Pure Land have received a lot of attention in English publications. Unfortunately, when the Japanese and Chinese masters along with English speaking scholars of this tradition began translating and explaining these Buddhist ideas, they chose Protestant theological terms thus confusing the situation. One can read of Buddha's grace, Amitabha saving people to the Pure Land, and other such expressions however untrue to the tradition. There is no concept of salvation or grace in Buddhism. The truth about this teaching is well illustrated in a famous picture that depicts Shakyamuni on the near bank of a raging river of fire and water pointing to the disciple to cross over a bridge. On the far bank is Amitabha signalling for the disciple to come. The disciple however, has to cross on his own. Shakyamuni does not deliver him to the other shore nor does Amitabha fetch him over. More recent publications have been correcting this misinformation but there are about one hundred years of misinformation already published.

Conclusion

The above has delineated that the distinguishing doctrinal characteristics circumscribing the concepts of "Christ" and "Buddha." Both are divergent and existing along very inimitable developmental lines. The conceptual connections between the notion of being anointed and thus chosen by God and the idea of "son of God" are not found in the connotations associated with a Buddha. A Buddha is not chosen by a god or by the God and does not claim or is not claimed to be the "son of God" in any of the literature. Buddhahood is open to all who are willing to transverse the path regardless of caste, wealth, point of origin or any other criteria. While the significance of the individuality of Jesus of Nazareth as the Christ and the plurality of Buddhas are different, in the Kingdom of God Christ also opened equal participation for all regardless of religious or economic marginalization, one's past or social standing. Buddhahood is understood as being determined by higher wisdom and compassion. Higher wisdom is the wisdom of what constitutes "reality" when our false constructs are removed, the true nature of self, and all necessary knowledge to be free from the cycle of rebirth. Compassion is the skilful activity, the actual enactment of wisdom, when one no longer functions from the central ground of "self."

The teaching of Christ or the Buddha in both cases draws upon the responsibility of the listener to investigate its meaning and implications. The most common mode of teaching utilized by Jesus was the parable. The parable is a mysterious narrative intended to elicit a deeper truth regarding God, humanity or the world. The Christian gospel narratives repeatedly recount how the audiences of Jesus were baffled, confused, or even angered by the potential of these stories. Even the closest disciples of Jesus would require special instruction after a parable was told in order to decipher its meaning. Similarly, the teachings of the Buddha are ineffable because of the impossibility of language to express and minds to comprehend. However, for the Christian there is always the attempt to grasp through speech and comprehension, and despite the ineffable qualities of God it is incumbent upon the Christian disciple to seek. It is likewise incumbent upon the Buddhist to seek meaning, but here in the role of guide taken on by the Buddha and the communication given has different limits and content. Nirvana's nature is beyond our intellectualization but very much an experiential possibility. Thus, Buddhist teachings are aids, indications, and act as a map, they are not the actual place.

Since the Buddhist "creation" story (more correctly origin story) has the genesis of the world system being driven by karma of those who will inhabit it, then the idea of the "Word was with God and the Word was God" is an unknown convention. As the former is entirely absent from the spiritual dialogue, the doctrinal construct supporting the concept of the "Word is made flesh" as John proclaims, is unnecessary and unknown. A Buddha is a manifestation of the absolute, as we all are, with the distinction being he is constantly aware of it whereas we are lost in our folly. That absolute is non-dual and carefully distinguished from any

Chapter 1

personification or individuation. It is not conscious, determining, directing or self-willed. A Buddha is fully human but outstanding because of his advance spirituality. Within the Indic spiritual dialogue, he was the most outstanding of all the yogis but not divine even though divine human forms were well known in India. For example, Rama and Krishna are both considered human manifestation of the supreme god Vishnu and called avatars.

The crucifixion and resurrection of Christ presented as a script in imitation of the animal sacrifice found in general and specifically within the Jewish tradition, finds no parallel in the Buddhist tradition although India too, in the Vedic religion, participated in the religious construct of animal sacrifice. Shakyamuni dies it would appear from bad pork unknowingly given by a donor. Although some traditions say it was a poisonous mushroom. Upon his death he was cremated and his ashes were distributed into eight monuments in the kingdoms he has visited during his life. Buddhists understand the sequence of events as a very concrete example of impermanence. Impermanence is one of the keystone doctrines within the tradition. There is no demonstration of divinity or miraculous powers, simply the death of another human however distinguished. His death is not the solution to the wrongs in the world or the gateway for the expiation of sin.

However, we can say that the "problem" of understanding "Shakyamuni" without the layers of the centuries of religious hermeneutics is a common problem faced by followers and scholars of both traditions in the modern period. As a person interested in explaining Buddhism to an audience who may be unfamiliar with this incomparable expression of spirituality, I have to ask myself if the enterprise of trying to flail off the "obfuscating husk" is even the appropriate approach one should take. The underpinning of the exercise seems to me to be secular humanism with the objective being finding the real Buddha behind the myth. This presupposes the more modern definition of "myth" as something untrue and fanciful. Certainly, many people have attempted this project for almost two centuries now. Yet, perhaps the best approach to the story of Shakyamuni is to understand that the idea of "Buddha" is the embodying of the *Dharma* or the teachings and praxis of the Buddhist tradition. Our scriptures state that to see the Buddha is to see the *Dharma* and to see (understand) the *Dharma* is to see the Buddha.

---

[1] For a historical and literary introduction to the Judges, see Richard D. Nelson, *The Historical Books* (Nashville: Abingdon Press, 1998), 93–108.

[2] Joseph Cardinal Ratzinger, *Introduction to Christianity* (San Francisco: Ignatius Press, 2004), 218–220.

[3] Flavius Josephus, *Antiquities of the Jews*, 13.5.9 in *The Complete Works of Josephus* trans. Wm. Whiston (Grand Rapids: Kregel Publications, 1981).

[4] Raymond E. Brown, *An Introduction to the New Testament* (New York: Doubleday Publishing, 1997), 74–83.

[5] The Temple was originally built ca. 537–516 BCE and stood until it was destroyed by the Roman Empire, thus crushing the Jewish revolt in 70 CE.

[6] Harvey Falk, *Jesus the Pharisee* (New York: Paulist Press, 1985). For a reading of the schools of Hillel and Shammai in understanding the Pharisaical heritage of the apostle Paul, see N.T. Wright, *What Saint Paul Really Said: Was Paul of Tarsus the Real Founder of Christianity* (Grand Rapids: Wm. B. Eerdmans, 1997), 26–35.

[7] Lawrence Briskin, "Tanakh Sources Of Judas Iscariot" *Jewish Biblical Quarterly* 32.3 (2004): 189–197.

[8] Richard A. Horsley, *Jesus and Empire: The Kingdom of God and the New World Disorder* (Minneapolis: Fortress Press, 2003), 29–30.

[9] See N.T. Wright, *Jesus and the Victory of God* (Minneapolis: Fortress Press, 1996), 89–98.

[10] See Jürgen Moltmann, *The Way of Jesus Christ: Christology in Messianic Dimensions* trans. Margaret Kohl (London: SCM Press, 1990), 73–78.

[11] For some connections between Word christology and the history of Israel, see Han Urs von Balthasar, *Truth is Symphonic: Aspects of Christian Pluralism* trans. Graham Harrison (San Francisco: Ignatius Press, 1987), 21–37.

[12] St. Athanasius, *On the Incarnation* (New York: St. Vladamir's Seminary Press, 1998), 29.

[13] For an excellent introduction to these ideas, see James D.G. Dunn, *A New Perspective on Jesus: What the Quests for the Historical Jesus Missed* (Grand Rapids: Baker Academic, 2005).

[14] T.W. Rhys Davids, *The Questions of King Milinda* (New York: Dover Publications, Inc. 1963).
[15] W. Holmqvist ed., Excavations at Helgö, I, report for 1954–56, Stockholm. As cited in: www.asianart.com/forum/takaki/dozen/Dozenns.htm
[16] A.L. Basham. *The Wonder That Was India*. (Calcutta: Rupa and Co., 1991).
[17] Akira Sadakata. *Buddhist Cosmology Philosophy and Origins*. (Tokyo: Kosei Publishing Co., 1999), 56 ff.
[18] For the sake of simplicity hereafter, the term "Shakyamuni" (Sage of the Shakyas) will be used to refer to Siddhartha Gautama Shakya.
[19] Akira Hirakawa. (trans. Paul Groner) *A History of Indian Buddhism from Sakyamuni to Early Mahayana*. (Delhi: Motilal Banarsidass Publishers, 1993), 37.
[20] There are some variances in different lists.
[21] N.H. Samtani. "Buddha: the Teacher Extra-Ordinary,"A.K. Narain. *Studies in Pali and Buddhism*. (Delhi: B.R. Publishing Corporation, 1979), 341-346.
[22] I.B. Horner, ed. *The Minor Anthologies of the Pali Canon, Vol. III: Buddhavaṁsa (Chronicle of Buddhas) and Cariyāpiṭaka (Basket of Conduct)*. (London: Pali Text Society, 1975).
[23] Hirakawa, *ibid.* 58-59.
[24] The Sanskrit "aryan" means "noble" and was the name of the large branch of Indo-European speakers who migrated to India. The word was taken by the Nazis and redefined.

Chapter 2
Religious Authority

The Pope

The role of Pope, the Bishop of Rome, has a long and storied history in Christianity.[1] Some Popes were saints (such as Gregory I, also called the Great, 590–604 CE) while others were accused of being egregious sinners (such as John XII, 955–964 CE).[2] Understanding who the Pope is requires a comprehension of the distinction between the office as the successor to the apostle Peter and the person occupying that role. Additionally, since the Pope is the Bishop of Rome, one must understand the relationship between the Pope and the other bishops. While the Pope is a sign of unity and human head of the Roman Catholic Church, it is essential to recall that Catholicism is a multiform and complex ecclesiastical, spiritual, and social reality that ought not to be equated with the papacy in a facile way.[3] In this brief description of the papacy there are two keys elements to consider. First, we must ask ourselves historical questions. How has the role of the Pope developed and changed over nearly two millennia? We must also inquire as to the role of the modern papacy. The Pope is claimed to be the successor of the apostle Peter as the first bishop of Rome. What is the historical connection between Peter and the current Pope? Second, we must ask ourselves the theoretical question of the role of the Pope and the religious views surrounding this office. To do this we must attempt to understand the office of the Pope both in terms of his primacy among the bishops and his collegiality with the other bishops and the wider church.

If the Pope's role in the Catholic Church stems from his connection to the primacy of Peter among the disciples and his bishopric in Rome, what historical and theological material is available to help substantiate this claim? It must first be recognized that Peter's primacy among the apostles is only present due to his connection to Christ and the role accorded him in that relationship. As such, Peter's ministry (and that of the Popes after him) is to facilitate a person's connection to Jesus Christ and not to be a self-referential affirmation of authority.[4] Peter is recognized in the New Testament gospels as being a central figure among Jesus Christ's closest disciples. Among the twelve disciples, eleven of whom would become apostles, one of whom would be instrumental in Jesus being handed over to the Roman authorities for crucifixion, there were three who are described as being especially close to Jesus. These three are Peter and the brothers James and John. Among these three, Peter comes to the fore on several accounts. It was Peter who first acknowledged Jesus's messiahship publicly where he is recorded as declaring, "You are the Christ, the son of the living God" (Matthew 16:16). The response of Jesus is poignant in understanding the biblical roots for the role of the Pope in the church in later generations. The gospel attests that Jesus responded in the following way: "Blessed are you, Simon son of Jonah, for this was not revealed to you by man, but by my Father in Heaven. And I tell you that you are Peter (Πέτρος), and on this rock (τῇ πέτρᾳ) I will build my church, and the gates of Hades will not overcome it. I will give you the keys of the kingdom of heaven; whatever you bind on earth will be bound in heaven, and whatever you loose on earth will be loosed in heaven" (Matthew 16:18–19). While varying interpretations of this passage are possible,[5] it is an entirely reasonable reading of the text to see the person of Peter as the one who is the rock upon which the church will be built. Additionally, Roman Catholics have interpreted the claim of giving Peter the

Chapter 2

keys to the kingdom of heaven as a statement of Peter's authority among the apostles. This authority appears to manifest itself in the Church's understanding of its earliest days as recounted in the first half of the biblical book of Acts.

Provided this biblical affirmation of the uniqueness of Peter's authority among the apostles is plausible, it still does not yet connect Peter with either the role of bishop in Rome or his successors. For this, one must turn to the available historical material to test the plausibility of whether Peter was in Rome as a leader of the Christian communities there. Christian tradition maintains that Peter was the first bishop of Rome and died there as a martyr. To corroborate this traditional claim, the documentary evidence must be examined. In a letter attributed to Peter and recorded in the Christian New Testament, Peter is located in Rome at the time of the letter's writing (ca. 63 CE). The letter closes by saying, "Your sister church in Babylon, chosen together with you, sends you greetings" (1 Peter 5:13). Babylon was a common codename for Rome among Christians who were at risk of persecution. While scholarship debates the genuineness of Petrine authorship for this letter, it does attest that by the early 60s CE it was understood that Peter was located in Rome.

Approximately thirty years later (ca. 96 CE), another bishop in Rome, named Clement, wrote the following words to the Church in Corinth:

> Let us set before us the noble examples which belong to our own generation. Because of jealously and envy the greatest and most righteous pillars were persecuted and fought to the death. Let us set before our eyes the good apostles. There was Peter, who, because of unrighteous jealousy, endured not one or two but many trials, and thus

having given his testimony went to his appointed place of glory (1 Clement 5:1–4).

While this passage does not offer a definitive statement of Peter's ministry and death in Rome, it does offer early textual evidence which may be understood in these terms. This document is in the first generation after the death of the apostle and became widely circulated. Approximately fifteen years after the writing of Clement, the bishop of Antioch named Ignatius wrote a series of letters when he was journeying to Rome, where he, too, would soon be martyred under Trajan (98–117 CE). In his letter to the Christians in Rome he writes, "I do not give your orders like Peter and Paul: they were apostles, I am a convict; they were free, but I am even now still a slave." While it is possible to interpret this passage as Ignatius saying he does not have the authority of Peter or Paul, given that he is writing to the churches in Rome it is reasonable to affirm that he is describing the historical ministry of both Peter and Paul. By the time of St. Irenaeus in the second half of the second century, it is virtually taken for granted that Peter ministered and died in Rome.

While these texts do not offer what might be considered irrefutable, empirical evidence, it does illustrate that from early on in the history of Christianity it was recognized that Peter had a ministry in Rome and died there. The earliest of this evidence occurs during a time when some of the contemporaries of these letters would have living memory of the events and people described. Coupled with the complete lack of extant materials contradicting this claim, it is indeed plausible to assert that Peter had a ministry of Rome. However, this does not yet make the case that Peter was bishop. The early Christian community in Rome did not have a centralized organization as other cities in the Greco-Roman empire apparently did.[6] However, given that Peter was already understood as a prominent leader, was an eyewitness and friend to Jesus, it is quite doubtful that Peter would not have exercised authority or influence in some manner over the varying communities. Therefore, while a centralized office of bishop was not likely exercised by Peter, it is incomprehensible that his leadership in Rome went unrecognized. In this more limited sense one may say historically Peter was the first bishop of Rome.

Given that Peter would have operated in a role of proto-bishop, the office in Rome, as elsewhere in Christianity, developed and became more centralized to provide for the unity of the local church communities. The office of bishop would organize ministries in a local diocese for the poor in a given city as well as settle theological disputes as they arose. Often theological disputes would also arise between bishops. During these conflicts the successor of Peter's See would offer judgments arbitrating the disputes. Eventually the role of the Pope as arbiter and judge in such disputes developed into the role of authoritative teacher. While the Petrine succession and authority for the bishop of Rome might not have been recognized by contemporaries of those persons in any conscious way, perhaps for several centuries, the practice of centralization and developing authority in matters of dispute and practice would express what would come to be recognized as papal primacy.[7]

During the sixteenth century, papal authority came to be criticized by the Protestant Reformation and figures such as Martin Luther (1483–1546). Luther's criticism of the papacy can be understood by reference to his broader theological concerns over what constituted the locus of a person's salvation. Luther sought to supplant the primacy of ecclesiology (the study of the Church) in medieval theology with soteriology (the study of salvation). In doing so, Luther's principles of sola Scriptura (scripture alone) and solus Christus (Christ alone) did not only relocate the discussion of soteriology outside of ecclesiology, but was a critical dispute against the function of ecclesiology within in the sixteenth century Church.[8] Luther argued that obedience to the Pope had supplanted the necessary role of faith in and obedience to Christ. He contended that the work of Christ and the authority of Scripture needed no other mediator and therefore the authority of the Pope was thought to be scandalous to Christianity. For Luther, the word of God was mediated in the proclamation of preaching, thus offering more direct access to the work of God. The teaching magisterium of the Church, and the authority of the Pope, became hindrances to the exercise of individual faith and the directness of the proclamation of Scripture. The response of the Catholic Church to Luther's challenge was to emphasize the historical role of the Church's teaching authority as the true instrument of authentic proclamation and practice.

Therefore, despite other reforms, and the consistent use of the word *reformatio* since the eleventh century, the Council of Trent (1545–1563) reaffirmed the authority and centrality of the Pope.[9] Responding to the Protestant Reformation, the *Catechism of the Council of Trent* argues that while Christ is the invisible head and authority of the Church, both history and scripture attest to the Pope being the visible head.[10] By the eighteenth century with Pope Benedict XIV's *Ubi Primum* (1744) the genre of communicating authoritative teaching was transformed from giving judgments to writing circular letters addressed variably to the bishops, the faithful, and to all people of good will. These letters were called encyclical letters and still operate as the primary mode of teaching from the Papal office.

If the Pope exercises primacy, including the primacy of authority, among the bishops, how may this authority to be understood? Most notably, how are Christians to see the infallibility of the Pope as described at the First Vatican Council (1868–1869)? It will be helpful to bear in mind the distinction between the office of Pope and the person occupying that office. Pope Pius IX, under whom the First Vatican Council was convened and the doctrine of papal infallibility gained dogmatic authority, was described in unflattering terms pertaining to his "authoritarian" approach to leadership and his tendency to "professional hypocrisy."[11] This control continued in influencing the council of Vatican I to accept papal infallibility as dogma. Infallibility was not originally placed on the agenda for the Council, but Pope Pius IX, diverging from the practice of previous ecumenical councils, forced the issue to be placed on the agenda and worked to assure its outcome.[12] The teaching of papal infallibility is definitively articulated in the dogmatic constitution of the First Vatican Council, *Pastor Aeternus*. It describes that when the Pope declares a teaching, faithful to the inheritance of the Church and officially pronounces a matter of faith or morals *ex Cathedra* ("from the chair"), then the teaching reflects dogmatic authority. However, this level of pronouncement (*ex Cathedra*) has been used rarely and does not reflect the status of normal papal teachings, pronouncements, writings, or views. Moreover, the Second Vatican Council's Dogmatic Constitution on the Church (*Lumen Gentium*) locates the Papal authority in connection with the collegiality the office of Peter has with the other bishops even while maintaining the supremacy of the Bishop of Rome.[13] The great Catholic theologian, Hans Urs von Balthasar writes, "Can we trust an authority that has failed so often, so humanly?...Infallibility, according to Vatican I, is not a personal trait of the empirical Church or of her representatives...it is...the merciful act of God."[14] The type of authority the Pope has is one in service to the faith to spiritually guide the members of the Church under its tutelage. Pope Gregory the Great stated that his ministry was to serve the servants of God (*servus servorum Dei*) and this was affirmed recently in an encyclical of Pope John Paul II in specifying the unifying and authority of the papal office.[15] The authority of the Pope is not that of a despot, but rather a spiritual authority although this spiritual authority may be exercised juridically. In the past, Popes have attempted to combine this spiritual authority with secular power, notably in the economic benefits of the old Papal States.

This affirmation of secular, temporal authority was thought to be based upon a document known as the *Donation of Constantine* wherein the lands outside of Rome known as the papal estates were "donated" to the Pope thus giving him secular authority over the Emperor. However, this document is now widely known to be a forgery and only surfaced in the middle of the eighth century to justify the increase in Papal power garnered from the donation of Pepin (father to Emperor Charlemagne). There have been times in history where the Pope exercised secular authority, but it was either based on false documents, a misunderstanding of the nature of Papal authority, desire for power, or at times the genuine need to care for the needs of the citizens of Rome with no other authorities operating. Catholic theology and teaching after the Second Vatican Council (1962–1965) have argued that such a combination of power is no longer a part of the apostolic mandate.[16]

There are two possible errors in conception when attempting to understand the authority of the Pope. They can be witnessed in the historical examples of Ultramontanism and Gallicanism respectively. Ultramontanism is a view within certain segments of Catholicism which assert supreme papal authority, even over temporal and secular authorities. It also affirms Papal authority over the ecumenical councils of the Church. This view was at a zenith in the nineteenth century and exercised in the declaration of Pope Pius IX of the Immaculate Conception of the Virgin Mary to be a part of the dogmatic deposit of faith. While the theological importance of Mary had always been present in Christianity as the *theotokos* (Mother of God), the dogmatic declaration by a Pope was an innovation. Ultramontanism maintains the authority of the Pope in isolation from both the college of bishops and the sense of the faithful (*sensus fidelium*). Additionally, Catholic theology within the last fifty years has predominantly argued that this misconstrues the authority of Pope as having autonomy apart from the development of doctrinal faith within the historical development of the Church and the Ecumenical Councils in particular. The Blessed Cardinal John Henry Newman consistently argued against the assertions of the Ultramontanists in the nineteenth century.

Gallicanism is the inverse of Ultramontanism. Gallicanism asserts that popular authority or the authority of the state over Catholicism is equal or superior to that of the Pope's. The Gallicans affirmed the primacy of the Pope over spiritual matters but denied his supremacy and certainly his infallibility. This was especially true in seventeenth century France. The Declaration of the Clergy of France (1682) maintained that the monarch may call a council, could not be excommunicated, and that papal Bulls and letters must be legitimated by a legal declaration of the monarch.

Both of these movements misconstrue the authority of the Pope. Ultramontanism isolates the Papal power while Gallicanism diffuses it to the point of dilution. In elevating Papal authority above that of the councils and apart from Church teaching, Ultramontanism disconnects the papal office from faithful adherence to the theological traditions of the Church and the life of worship and sacramental practice by which it is connected to Christ. In devaluing the papal office, Gallicanism negates the historical origins and practice which gave the Bishop of Rome a particular standing among the bishops and also doctrine of apostolic succession as it pertains to Peter's See. The contribution of the Second Vatican Council, particularly in the document *Lumen Gentium*, was to affirm the primacy of the Pope in line with Vatican I while reorienting the Church's understanding of the Pope's connectedness and collegiality with the bishops and the Church as a whole.[17]

The Church is not only a spiritual reality but one of flesh and bones. It is real people and real ecclesial communities. Therefore, the Pope plays an essential role in facilitating and fostering the visible unity of the Church. The Pope "is the first servant of unity."[18] This service of unity is exercised not as despotic power, but as a calling and peaceful vocation. Spiritual authority is necessary for the role, but the authority is derivative of grace in connection with Jesus Christ. While some historical Popes have abused power, one must properly distinguish between the Chair of authority and the individuals occupying it (between the *sedes* and the *sedens*). The ministry of unity can perhaps best be seen, not only in the collegiality of the college of Bishops, but also in the unity with the poor. This is what the current Pope, Pope Francis, brings to the fore in his writings. In his Apostolic Exhortation, The Joy of the Gospel (*Evangelii Gaudium*), Pope Francis speaks of the need for "a conversion of the papacy" where the centralization of authority "rather than proving helpful, complicates the Church's life and her missionary outreach."[19] Here Francis emphasizes the imperative of dialogue in the hierarchical structures of the Church and this includes the necessity of collegiality between the Pope, the bishops, the non-clerical members of the Church, and all people of good will.

The Dalai Lama

In order to begin to understand the unique role that His Holiness the Dalai Lama has at present we first need to understand how Buddhist authority is structured in general, how this developed in the Buddhist world, the history of religious authority in Tibet and finally, the history of the Dalai Lama. As each of these topics are worthy of a book length study, our material here will be general and summary in presentation.

Chapter 2

The Buddha Shakyamuni was born in one of the republics in ancient India. His kingdom was one of the minor republics when viewed in terms of territory under its control and the general significance it held within the social-political world of his day. However, his kingdom was not alone, and several great neighboring kingdoms were also republics. These republics were clearly the equal to ancient Rome and Athens in terms of the liberties and responsibilities that were enjoyed by the elite members of society and probably to the general members of society although the latter cannot be proven as there is little evidence for this group.[20] Thus, when Shakyamuni came to organize his quickly growing monastic community, he utilized the store of knowledge he had gained growing up as a favorite son of his kingdom. That is, he organized his community of monks and nuns along democratic lines.

Buddhism has several different categories of community members. These are the fully ordained monks and nuns, the novice monks and nuns, lay men and women holding vows and supporters in general (together called the *sangha*). The supporters and the vow holding laity are free to conduct their own affairs as they see fit but of course, they are constrained by social custom and the law of the land. If a person in these categories were to act in such a way as to violate Buddhist moral principles to the extent that it reflected poorly on the monastic members, the monastic members can refuse to accept him or her into their company. However, there is no ecclesiastic act the equivalent of excommunication. Such a person upon repenting and rectifying his or her behavior would be welcomed once again. Dependency on being acceptable by the monastic community is not required to be seen as an authority on either doctrine or practice. There are historic cases of individuals who were found not acceptable by the monastic community who were famous teachers with scores of followers.

In general, fully ordained monks and nuns were considered the better educated and more experienced members of the larger community and therefore could speak with authority on the teachings. This was not officially designated as their preserve and there are cases of well-educated laymen also speaking with authority on the teachings. In many ways the spreading of understanding of the teachings was up to the individual based on his or her education and experience. The monastic structure however did act as an underpinning in sanctioning or rejecting different views along informal lines more so than as official acts. Further, as each monastery was a self-contained unit supported by its locale, there was no overarching structure for institutional political or doctrinal control. According to a Chinese Buddhist traveller in India in the medieval period, it was common to find within the walls of a particular monastery various interpretations or philosophical school of Buddhism. What unified the monastery was not the doctrine but the particular monastic code that was adhered to by the residents.[21] There are only a handful of monastic codes which generally agree upon the rules and encoded culture but contained minor differences.[22]

Thus, Buddhist institutional authority was horizontal in structure with each monastery the most important determining factor. Within each particular monastery the fully ordained monks or the full ordained nuns (if a nunnery as these were kept separate) were to meet on a regular basis to determine the business of the monastery. The Buddha Shakyamuni had required that these members first attempt to reach a unanimous decision on the business at hand (which could include disciplining members who broke the rules). If unanimity was not possible, then each member was to cast a vote, yea or nay, on motions put forward. The vote was cast by chits that were collected and counted. We can see here the reflection of the democratic government as found in those

Chapter 2

ancient republics mentioned above. There are several points in this that are of significance that need to be highlighted.

After Shakyamuni's death, and after the division of Buddhism into different sects, the monastic members were only dealing with business of their particular institution and were not making decisions that would necessarily affect other institutions. One group of monks did not have the authority to tell another monastery what to do. Second, decisions were generally on non-philosophical issues. As far as I know in India, there was not a case where some group of monks or even a group of monasteries held a vote to determine "orthodoxy" with regard to doctrine and then all Buddhist were required to accept. In fact, if one group could not accept the teachings of someone or some other group, they usually just broke away forming a new sect. This is not to say that doctrinal debates did not take place. India enjoyed a very lively philosophical atmosphere with kings sponsoring debates and awarding considerable prizes to the victors. Further, we can easily trace some of the philosophical debates which took place in treatises after writing became popular. Not only did particular Buddhists master produce tract critical of various Hindu schools of thought or positions, but they were highly critical of each other as well. Third, there are conflicting traditions regarding the Buddha Shakyamuni designating one person to be the head of Buddhism after his demise. The Buddha definitely rejected selecting his cousin as the future leader even though his cousin wished to be so named. According to the Theravada school (now found in Sri Lanka, Thailand, etc.) no person was selected. However, according to other traditions someone was designated. Whatever the situation in primitive Buddhism may have been, by the third century after the *parinirvana* (i.e., the death) of the Buddha, Buddhism had divided into several schools and had reached widespread distribution across India so central control became completely impossible. Although in some locales groups of monasteries that followed the same monastic code may join together in a union. The important thing about any such union is that its authority was only local. We can see this still in Kathmandu where the many Buddhist temples each independent have been in union for centuries. Within the Kathmandu union each representative again has one vote when deciding the business of the entire Buddhist community housed in Kathmandu.

There were a few attempts to unify Buddhism in the early centuries after it began forming different sects. These failed in the long run. There was at least one attempt to make a comprehensive approach to the doctrine. In this example, masters holding many different positions and positing diverse tenets but all within the general parameters of Buddhist doctrine, produced a work.[23] In this work the majority opinion was determined but other views were noted and as I understand it members of the greater Buddhist community were not forced to follow some determined orthodoxy.

Further complications were introduced within a century or two of Shakyamuni's *parinirvana*. As noted above at the time of the Buddha, India had several republics, but this situation rapidly changed after his death. His own kingdom was conquered, and the other republics were conquered by true monarchies one after another. This changed the model of authority as understood in India in general and we can see this influence within the Buddhist community as well. Within the monastic institutions more influence was being recognized as belonging to the "elders" and shifts in institutional day to day control can be noted in the evolution of the monastic regulations. This may have been a significant contributing factor in the first major division of the Buddhist community that formed two distinct schools. The two groups that formed called themselves the "followers of the elders" (Sk. Sthaviravada) and the "majority" (Sk. Mahasanghika). Eventually this shift in organization structure would affect the whole of

Chapter 2

Buddhism in India. In addition, there were groups of Buddhists who were associated with particular teachers that lived in forest community in small groups and there were bands of monks who wondered continually except during the monsoons. Regardless of whether one was a member of a monastery, nunnery, forest community or wondering band one was free to leave at any time and live alone or join another Community. This overall picture shows both that the institutional situation for Buddhist in India was very dynamic and that institutional authority was non-centralized.

At first, as Buddhism spread into China, this same horizontal structure was developed. This would remain the case but there was a change in the terms of affiliation and the pinion of centralization. During the early centuries of the spread of Buddhism in China all but one of the different forms of monastic codes were translated and found adherents. This changed when Emperor Tang Zhongzong[24] ordered the monks and nuns of China to follow only one particular code in the first decade of the eighth century. The other codes soon became only texts that were studied by special-ists and had no living representatives. In India, monks and nuns were seen as outside the social order as they had the ability to renounce earthly pleasures such as family, wealth, and so on. Because of this, even kings and emperors would place them on high and offer praises humbling their royal selves in the presence of such masters. In China, all things were under the emperor and this included the monks and nuns. Because of this, the permission to ordain came under central authority of the court. Thus, monastic institutions were independent of each other being constrained by the current master, school affiliation, and their patrons although a select few were patronized by the emperors. However, the court continued to be an overarching control on the monastic community. There is even a saying about how independent each monastery was in China: "No mountain has two tigers." This is understood to mean that no locale had more than one authority, but that authority only extended to one locale.

In Japan, the situation was very different. They inherited the single code already popular in China and the introduction of living traditions of the different codes did not seem to have occurred. However, in addition to the monastic code there had developed in many Buddhist countries another code called the Bodhisattva (those training to be Buddhas) code. In general, these distinct types of codes were seen as complementary, and since both monastics and laity could hold the Bodhisattva code, we find many monks and nuns holding both. In Japan these became separated and some would hold the monastic code and other the Bodhisattva code. Over the centuries, the Bodhisattva code became more popular until the monastic code died out. Buddhism in Japan was highly influenced by the clan orientation of that society and so the different sects that had originated in China and the one that originated in Japan were more centralized to begin with as important members of a clan became authority figures in their clan supported Buddhist school. In this way the head of a Japanese Buddhist school could exercise authority by means of ordination, transmission of authority to teach, and the general feudatory system of obligations. As a side note, since the Bodhisattva code does not require celibacy as does the monastic code, Japanese Buddhist priest are allowed to marry. Although this Japanese expression is unique to that country, in India in the later period of Buddhist history, many followers no longer ordained in the monastic code but instead followed secret codes as propagated in particular teachings called *Tantras*. These codes too allowed masters and followers to have wives or husbands.

In general, in the current Buddhist world, the Japanese Buddhist do not follow the monastic code but follow the Bodhisattva code as understood and determined by the school membership (e.g., Zen, Pure Land, etc.) a *Tantric* code is also found. The Chinese continue to follow one monastic code upheld by monks and nuns complimented with the Bodhisattva code. In addition, lay people also hold the Bodhisattva code. In Sri Lanka, Thailand, Myanmar, and elsewhere the monks follow their monastic code, which is different from the one found in China, but which dates back to India. The nun tradition has died off centuries ago and there is no recognized Bodhisattva code or *Tantric* code. The Buddhism as followed in modern India and Vietnam are mixed in their approaches. Excluding Tibetan Buddhism, in the rest of the world authority is understood according to the school of Buddhism that is being followed. That is for example, in North America and Europe, a Theravada monastery affiliated with Thailand will follow Thai customs and a Zen monastery will follow Japanese customs with regard to authority. Many non-sectarian organizations have reverted to the more democratic approach of institutional organization, yet the teacher(s) will still hold authority in terms of the teachings.

Tibet has a far more complex situation. In the mid centuries of the first millennium of the current era, Tibet was a powerful empire controlling parts of the Silk Route, sacking the capital of China and Nepal and flexing its muscle all the way into the Gangetic plain of India. At that time, Tibet started importing Buddhism with the emperor's support. The *Tantric* form of Buddhism became the most influential and, in this form, it is the guru (either lay or monastic) who is the final authority. Guru in Tibetan is *"lama"* and each lama was considered a separate authority. After the empire collapsed, there begins the formation of different schools of Buddhism based on a lineage of gurus/lamas who could trace their teachings back to India. The empire was formed when the king of the central district was able to organize or subdue the other petty kings. When the empire fell, Tibet reverted into regions governed by petty kings. Although some of these kept alive the model of trying to unify the country.

Over time connections between the growing Buddhist schools and particular noble families formed.

As we enter the thirteenth century there began to emerge four major Buddhist schools. These are the Nyingmapa (Ancient Ones) who are really an amalgam of the Buddhist teachings transmitted to Tibet before the eleventh century, the Kargyupa (Whispered Lineage Followers) which stated with Marpa (1012–1097) a lama who traveled to India and brought back a particular line of teachings, and the Sakyapa (Pale Earth {place name} Followers) representing a different line of tantric teachings originating with other gurus in India than the Kargyupa. The final school called Gelugpa (Virtuous Way Followers) does not form until the fourteenth century following the teaching of a Tibetan master. Because of the fractured nature of Tibetan politics, the monasteries with their connected nobility increasingly unified religious, political, and economic authority in the isolated valleys of Tibet.

By 1240 CE, Mongolia extending its empire had already conquered Northern China, all of Central Asia, and was knocking on Europe's door. At this date, approximately 30,000 Mongolians also invaded Tibet and eventually gained rule over the many different small kingdoms. The sixth head of the Sakyapa School was invited by the Mongolian Buddhist general and began the process of converting the Mongolians to Tibetan Buddhism. Previous to this, they were already influenced by Central Asian Buddhism. Sakya Pandita was an outstanding scholar, medical doctor, and practitioner who not only cured the Mongolian prince but invented the Mongolian alphabet and provided the imperial court with advanced Buddhist teachings, rituals, and much more. As a reward for his service to the empire and the imperial family, he was granted authority over Tibet. Sakya lamas became teachers of the great Khans. Sakya Pandita is the first example of a Tibetan Buddhist monk gaining secular authority over the country and his

Chapter 2

successors would continue to rule for several generations. In the fourteenth century the Sakyapa lost political control to a branch of the Kargyupa School and shortly the head of the Kargyupa was granted rule over Tibet by the Mongols and also acted as spiritual counsel to the Khans.[25]

In a monarchy, political and economic power is normally transmitted to blood descendants; this presented a problem in Tibet when monks became rulers. As monks are forbidden by their vows to procreate, another mechanism needed to be established. This was accomplished in Tibet by the idea of the *tulku* or reincarnated past master. Tibetans claim that this idea goes back to the beginnings of Buddhism. The oldest line of these *tulkus* is the head of the Kargyupa School. Although there are various means for determining if a child is a *tulku* including visions by masters and prophecy, being declared a *tulku* often brought about not only prestige but political, economic, and spiritual authority at least at the local level and gave one some standing in the national hierarchy. This demonstrates that there is no recognized distinction between the office of whatever *tulku* and the person who holds it. The current person who is entitled is the reincarnation of the previous person who held that position.

Tulkus in some cases are not only understood as being the reincarnation of a famous past master, but also a manifestation of a great Bodhisattva or a Buddha. Buddhists recognize that there are or were many Buddhas. Shakyamuni was only one, the last one, on earth. Before him there were others and in the future there will be more. Also, since Buddhists recognize that other planets or realms exist in the universe, those people will have their own Buddhas. Some of these realms are accessible via meditation and so some Buddhas in other realms are known. In addition to Buddhas, Bodhisattvas are advanced followers who are only slightly below a Buddha. These Bodhisattvas continually aid the Buddhas in their teaching and compassionate activity. They manifest on earth from time to time although people usually do not recognize them to be such until long after they are dead or gone. Hence, the head of the Kargyupa is seen as one manifestation of the Bodhisattva Avalokiteshvara (The Lord who looks down {out of compassion onto the world}). Other *tulkus* are understood to be manifestations of different Bodhisattvas although a Great Bodhisattva can have more than one manifestation. The chief rival to the Dalai Lama for political power is understood to be a manifestation of a Buddha.

Alta Khan, a descendent of Kublai Khan, an usurper and leader of one branch of the Mongolians, invited a Gelugpa lama of considerable scholastic fame to come to his lands. This lama declared Alta Khan to be the reincarnation of Kublai Khan helping to legitimate his rule and the Khan declared him to be the Dalai Lama. The new Dalai Lama declared his two previous *tulku* predecessors to also be "Dalai Lamas" and thus he was the third in the line. The fourth Dalai Lama was the son of a Mongolian chieftain, born in Mongolia and the great-grandson of Alta Khan. This fact united the Mongolians with the Dalia Lama in a manner unknown by the previous incarnate lamas of Tibet. The fifth Dalai Lama was enthroned as the ruler of Tibet with the support of the Mongolians. The doctrine of the Dalai lamas from this time on included Nyingmapa teachings because he came from a Nyingma family, but he is a member of the Gelugpa. The Dalai Lamas are fully ordained monks, holders of the Bodhisattva code, *tantric* code and are tantric gurus. In addition, they hold advanced degrees roughly equivalent to a Ph.D. in the western university system. Since the seventeeth century the Dalai Lamas have ruled Tibet. We are currently living in the time of the 14th Dalai Lama. The 14th Dalai Lama's personal religious name is Tenzin Gyatso although he was born Lhamo Dondrub on July 6, 1935. He was unofficially declared the *tulku* of the thirteenth Dalai Lama when he was two years old and officially enthroned when he was fifteen years old. The process of selection included omens, visions by the Regent, and a test of the small child where he had to select items that belonged to the 13th Dalai Lama out of a group with mixed in decoys.[26]

The relationship between Tibet and China is a highly disputed topic but shortly after the Communist government of China (People's Republic of China) gained power it asserted China's claim on Tibet. Armed conflict between Tibetans and Chinese troops began in the outer provinces of Tibet in 1956 and in 1959 Tibet had an anti-Chinese uprising in the capital. The Dalai Lama, his court, the heads of all the schools of Tibetan Buddhism, hundreds of lamas, and approximately 100,000 Tibetans fled to India, Nepal, and Bhutan. A couple of thousand each year continue to flee.

The 14th Dalai Lama at the age of 24 years was thrust into an extreme critical political situation with international powers. Tibet's southern neighbors did not hold a significant position on the international stage and were too busy with their internal problems to be able to help the Tibetans more than offering refugee status. Britain, the USA, the USSR found no reason to do more than protest and condemn. Thus, the young Dalai Lama was on his own in trying to organize and consolidate the Tibetans in exile. Because of the severity of their situation, the sectarian rivalries had to be deemphasised and fellowship fostered. The 14th Dalai Lama as the political head (now in exile) and as one holding teachings from two schools was in the best position to do this. Whereas the heads of the four schools were in less advantageous positions as they had to focus on the survival of their individual schools.

Basing himself on a non-violent approach to problem solving, the 14th Dalai Lama has promoted the plight of the Tibetans since his exile. He uses mostly unofficial dialogue with the People's Republic of China, but this approach has produced little results to date. He has also taken his case to the people meeting political, religious, and civic leaders all around the world. At times he is spreading the teachings of Tibetan Buddhism (with lectures, rituals, over 45 publications), at times he teaches world peace, and at times he is trying to advocate for the Tibetan cause. He has been awarded the Nobel Peace Prize, Congressional Gold Medal (USA), Honorary Citizenship (Canada), the Ramon Magsaysay Award (community leadership), the Christmas Humphreys Award (from the Buddhist Society, UK), 40 honorary Doctorates, 2 other honorary degrees, Honorary Citizenship (Huy, Budapest, Warsaw, Paris, Venice, Rome), and numerous awards for peace, human rights, leadership, non-violence, democracy, freedom, and much more. The 14th Dalai Lama is a truly exceptional individual by any measure and yet when speaking with him he is a humble monk with a wonderful sense of humor. One walks away feeling that being a world icon was not his choice but his karma.

Be this as it may, the Dalai Lama is not the pope of Buddhism. His authority is actually limited. The heads of the four schools of Tibetan Buddhism are not compelled in any way to do as he may ask. Even less well-placed lamas have openly rejected his suggestions. Outside of Tibetan Buddhism, although he is recognized as a great spiritual leader, he has no authority official or otherwise over Sri Lankan, Thai, Chinese, Korean, Vietnamese, Japanese, Burmese or other forms of Buddhism. He is charismatic, highly educated, articulate, and respected but he can only rely on his ability to convince and his collegiality to influence world leaders as well as Buddhist leaders.

Conclusion

Within the Christian tradition, the Pope has a unique history and role that is dissimilar to any authoritative figure in Buddhism.

Chapter 2

One must clearly distinguish between the office and the incumbent of the office as the first endures through time with an unchanging foundation and the incumbents have their own personality, inclinations, and manner of facing the challenges of their time. Further, as the Bishop of Rome the relationship between the Pope and other bishops is essential to understanding the significance of this chair. In the present chapter the role of the Pope has been placed within the historic development of this institution and secondly analyzed in relations to his primacy and the collegiality with other bishops in the greater church.

The Pope is the successor to the apostle and martyr St. Peter and his particular status is directly drawn from the primacy of Peter among the original disciples of Jesus. Its localization in Rome is also due to Peter's mission to the Eternal City. Originally based on the accounts in the gospels and followed with information from the first centuries of Christianity, Peter was understood to be the foremost of the disciples and to have ministered to the congregations in Rome. Because of this, the bishops of Rome not only served the local parishes but was also involved in the wider community and in particular in adjudicating in doctrinal disputes and concerns of practice. This role of adjudicator developed into the issuing of encyclical letters which are teachings from the Papal office.

In *Pastor Aeternus*, the constitution of the First Vatican Council, the infallibility of the Pope is laid out. However, this doctrine is far more complex that the term "infallibility" would imply and is expressed as a merciful act of God, in collegiality with other bishops, and spiritual guiding the faithful. Historically because of the role of the Pope as the head of the Vatican States, there developed two different ideas of the authority of the Pope and the chair's relationship to secular power. Ultramontanism holds that papal authority is over both temporal and secular authorities including the ecumenical councils of the church.

Gallicanism holds that state authority over Catholicism is equal or superior to that of the Pope. The Pope's authority is over spiritual matters but denies his infallibility and supremacy. These two understandings to the question of papal authority are products of their times and have to be rejected as both have significant doctrinal lacunae. Presently, the Pope is seen as the "first servant of unity" a calling and peaceful vocation by the grace of Jesus Christ.

In order to appreciate the role of the Dalai Lama one has to understand the structure of Buddhist authority, its historical development, religious authority in Tibet and the history of the Dalai Lamas.

Shakyamuni the Buddha organized his community along democratic lines a model he borrowed from his own kingdom. In general, authority in Buddhism is only extended over the monastic community and lay individuals are only subject to secular authority in the Indian setting. The monastic members were outside of society because they had renounced it. Except in extreme cases, most rulers allowed the monasteries to conduct their own affairs. Because the monks and nuns were better educated and more experienced, they could speak with authority on the teachings, but others were not prohibited from teachings what they knew. Monasteries were self-contained and often had individuals holding diverse philosophical views but were united by the monastic code they followed. There were several monastic codes in ancient India. Because of these factors institutional authority was horizontal, and the individual monastery became the predominant factor. As time advanced, the democratic structure in the monasteries weakened and greater authority was garnered by certain members in the role of administers.

Although the horizontal structure as found in India first spread to China, later the government took control over who could ordain and placed the entire edifice of Buddhism under bureaucratic control leading to all monks and nuns only ordaining in one of the

Chapter 2

monastic codes. By this time, ordination into the Bodhisattva vows had already spread to China, but this was open to both monastics and lay followers. Japan at first received both traditions from China but because of the unique culture of Japan, the monastic code tradition died out and only the Bodhisattva code continued.

Tibet received a different monastic tradition from India than did the Chinese. They also received the Bodhisattva code and *Tantric* code. In addition, they received a third set of teachings, the *Tantras*, and in this tradition it is the guru who holds authority. The guru or lama developed connections with the noble families and in this way gained more than mere spiritual authority. Eventually four major schools of Tibetan Buddhism developed. As the Mongols were gaining power in Central Asia then converted to Tibetan Buddhism and gave Tibet to one of the great lamas to rule. This rule changed from the head of one school to another until finally, the Dalai Lama gained ascendency with the help of the Mongols.

A ruler can pass authority to his offspring but some of the rulers in Tibet were monks who are prohibited from reproducing. To address this difficulty in the smooth transition of power between generations, the office of the *tulku* was established. A *tulku* is a reincarnated lama, Bodhisattva or Buddha. This nullified the distinction between the chair and the person as in each generation it was the same person holding the chair but in a different body. Being declared a *tulku* gave one political, economic, and spiritual authority.

His Holiness the Dalai Lama is a *tulku* in the Gelugpa School whose previous incarnations were given Tibet to rule by the Khans. He is a monk, a holder of the Bodhisattva code, the *tantric* code, a tantric guru, and holds the equivalent to a Ph.D. Since the seventeeth century the Dalai Lama line of incarnations have ruled Tibet as king. The current Dalai Lama is the fourteenth. When the

Communist government of China exerted its claim (disputed by others) over Tibet and Tibet not having an army, the Dalai Lama, the heads of the four schools, and about 100,000 refugees fled to India and neighboring countries. The 14th Dalai Lama has endlessly promoted for the Tibetan people, advocates peace, and gives Buddhist teachings around the world. He has been honored in many countries, and the Buddhist world see him as a great Buddhist teacher, but he has no authority in Buddhism resembling that of the Pope. Chinese, Japanese, Thai, and others benefit from his teachings, but he can only inspire them if they wish to be inspired. Even within the Gelugpa School other lamas disregard his inclinations and requests.

---

[1] See Eamon Duffy, *Saints and Sinners: A History of the Popes* 3rd Edition (New Haven: Yale University Press, 2006); John W. O'Malley, S.J., *A History of the Popes: From Peter to the Present* (Plymouth: Sheed and Ward, 2010).

[2] This is according to Benedict of Soracte, who was a tenth century Italian chronicler and Benedictine monk.

[3] For a fulsome description of Catholicism, see the classic work, Henri de Lubac, *Catholicisme: Les aspects sociaux du dogme* (Paris: Les Éditions du Cerf, 2009).

[4] *Catechism of the Catholic Church,* nos. 874–875.

[5] For example, it could be read that it is the content of Peter's confession rather than the person of Peter upon which the church will be built.

[6] This is likely due to the differentiated governance of the Jewish synagogues in Rome during the first century. See Raymond E. Brown and John P. Meier, *Antioch and Rome: New Testament Cradles of Catholic Christianity* (New York: Paulist Press, 1983).

[7] Klaus Schatz, *Der Päpstliche Primat: Seine Geschichte von den Ursprüngen bis zur Gegenwart* (Würzburg: Echter Verlag GmbH, 1990).

[8] Kimlyn J. Bender, "Martin Luther and the Birth of the Protestant Ecclesial Vision," *Perspectives in Religious Studies* 41.3 (2014): 257–275.

[9] John W. O'Malley, *Trent And All That: Renaming Catholicism in the Early Modern Era* (Cambridge: Harvard University Press, 2002), 130–134.

[10] J. Donovan (trans.), *Catechism of the Council of Trent* (Charlotte: Saint Benedict Press, 2006), 94–96. These arguments occur in questions 11 and 12, under the ninth article in part 1 of the catechism.

Chapter 2

---

[11] August Bernhard Hasler, *How the Pope Became Infallible: Pius IX and the Politics of Persuasion* (New York: Doubleday, 1981), 114–123. See also, Richard F. Costigan, S.J., *Consensus of the Church and Papal Infallibility: A Study In the Background of Vatican I* (Washington DC: The Catholic University of America Press, 2005).
[12] Hasler, *How the Pope Became Infallible*, 129–145.
[13] Second Vatican Council, *Lumen Gentium*, nos. 22–25.
[14] Han Urs von Balthasar, *The Office of Peter and the Structure of the Church* (San Francisco: Ignatius Press, 1986), 19.
[15] Pope John Paul II, *Ut Unum Sint*, no. 88
[16] Balthasar, *The Office of Peter and the Structure of the Church*, 32.
[17] See John W. O'Malley, *What Happened at Vatican II* (Cambridge: The Belknap Press of Harvard University Press, 2008); Margaret Lavin, *Vatican II: Fifty Years of Evolution and Revolution in the Catholic Church* (Toronto: Novalis Press, 2012), 13–37.
[18] Pope John Paul II, *Ut Unum Sint*, no.94
[19] Pope Francis, *Evangelii Gaudium*, no.32
[20] Mizuno Kogen, *The Beginning of Buddhism.* (Tokyo: Kosei Publishing Co. 1987), 9-10.
[21] Samuel Beal, *Si–Yu Ki Buddhist Records of the Western World* (Delhi: Motilal Banarsidass, 1981).
[22] Mizuno *Essentials ibid.* 81-82.
[23] The *Mahavibhasha;* no English translation available.
[24] 656–710 CE.
[25] David Snellgrove, *Indo-Tibetan Buddhism Indian Buddhist and their Tibetan Successors.* (Boston: Shambhala, 1987), 381 *ff.*
[26] http://web.a.ebscohost.com.ezproxy.lib.ucalgary.ca/ehost/detail/ detail?vid=2&sid=f478f4ee-dbfb-4a7e-83ef-f0a47bd33a9f%40 session mgr4008&bdata= JnNpdGU9ZWhvc3QtbGl2ZQ%-3d%3d#AN= 21954084 &db=f5h.

Chapter 3
Sacred Texts

The Bible

Christianity contends that it is a religion of revelation. That is to say, it holds that God has revealed the divine self in relationship with humanity in history and that the unfolding of that history relays the content of divine work in the world.[1] In the ancient world history was often communicated in mythological language, polemical discourses and narratives, or through etiological narratives.[2] They do not conform to modern critical methodologies of historiography. However, the ancient near eastern writers understood the literary form attached to their work and saw themselves as artistically communicating the histories of a given people. The texts that are central to the Christian understanding of this history are contained in the compiled work known as the Bible. The word "Bible" (taken from the ancient Greek word for "book") may be a misleading nomenclature since it is not a single book, but is rather comprised of several texts written, edited, and compiled over centuries. The Christian Bible has two primary divisions, which may then be subdivided into further categories. The two primary divisions are the ancient Hebrew scriptures known as the Tanak (what Christians often refer to as the "Old Testament") and the Greek writings of the early Church (what Christians refer to as the "New Testament"). We will explore each of these in turn.

The Tanak is comprised of three main bodies of literature: the Torah, the Neviim (the Prophets), and the Ketuvim (the Writings). The Torah, also called the Pentateuch, is the opening five "books" of the Hebrew Scriptures (Genesis, Exodus, Leviticus, Numbers, and Deuteronomy). Torah simply means "teaching" or "instructtion." These works are named as such due to their traditional association with Moses, to whom the liberation of ancient Israel from bondage in Egypt and the giving of the Israelite law are attributed. Modern scholarship has shown, however, that these texts are not the product of a single author or editor. Rather, these works have been skillfully woven together from disparate sources who themselves drew on oral traditions which had been passed down through generations. In the five books of the Torah, scholars have commonly referred to four distinct, and authorial voices or sources, which narrate the material. These sources are the Yahwist (J), the Elohist (E), the Deuteronomist (D), and the Priestly source (P). These sources are then often reworked by editors called redactors who impact the final product of the written sources over time.[3]

The Yahwist is so named because in the J materials the proper divine name is predominantly used to refer to God. The Yahwist is thought to be a Judean source (from the southern Kingdom) writing and compiling materials in approximately the ninth century BCE. J-source materials feature a literary style consisting of folklore and epic narratives. The divine is typically featured in anthropomorphic ways. The Elohist material is thought to be written by an Israelite from the Northern Kingdom in approximately the eighth century BCE. The E-source is so named because the prominent way of referring to the divine in these texts is with the generic word for God: El. These texts are typified by their moralistic and prophetic material and prominently feature narrative action of characters that represent the northern tribes of Israel. The Deuteronomist is likely representative of a school of thought rather than a single representative author. The D-source is thought to have produced the book of Deuteronomy during the reign of King Josiah in the Southern Kingdom (630–600 BCE) and is characterized by covenantal themes and an interpretation of Israel's history consonant with the blessing/cursing motifs found in the latter portions of the book of Deuteronomy. Finally, the Priestly source is the latest material found in the Tanak (ca. 550–450 BCE) and is distinguished by its uniform style and orderly arrangement of material. The P-source material contains liturgical and ritualistic texts as well as genealogical tables, statistics, and prescriptive laws. It is likely that a priestly source or school operated as the final editors, not only of the Torah, but the Tanak as a whole after the exile.[4]

In the Jewish tradition, the Neviim, consist of the historical narratives of Israel (called the Former Prophets)[5] and the orations of the literary prophets (called the Latter Prophets) which are recorded as given by various figures in the Northern and Southern kingdoms, before and during the exile. The history of the former prophets describes, through its narratives,[6] the tension Israel felt between the anarchic leanings of its identity as a nomadic, shepherding people, and the totalitarian leanings of its monarchies which is metaphorically viewed as a return to its early slavery in Egypt described in the Torah. The anarchic tendencies are seen in the troubling times of the Judges wherein the tribes were disparate, disunified, and violent. The threat and enactment of civil war was constantly on Israel's doorstep. The totalitarian threat is seen in the building projects, great wealth, political marriages, and military growth of Solomon (contrasted with the critique of Solomon and image of the ideal king found in Deuteronomy 17). This is followed with the division of the unified kingdom into two, separate states after Solomon's death and the stubbornness of Solomon's son, Rehoboam. The remainder of Israel's history is an account of the devolution of both kingdoms through cycles of violence and what the texts convey to be false worship through idolatry, repentance, and return to unjust living until the eventual exile and dissolution of the Northern Kingdom under the Assyrian Empire (722 BCE) and the Southern Kingdom under the Babylonian Empire (587 BCE).

The orations of the Latter Prophets give poetic expression to the critique of both the anarchic and totalitarian tendencies of Israel's leadership leading up to the exile, interpreting the rationale for the exile in the midst of it, and returning after the exile under the Medo-Persian Empire (538–397 BCE).[7] The Latter Prophets may be further divided into two major groupings. These are the Major Prophets (Isaiah, Jeremiah, and Ezekiel) and the Book of the Twelve (Hosea, Joel, Amos, Obadiah, Jonah, Micah, Nahum, Habakkuk, Zephaniah, Haggai, Zechariah, and Malachi). American scholar Walter Brueggemann has described the twofold function of the literary prophets, so called because their poetic orations take literary form. The function of these prophets is to criticize and to energize.[8] The role of criticism is to penetrate the self-deception of power located in the monarchy. It is achieved by confronting the self-satisfaction of the monarchy and the horror of the people by bringing to expression the fears and terrors of injustice, and by utilizing metaphorical images and literal attestations to speak of the ill effects these have on the people. The energizing role of the prophets is to offer symbols of hope which counter situations of travesty through the imaginative possibilities recounted in the history of the people. Both of these can be found in the Latter Prophets.

The final major division of the Tanak is the Ketuvim, or the Writings. The Ketuvim consists of diverse literary types. The Psalms is the largest book in the Writings and is a collection of the hymnody and liturgical poetry of ancient Israel. The Writings also consists of an extended love poem (Song of Songs), wisdom sayings and social commentary (Proverbs and Ecclesiastes), a dramatic work on the relationship between God and human suffering (Job), narrative and apocalyptic material (Ruth, Esther, Daniel, Ezra-Nehemiah), a lament (Lamentations), and an alternative account of Israel's monarchial history (Chronicles). The diversity within the Ketuvim means these works are read as moral philosophy, prophetic orations, moving poetry, and historical hermeneutics. They work together with the Torah and Neviim to offer an ongoing debate within Israel and, subsequently, within the early Jewish-Christian communities in discerning the manner in which the people can conceive of the interaction between divinity, history, and national and religious identities. All three major divisions in the Tanak contain varied, complex, and at times competing, accounts intended to offer to their readership an invitation into an ongoing discussion of what it means to interact with what was understood to be its life with God and the world.

In addition to the Hebrew Scriptures, the Christian Bible contains the writings of the early communities who identified themselves as followers of Jesus and who professed belief in the resurrection of the crucified Rabbi of Nazareth. This collection of writings, called the New Testament, consists of four narrative accounts of the ministry, execution, and testimonies to the resurrection of Jesus. These are followed by a narrative account of the earliest days of the Christians, a collection of letters from Paul of Tarsus, a smaller collection of letters from various authors known as the pastoral epistles, and a visionary apocalyptic piece critical of the Roman Empire. The earliest material written in the New Testament are the letters of the Pauline corpus.

The central political reality for the New Testament was the dominance of the Roman Empire.[9] Once more Israel found itself under the thumb of another Imperial power. However, in contrast to the destruction and exiles that occurred under the Assyrian and Babylonian empires, Roman practice was to install local leaders to rule on their behalf and control these rulers through the bestowal of political benefits and the threat of destruction. It was the expansive Roman Empire, with its developed road systems and large urban centres which allowed the apostle Paul's reach to be so extensive and allowed for the spread of early Christian belief and practice throughout the empire. It was the local communities established in these urban centres, often as offshoots of local Jewish synagogues, which constitute the recipients of Paul's letters in the New Testament.

The Letters of Paul are the earliest writings in the New Testament and can be dated to the 50s CE. The letters of Paul, whose authorship are not disputed among scholars, are Romans, 1 and 2 Corinthians, Galatians, Philippians, 1 Thessalonians, and Philemon. The letters follow the same structure as any letter in the Greco-Roman world, though several of Paul's letters are of much greater length. They begin with a salutation, which identifies both the author and the addressee and is followed by a prayer or blessing which wishes well for the recipients. After this opening the body of the letter occurs with the standard rhetorical conventions for the expressed purpose of the letter. Finally, the letters will close with a greeting to particular people associated with the addressee and a brief closing.[10] There are other letters attributed to Paul, but whose authorship is disputed for various reasons. These are often referred to as the Deutero-Pauline corpus. These letters include 2 Thessalonians, Ephesians, Colossians, 1 and 2 Timothy, and Titus. These letters exhibit a differing linguistic style along with varying and, at times, contrasting theological motifs from the undisputed letters. Additionally, some of the letters (for instance, the letters that bear the name of Timothy) describe a developed ecclesial structure which did not historically occur until a later time.

The primary narrative materials of the New Testament can be found in the four Gospels and in the companion volume to the Gospel of Luke called the Acts of the Apostles. While there is scholarly debate around the dating of these works, the Gospel according to Mark is traditionally viewed as the earliest of the gospels and provided key source material for the Gospels of

Chapter 3

Matthew and Luke. It is hypothesized these three synoptic gospels (synoptic meaning "viewed together" due to their similarities) also made use of a common collection of sayings material circulated among early Christians as a teaching resource. This sayings material has been named "Q" by scholars from the German word "Quelle," meaning "source." While the Q hypothesis has been debated recently among scholars, it is still the most widely held account of synoptic development.[11] The Gospel according to John is generally held to be the latest of the four gospels (ca. 95–125 CE) and it is the gospel which contains the most material that is unique to itself, both in style and content. There is evidence that the work went through different revisions as is evidenced by its multiple endings (the original ending at the conclusion of chapter 20 with the apparent later addition of chapter 21). The fourth gospel is thought to be the primary document from what is called the Johannine community. There are three letters in the New Testament which are also thought to be the products of this community (1, 2, and 3 John).

The Johannine epistles, together with the letter to the Hebrews, James, 1 and 2 Peter, and Jude, are called the general epistles. The Johannine epistles are letters expanding upon themes in the gospel but within the context of responding to the issue of division within the community. The letter to the Hebrews examines the nature and function of Jesus and his faith within the context of the narrative history of Israel.[12] The epistles named for the apostle Peter examine what it means to be an early Christian community of the diaspora in the Roman Empire. It poses the question of what it means to live as aliens within the context of empire and employs the motifs of exile found in the Tanak.

The final book of the Bible also poses questions about the role of Christian faith within the context of the Roman Empire but utilizes the symbolic and metaphorical literary features of ancient apocalyptic.[13] The book of Revelation has created much imaginative and fanciful literature engaging in speculative attempts to divine the future. However, like all the ancient writings in the Bible, Revelation too is a literary work firmly rooted in its own time. The dating of this work is largely dependent on the scholarly determination of which emperor is connected with the work. If Revelation is connected with the emperor Nero, then it can be dated in the 60s CE. More likely, the work is to be understood as referring to the emperor Domitian and dated in the mid-90s CE, even if Domitian is symbolically portrayed with imagery intended to recall Nero by way of analogy for its audience. Central to this work is the symbolic portrayal of worship and what it means to worship a figure who was crucified as an enemy of the state in the midst of an Imperial power which claims divinity for itself. Hence, the imagery of the sacrificed lamb is a central motif in this vivid literary piece.

This collection of works found in the Tanak and the New Testament comprise what is found within all Christian Bibles. However, there are some Christian traditions which include works not heretofore mentioned. Roman Catholics and Eastern Orthodox traditions contain additional works in their scriptures which are not located within the Bibles of Protestant Christians. These are early Jewish works and are located chronologically in their respective places within the Roman Catholic and Orthodox canons. These works are Tobit, Judith, additions to the book of Esther, 1 and 2 Maccabees, Wisdom of Solomon, Sirach, Baruch (Letter of Jeremiah), and additions to the book of Daniel. Eastern Orthodox Bibles also contain 4 Maccabees as an appendix. It is important to recognize that these were not additions to the Christian Bible. The earliest Christians utilized a Greek translation of the Hebrew scriptures call the Septuagint (LXX). It was most commonly this Greek edition of the Hebrew scriptures which are referred to or quoted by the authors of the New Testament. The works, which later became known as the Apocrypha, remained in

Chapter 3

the biblical literature and was recognized as useful for the edification of Christians and the piety reflected within its writings. This was the case until the sixteenth century when Martin Luther relegated these texts to an appendix in his translation of the Bible and later criticized the works as upholding Roman Catholic doctrine. Subsequently, Protestant Christian Bibles no longer contained these works, but they remained in the Roman Catholic and Eastern Orthodox Churches. Responding to the Protestant Reformation and the historical alteration of the biblical text, the Roman Catholic Church affirmed the works to be a part of the canon of Scripture at the Council of Trent (1545–1563). Luther also considered particular texts of the New Testament (Hebrews, James, Jude, and Revelation) to be of inferior value because they could not be easily used to support his doctrine of justification through faith alone, though he allowed them to remain.

The controversies over the texts of Christian scripture found in the sixteenth century cannot easily be transposed onto the debates in the early Christian Church. However, it does open the question as to how it came about that Christianity has a sacred text such as the Bible. In the first four centuries of the Church there was neither the doctrines of "Scripture alone" (*sola scriptura*) nor "Tradition alone" (*traditio sola*) as was seen in the sixteenth century. The Christian reception of Hebrew scriptures is rooted in the Jewish origins of Christianity in Palestine in the first century. While the most commonly used translation by the earliest Christians was the Septuagint, debates surrounding the primacy of varying texts continued for centuries. This is exemplified in the differences between Jerome, who translated texts into the Latin Vulgate and advocated for the truth of the Hebrew text (*veritas hebraica*), and Augustine who advocated the authority of the Septuagint as late as 400–405 CE. When it came to the formation of the New Testament several criteria were employed, and these are also noted in Augustine. The three primary criteria were:

apostolic tradition (texts had to be associated with an apostle, either as author or source), unbroken transmission through the succession of bishops, and the consent of the major Churches. Of these three, apostolicity occupied the place of primacy and was used to verify the other two. This principle, however, did provide some controversy for certain texts. For example, the epistle to the Hebrews was contested by the Latin West, whereas the book of Revelation risked exclusion in the Eastern Churches because it was assumed to advocate millennialism, which was regarded as a heretical doctrine. Conversely, certain texts were regarded as authoritative due to their usage and unbroken succession, such as the *Didache*, the *Shepherd of Hermas*, and the *Apocalypse of Peter*. In 405 CE, Pope Innocent I sent a letter to a Gallic bishop enumerating the number and list of canonical texts which appeared as modern lists do today. Some debate surrounding the book of Revelation continued, but the matter is of its inclusion was relatively settled by the fifth century.

The history of canonization, along with the criteria and controversies ensuing from that history, illustrate the importance of the biblical texts for Christianity. This is because these texts operate as sacred scripture for Christianity and this important category must receive some explication. What does it mean for this collection of texts to be considered scripture? For Christians, the role of the Bible as scripture is connected at the outset with an understanding of revelation. Christians affirm that in one way or another the character and truth of God is revealed within the pages of scripture. The difficult task is to understand the relationship between the human writing, editing, and collecting of these texts, which can be understood in naturally historical ways, and the contention that these texts are a part of God's revelation. Christianity affirms both the human origin and divine influence in these texts. How does the text relate to the tradition within which it arose?

We have already noted the Protestant formula of *sola scriptura* found in Martin Luther. However, Luther did not conceive of *sola scriptura* operating apart from his other doctrinal affirmations of *solus Christus* (Christ alone) or *sola gratia* (grace alone). The Protestant Reformed theologian, Nichaolas Wolterstorff, has suggested that one possible way Christians may understand the relationship between the Bible and God is to speak of the divine annexation of human texts, where God deputizes or appropriates human discourse, thus sanctifying such utterances with the authority of divine speech.[14] To speak of scripture in this way is to acknowledge the human tradition, writing, editing, collecting, and interpreting of these texts in ways accessible to the rigour of historical critical analysis. It simultaneously locates these texts as Scripture and recognizes that these texts have a unique status within Christianity apart from their instrumental value in communal readings. On the one hand, in affirming the human and divine roles in the Bible in this way, Christians are able to avoid fundamentalist assertions of inerrancy. On the other hand, they are also able to maintain the central, formative place of scripture within the Church due to recognition of divine authority which may be assented to.

Protestant evangelicals are unique within global Christianity in affirming belief in the inerrancy of the Bible as a theological distinctive. The notion of biblical inerrancy or infallibility, upholds that divine inspiration and influence guided the composition of the biblical texts in such a way that the Bible is without error of any kind—historical, scientific, its own literary origins, moral, theological—and this extends to the individual words used in the text (known as verbal inspiration). The most prominent expression of the evangelical notion of inerrancy is expressed in the Chicago Statement on biblical inerrancy drafted in 1978. The Chicago statement minimizes the role of the Church and the historical process of canonization and emphasizes the importance of the original documents. Perhaps oddly, it recognizes the original texts, written by the authors, have been lost to history, even while affirming that the copied editions and translations maintain the authority of the originals and are continuous with them. This neglects the textual variants in the extant manuscripts which, on rare occasions produce theologically significant variant readings. This is particularly true of the extant manuscripts of the New Testament. The Chicago statement denies that inerrancy is problematized by a lack of technical precision in the texts that may be understood with reference to culture, history, or genre. More recently, Protestant Evangelicals have engaged in debates surrounding the understanding of scripture's inerrancy,[15] but the term and what it signifies remains significant for Evangelicals and is often argued to be a necessary belief for Christian communion. However, the doctrine of biblical inerrancy (or infallibility) as understood by Evangelicals is of recent origin in Christian belief and is anomalous in historical and global Christianity.

Recognizing that the processes of writing the New Testament documents and of canonizing those texts arose from within the Church recognizes both humanity's and divinity's relationship to the Bible and is one way of understanding the Roman Catholic affirmation that Scripture and Tradition—together—form "a single sacred deposit of the word of God"[16] as was formulated at the Second Vatican Council. A primary metaphor used by Roman Catholics is that Scripture and Tradition form a mirror and they cannot stand apart from one another. This differs, for example, from the metaphor of the Wesleyan quadrilateral, which envisages Scripture, Tradition, Experience, and Reason as forming varying loci which distinctly, though cumulatively, inform Christian teaching. With Roman Catholicism's contention that Scripture and Tradition are, together, one source of revelation, there is recognition of the necessity of historical-critical approaches to the text, which use scholarly methods to understand the Bible as a collection of ancient texts. There is also recognition that the normative role of these texts is derivative of their location within the divine working within the world. Christians acknowledge the naturalness of the texts as productions that are inextricably conditioned by their own historical location. As such, they are best understood through critical analysis of literary genre (myth, narrative, poetry, oration), history (as texts conditioned by the politics, science, and worldviews of their day), and their source material (both internal to Israel as well as borrowing from other cultures contemporary with the authors and editors). However, for Christians, they cannot be understood as only this. They cannot because Christians view in these texts the communication of God. As such, Christians view the Bible as derivative of God's gracious working within the world.

Buddhist Texts

Origins:

After the teachings of a Buddha disappear, it is the responsibility of the next Complete Perfect Buddha to reintroduce the teachings. This means that any particular Buddha provides his own expression of the universal truths that is particularly suited to the time, place and disposition of his audience. Shakyamuni Buddha after achieving awakening began his teaching career which lasted forty-five years. This provided his followers a large body of teachings. However, his teachings were not just limited to those people and that place but are understood as being applicable to all humans on Earth. Further, as Buddhism has an expansive cosmological view, the time frame for the teachings is measured in millennial terms in the sense that the duration is a long period, the end of an era coincides with the fading of the teachings and a new era will begin with its future Buddha providing the teachings anew.

According to the custom of the day and because of necessity, Shakyamuni travelled to the many towns and cities from the foothills of the Himalayas to regions in the water shed of the Ganges River. He gathered a very large following of disciples. These disciples included nobles like King Bimbisara who expanded his kingdom into an empire, princesses, oligarchs, village heads, craftsmen, townsfolk, farmers, courtesans, and others. There was also a large group of monks and nuns that formed.[17] In addition, the texts inform us that other non-humans also frequented the Buddha's teachings. This included the gods headed by Indra (=Jupiter) and various *nagas* (often translated "dragons") as well as others.

Just as we can still see today in Thailand or in Japan, the monastic members of the Buddhist community often beg. The usual form of this begging at the time of the Buddha was for groups of monks and nuns to wander from village to village and each morning go house to house where people would fill their bowls with food. Sometimes a householder would invite a monk or nun inside providing them with a lit lamp to illuminate the room, water for rinsing off their feet, drink, food etc. In this situation the monk or nun would give a teaching to the householder. This is what the Buddha often did. Wealthy people could afford to invite the Buddha and his immediate followers. However, the number of monks and nuns travelling with Shakyamuni soon grew so large that villages could not afford to host the troop for long. So, under the direction of leading disciples the early Buddhist community divided into bands which would wander in different areas and thus not overly tax the people's resources.

As Shakyamuni's years of teaching lengthened, more individuals were not always personally attending him. Because of this, few individuals had heard all the teachings. There was one individual however, who had. This was the Buddha's cousin Ananda,[18] who also acted as his personal attendant. Ananda is also credited in the texts as having perfect auditory memory rather like a photographic memory.[19] After the Buddha entered into complete nirvana (i.e., he died), a council was held with all willing monks and nuns attending. At that time, Ananda recited all that he had heard. When we read in the *sutras* (the discourse of the Buddha), "Thus have I heard, at one time the Lord was dwelling at..." it is Ananda's voice. Further, a monk named Upali was a master of the monastic code,[20] so he was asked to recite those teachings. At this first council the teachings were recited and rehearsed until there were many who had memorized them. Following this event, generation after generation of the monastic members spent their years memorizing the teachings until they were written down around the first century BCE.[21]

The Texts:

Although in English Buddhist texts have been referred to as "sacred" this is a misnomer of sorts. The texts are not understood as being the words of a god or gods, they are not associated with a god or gods, and they do not in the main teach about a relationship with a god or gods. They do mention that there are gods, but they are not important in the nirvana project as stated before. These teachings are understood as given by a historic individual. The texts are deeply esteemed and even have offerings placed in front of them out of respect for what they contain. The contents of the texts are not understood as revelations but as a particular expression of an eternal truth.

The expression we now have was enunciated by Siddhartha Gautama the Buddha (6th to 5th c. BCE) but he was not the first to "reveal" these truths nor will he be the last to expound them. He is the person responsible in this cycle of time and place for providing this help. It is recognized by the tradition that none of the teachings were written down at the time of Shakyamuni Buddha but only centuries later. It is also recognized that India has a long tradition of memorizing and orally reciting texts in a method that permitted few mistakes. That is the magic power associated with some non-Buddhist texts was such that if mistakes were made in the recitation of the texts, the magic backfires on the errant priest. This thought generated a high degree of accuracy in the memorization of texts. Buddhist texts are divided into two broad groupings of canonical and post-canonical texts. There were many different schools of Buddhism in ancient India and not all of them had exactly the same texts in their respective canons. For the most part there is agreement across the canons but there are also some differences.

The language of Shakyamuni Buddha was most likely Magadhi (*aka* Magadhi-Prakrit). This is one of the Prakrits or common languages spoken in India in those ancient times that were derived from Sanskrit. Although, it is also possible that Shakyamuni spoke Sanskrit as many of the nobility and the Brahmins used this language, but Sanskrit was not spoken by the common people. Shakyamuni specifically instructed his disciples to teach in the language of the people. Over the centuries the way leading Buddhist looked at Sanskrit and its use in society changed. This led to the teachings being translated into Sanskrit roughly in the first centuries of the current era. Be this as it may, currently we do not have a canon in Magadhi. We do have a canon in Pali, a sister Prakrit, in Chinese and Tibetan both translated from the Sanskrit canon or mixed Sanskrit-Prakrit collection. We also have an incomplete canon in Sanskrit. This disappearance of the Magadhin canon and most portions of the Sanskrit canon is not surprising. In ancient times the writing materials in use in India were highly perishable. Most of what we do have of the Sanskrit canon was either preserved in Nepal where conditions

Chapter 3

are different or where archeological finds preserved in the desert like areas of India. The Pali canon was preserved in Sri Lanka. Modern translations into European languages now exist. Almost all of the Chinese Canon (see below) has been translated but still awaits publication. Only a small portion of the Tibetan canon has been translated and published so far but more texts appear each year.

Although the account of the origin of the teachings provided above exists from early times, actual collections were always sectarian in nature during the historic period. In other words, that which one Buddhist school considered to be the "canon" was different from what another school included in their "canon." Although there was agreement on most titles. Our current notions of a Buddhist canon have been influenced by collections made in Sri Lanka, China and Tibetan in previous centuries. An elevation in the status of these collections as a collection, may have been influenced by Christian missionaries' notions of the status of the Bible in the last two centuries. Given the large body of texts considered Buddhist by followers, most schools had a more manageable grouping that they considered authoritative for their individual tradition. This grouping would include *sutras* (or *Tantras*), commentaries and sectarian works, and may include a *Vinaya* tradition, and an *Abhidharma* tradition. We know from foreign travelers to India in the early centuries of the current era that not every monastery kept a complete set of all texts. The travellers who came in search of texts often had to go to multiple monasteries seeking the teachings of their quest.

For the sake of understanding, we can divide the canon into two major sections which we can call the early texts and the *Mahayana* texts. This grouping is not traditional but is commonly used by modern scholars. The early texts of the cannon are divided into the Three Baskets (Skt. Tripitaka). These are the *Sutras* (discourses given on occasion), the *Vinaya* (encoded Buddhist culture) and the *Abhidharma* (systematic teachings). All three sections are considered the Buddha's word by disciples although most modern scholars doubt that any of these texts actually are a word-by-word dictation. Traditionally, the teachings found in the canon are understood as having twelve divisions. These are: prose, verse restatements, predictions of disciple's awakening, verses, spontaneous teachings, explanations, tales of previous lives of others, tales of the Buddha's previous lives, discourses, extensive doctrinal teachings, recounting events of the Buddha and major disciples, *sutras* (with prose, verse or mixed).

The *Sutra* basket of the early texts was organized by length. This was to aid in their memorization. A *sutra* is a teaching given by a Buddha or authorized by him, given upon a particular occasion. The texts often list the place and some of the events surrounding the delivery of that particular teaching. As Shakyamuni traveled his entire life, many different places are mentioned. Some of the teachings were given because of being requested and some were spontaneously given by the Buddha. The *Sutras* are divided into the "Long Discourses" (34 titles), the "Medium Length Discourses" (152 titles) "Connected Discourses" (Kindred Sayings/ thousands of *sutras* under 5 headings), "Gradual Discourses" (Numerical Discourses/ thousands of *sutras* under 11 headings), and "Minor Discourses" (18 titles). There are over 10,000 *sutras* in this basket but most of them are rather short. These teachings cover Buddhist meditational practice, philosophy, morality, general advice on living, financial advice, advice to kings, advice on government and much more. Although they are critical of particular activities by kings or governments, they are not anti-government. Further, even though there is an emphasis in some texts on the monastic life, the texts on a hole are not anti-family. They sometimes do not work out the details of the teachings nor are they presented in a systematic manner.[22] This is the role of the *Abhidharma*.

Chapter 3

The *Vinaya* basket contains the rules for the monks and nuns and important other materials. In addition to the hundreds of rules that a full monk or nun must follow, monastic governance, transgressions, regulations for taking care of the monasteries, explanations of ecclesiastic acts, the rules for novice monks and nuns, and other information is provided. However, the *Vinaya* collection differs from one school to another. We are aware of at least six different *Vinaya* traditions. In the School of the Elders (*Theravada*) now found in Sri Lanka, there are five books: the first book deals with major, secondary, indefinite, and greed related transgressions. The second book deals with speech offences, behavioral offences, settling disputes, and all other rules. The third book includes a portion of the Buddha's biography (or hagiography) as well as teachings on such topics as the path, factors of awakening, meditation, spiritual powers, etc. The fourth book is on etiquette and duties, procedures, and early history. The final book includes a summary of the rules, analysis, lineage information, ecclesiastic acts and other information.[23] The various sectarian *Vinaya* traditions mostly agree on major points but differ on minor points such as eating times. The arranging and editing of the *Vinaya* texts differ amongst the schools as well, with the Great Community School (*Mahasanghika*) collection seeming to be earlier than the School of the Elders.

As with the Catholic Church, the institutional elite have a significant influence on the whole of Buddhist spiritual culture. The lay members of the community try to incorporate not only the orientation of the monastic community but also many of the manners and ways of organizing their life. This includes following some of the same daily rituals as keeping a shrine at home, following the religious calendar, leading a simple life, etc. This is in addition to maintaining the most important of the vows (not killing, not lying, etc.) and many followers even practice meditation and other rituals daily. Because of the lay members ordering their lifestyle along the lines inspired by the monks and nuns, this basket really acts as the encoded spiritual culture for the Buddhist tradition. At the most enmeshed one finds the full monk or nun, then the novice monks or nuns, lay precept holders, and at the low end the general followers.

Abhidharma is accepted by most of the schools as the words of the Buddha. Modern scholars understand that this literature grew out of seminal texts over the centuries. Unlike the *Sutra* basket and the *Vinaya* basket where the differences between the sectarian literatures are minor in nature, the *Abhidharma* basket has major differences. "*Abhidharma*" can be translated as either "Higher Teachings" or as "About the Teachings." In general, it is a systematic listing, summary, and working out the details of many of the doctrinal issues. The books of the *Abhidharma* Basket according to the School of the Elders are: Psychological Ethics (enumeration of factors), Analysis, Discourse on Elements, Designation of Human Types, Points of Controversy, The Pairs (interrelated points), and the Conditional Relations.[24] However, according to the All Exists School (Sarvastivada) the books are: Discourse on Gathering Together, Aggregation of Dharmas (i.e., the fundamental elements), Treatise on Designations, Body of Elements, Body of Consciousness, Expositions, and Foundation of Wisdom.[25]

With wandering bands of monks or nuns, with that ritual practice being weighted heavier than textual studies, with the oral nature of the teachings in the first few centuries, and considering that India at this time was communities separated by jungles, mountains, and deserts it is not surprising that different schools arose. A number of the changes we find in the *Vinaya* of these schools can be understood as adaptations to local conditions and local views. There did develop a methodology for determining if a teaching was Buddhist or not. Of course, if someone heard it directly from the Buddha or heard it from someone who had directly heard it from the Buddha it was acceptable. Also, if the teaching came from a group of elder monks or nuns, or from a monastic member who specialized in the mastering (memorization) of a text, these were acceptable if they conformed to the known body of teachings. In addition, at least according to some traditions, one should rely on the teachings not on the person teaching, on the meaning not on the words, on *sutras* defined as explicit and not on *sutras* defined and implicit and one should rely on direct insight and not on conventional learning.[26]

It is in this somewhat disjuncted environment that we see the beginnings of *Mahayana Sutras*. These *sutras* too are placed in the mouth of Shakyamuni Buddha. Some are said to have been stored in the realm of the *nagas* or dragons by the Buddha, others were held in safe keeping by the gods. After the time of the Buddha, these teachings were then spread amongst humans. Like in Greece, the Indians believed that the gods frequented the earth and interacted with humans. Thus, teachings being held by the gods and later given to humans is not a large jump in imagination. The "dragons" are a different story. *Nagas* are understood in Indian culture as a type of demi-god associated with water, treasures, secret lore and having powers like shape-shifting and flying.

Even today in India there are tribal peoples called *Naga*. Once they were far more plentiful on the India subcontinent. Buddhist to this day maintain a hermit tradition. This is sometimes referred to as "forest dwellers." This could be an individual or it could be a small group of monks or nuns who isolate themselves from society. Although they are still dependent on society to donate food. Such forest groups would have certainly come into contact with the tribal people also living in the jungles. Whether or not they preserved some teachings given to them by Shakyamuni is unprovable. However, saying that some teachings came from the *nagas* did not sound as farfetched in ancient times as it does today.

Thus, a connection between these peoples and the mythic demi-gods may explain the accounts found throughout Indian literature. Alternatively, awakened individuals with a status below that of a Buddha (i.e., *Arhats*) were also called *"nagas"* these teachings could have developed among such individuals.

Given the differences mentioned above, these three baskets are accepted by all of the various schools of Buddhism. Some schools had other baskets, but these were not accepted by all. The most important collection of texts not accepted by all, were the *Mahayana Sutras*. Modern scholars state that the *Mahayana Sutras* developed a few centuries after the early *sutras*. They were accepted by some communities but were rejected by others in India. One could argue that these texts did conform to the standards of determining acceptable teachings of the Buddha. All of them were accepted in Nepal, Tibet, China, Korea, Vietnam, Mongolia and Japan. In fact, the schools of Buddhism that arose in those countries are more closely affiliated with the teachings as found in the *Mahayana Sutras*. There are a great many of these *sutras* with disparate teachings therein. Some of these are collected into Higher Wisdom *Sutras*, Extensive *Sutras*, The Jeweled Collection, the Flower Adornment *Sutra*, and many more. If we look across the entire collection of early *sutras* and compare them with the *Mahayana Sutras*, we can generalize in saying that the philosophical tone and underpinnings between these two collections is different without being antagonistic. This is why the Mahayana schools did not reject the early *sutras*. In additions, the Mahayana schools also accepted the early *Vinaya* and much of the *Abhidharma* that had developed earlier.

The post-canonical texts form a large collection that is basically sectarian in nature. These contain commentaries to specific texts (e.g., *The Lotus Sutra*), groups of texts (e.g., the *Abhidharma*), various topics (e.g., karma), practice manuals (e.g., meditation instruction), laudatory verses, liturgies, ritual manuals

Chapter 3

(e.g., vow transmission), art and architecture descriptions, and much more. Some of this material is in verse form and others in prose. Some are highly philosophical and some incredibly inspirational. These are composed by known historic figures for the most part with much written by the many luminaries that fill the pages of Buddhist history over the last 2500 or so years. We have such works in Pali and Sanskrit as well as in their Chinese and Tibetan translations. In addition, the Chinese Tripitaka and the Tibetan Tripitaka contain works by masters from those countries respectively. Hence, the Chinese and Tibetan Tripitakas are larger than the Pali Tripitaka because of containing Mahayana works as well as containing secondary works by various masters over the centuries. There are also significant works in Japanese, Vietnamese and Korean added to the collection.

Understanding this large collection of text is no small matter. In the early centuries, people would memorize a few *sutras*, perhaps the rules for the monks or nuns, or particular collection like the *Long Discourses*. A few very talented individuals would memorize all of the Buddha words as found in the *Sutras, Vinaya* and *Abhidharma*. These individuals were called Tripitaka masters. After texts were committed to writing, people still memorized texts because they were often chanted—a custom that reaches back to the first days of Buddhism.

The Chinese Canon:

Buddhism following the Silk Route enters Chinese territory somewhere around the beginning of the current era. At first, it was a spiritual tradition of foreign merchants, caravan members and diplomatic dignitaries. The Chinese soon took an interest. It is claimed that Emperor Ming (28–75 CE) had a dream of a golden man. He then sent out an envoy who returned with teachers, texts, and Buddhist art. These were housed in the monastery he built named White Horse Monastery because a white horse was carrying these treasures. This monastery still exists. This story is most likely a myth and there is evidence that Buddhism was known in China before Emperor Ming. It does illustrate that texts played an important role in the spread of Buddhism from its introduction into the Middle Kingdom.

In the one-thousand-year process of collecting texts and translating them into Chinese, there were only about 200 individuals who could speak authoritatively about Buddhism in India and to a lesser extent Central Asia wherein all the kingdoms were Buddhist.[27] That means that the average Chinese person's encounter with Buddhism was more likely through a Chinese teacher working with texts than with an Indian master. Those texts may have been memorized, written down, or printed (printing was invented in China and the first text printed was a Buddhist *sutra*).[28] The translation of Indian texts into Chinese was not always a smooth process and was fraught with the many problems that any translation effort must encounter. This was made even more difficult by the considerable differences between the Indo-European languages used in the Indian or Central Asian Buddhist texts and the Chinese language. For example, Chinese writing is not alphabetic and is monosyllabic. Thus, transliteration of Buddhist pronouns and Indian place names became difficult as Chinese could not always accurately represent the word's sound and things like consonant clusters were particularly problematic.

Yet, over the centuries, methods were devised to deal with various problems in translation. Sometimes an Indian or Central Asian Buddhism master would work with a small group of disciples in translating texts he had brought with him under spartan circumstances. Sometimes the master would receive support from local elite during his labors. The real innovation in this massive project was the development of the Translation Bureau under the direction of the Imperial government. In this setting the Indian master would work with hundreds of scholars to produce

Chapter 3

translations. A great example of this was the Central Asian monk Kumarajiva (334–413) who was educated in India. In China he was the head of the Translation Bureau and is credited with translating or composing approximately 52 works. This includes many of the *sutras* that would play a seminal role in Chinese Buddhism and a number of texts that are quite long. Some single *Mahayana Sutras* are equal to several Bibles in length.

The Chinese being demanding scholars edited various texts over the centuries, but this was not a single effort. In addition, the collection of the texts into one vast body also required repeated efforts. This is because monasteries across the country had different translated texts. Some were produced locally, some were preserved in one place and lost in another and because of the vagaries of history stretching across a couple millennia. We find canons "published" from the earliest in seventh century and in the centuries that follow. These are not simple later editions but contain difference of note. Except for the collection made in stone, these were usually hand carved woodblock prints until the modern period. Some of these were preserved in China but others were in Korea and Japan where the Chinese language canon is used. A standardized critically edited version was produced in Japan called the Taisho (Japanese era 1912–1926) Tripitaka. This was published in western style format in the beginning of the twentieth century. It contains the early texts, *Mahayana* texts, commentaries, and works of famous East Asian masters. It is this version that is translated into English and awaiting publication. Yet, even this version does not contain all of the known texts.

In the beginning of the twentieth century Sir Aurel Stein (1862–1943) a British archaeologist during an expedition sponsored by the British government in India, discovered a treasure trove in a cave monastery on the edge of China and Central Asia near Dunhuang. The Dunhuang cave held thousands of texts and other artifacts in a well-preserved state because of the dry conditions.[29] A considerable number of these texts were Buddhist in such languages as Chinese, Tibetan, Sanskrit, Prakrit, Turkish, and others. It was a much larger find that the Dead Sea Scrolls. Many of these texts were not included in the Taisho canon and scholars are currently studying these texts.

The Tibetan Canon:

The Tibetans were benefited by the work on the canon done in China and the close proximity to India. Although there was no written language in Tibet at the time of their first encounter with Buddhism, the Tibetans adopted one of the Sanskrit scripts and quickly developed their language with the help of Sanskrit linguistic. In this manner they created a language specifically well designed to translate Buddhist texts. There were individual Tibetans who worked with Indian and some Chinese masters to make translation of important texts, but many texts came from the Imperial sponsored translation groups somewhat similar to the situation in China. We can see an increase in translation activity in the eighth century. In the ninth century there is a major editing of many texts. A new style of translation developed beginning in the eleventh century. It was not until the fourteenth century that the texts were collected and organized into a canon. Before this different groups had separate sections or smaller collections of the texts that were important to their school or individual tradition. The largest collection which includes both the old translation and the new translations was published in western format in Taiwan in 1991.[30] The Tibetan Tripitaka contains early texts (but less than found in the Chinese canon) *Mahayana* texts, commentaries, and *Tantras* along with their ritual sub-texts. *Tantras* are similar to *Sutras* but focus on elaborate rituals. Scholars consider them a product from the last period of Indian Buddhism, they are also found in Sanskrit and Chinese translation.

Chapter 3

Buddhist Sacred Texts:
With the advent of written Buddhist texts, the book brings together two currents already present in Buddhism. The first is the veneration of the Buddha teachings. People approached the listening to a teaching with different behavior than listening to secular oral literature. The texts were to be memorized, thought through, implemented and the principles realized. However, it was recognized that without reverence for the teachings the other aspects rarely follow. Second, there already existed in India shrines by the time of the Buddha and he did not cast these down. Instead, he instructed his disciples to create new shrines to contain his cremated remains. These shrines are called stupas and they dotted the landscape of India. The written Buddhist texts is both a teaching and a physical relic representing the eternal teachings and thus is twice worthy of veneration. This is why the *Mahayana Sutras* often declares that someone who engages in the study, remembering, reciting and explaining, of the *sutra* gains the most merit and will arrive at nirvana. Because of this those people are worthy of veneration and the place of teaching too is worthy of veneration. Thus, the text comes to be respected similar to a stupa.

Conclusion

In viewing the canon of each religion, we see considerable divergence and yet some similarities remain. The cultural and historical context in the formative years for the Hebrew Scriptures used by Christianity (the Septuagint) and the Buddhist texts were vastly different. However, the formative years of early Christianity seems much closer to the Buddhist situation. Buddhism began as the full implication of steel technology was manifesting in the jungles of India leading to rapid social-political and economic changes. The economy was booming but this led to the small kingdoms becoming absorbed into empires. Whereas the Jews were always in a precarious situation with regard to the empires of Egypt, Assyria, and Babylonia. Shakyamuni Buddha was the teacher of kings and thus maintained good relationships with the kingdoms and the fledging empire of his day. In the first century of Christianity the Roman Empire was on the verge of reaching its greatest expansion under Emperor Tarjan (r. 98–117). Even given this, the New Testament incorporates an anti-Rome rhetoric wherein the early Christians see themselves as being in a similar situation as the Jews portrayed in the Old Testament and the Apostles were apprehensive of the political elite. The disciples of the Buddha continued through the ages to maintain relations with the powerful, but it took generations before the Christians would establish similar relationships. In India, kings generally supported all the major religions although showing favor to one or the other. They did not demand their citizens convert nor did they prevent it. In the ancient Mediterranean a religion could be determined as subversive by the empire.

The Bible, although now translated into every language, was originally composed in ancient Hebrew for the Old Testament and classical Greek for the New Testament. This interesting fact testifies to the Hellenistic influences in the eastern Mediterranean that was undeniable even to the Jews. It also speaks volumes as to how the teachings of Jesus was able to spread across the empire. The teachings of Shakyamuni Buddha although probably spoken in Magadhi were transmitted in various related regional languages as the Buddha's disciples came from various kingdoms. Thus, there was from the beginning no scriptural language that received exalted status. As the teachings spread across India they were broadcast in the language of the people although over the centuries this included Sanskrit the language of the elite in India.

The scriptures held dear by Christians are understood as being "revelations" that is the inspiration of God guided by the Holy

Spirit as recorded by people at first through oral traditions and later written down. They present substantial information that is crucial about the Divine self and that self's relationship with humanity. In part, the Old Testament developing from disparate sources and pulling together different voices helps provide an identity for God's chosen people—the Jews. The New Testament through its four primary religious narrative with Mark being the earliest and John the latest, as well as additional materials and in particular the Pauline Epistles, provide for a Christian identity. The Buddhist materials have a complete division of the canon that is the encoding of Buddhist culture both monastic and lay. This clearly is designed as an orthodox expression (however orthodox is understood by each school) but it is also the ideal to which all should aspire. Studies have shown that in ancient times the reality of Buddhist culture may have been different than the ideal upheld in these texts.[31] Be this as it may, the type of in-depth analysis of the source materials that has occurred for over a century in regard to the Bible has just begun with the Buddhist canon. Partly this is due to the fact that this type of analysis is very much a western development. It is also partly due to the fact that research in Buddhist Studies has been focused on simply making the information in the texts assessable. This would include publishing the canon in standard formats, making critical editions of texts, and much energy has been spent on translations.

The theological difficulties encountered with understanding the exact nature of Christian scripture, its divine origin, its human transmission, and its connection with the historic tradition is a very complex and profound topic to plumb. The Catholic idea of scripture and tradition being a single deposit of the word of God is a very successful attempt to both provide a valid approach and to simplify the theological complexities. The Wesleyan quadrilateral approach placing in relationship scripture, tradition, experience and reason is another. There is no equivalent to this problem in Buddhist doctrine. Buddhist scriptures have from the beginning been understood as universal truths spoken by a human in a skillful manner suitable for humans on earth. The texts are an aid to the nirvana project, but the meaning of the teachings should be adhered to and not the words. Nirvana is only approachable through experience and no amount of study and legalistic arguments will move an individual closer to the goal. Although tradition was seen as important, it was not as important as skillful means. Thus, the rituals and traditions of Japanese Buddhism are vastly different than those found in Sri Lanka because of adopting local customs skillfully to the use of Buddhism.

The creation of the Buddhist canons as we now have them was a gradual process as the thousands of teachings were gathered, organized, edited and "published." Records on some of the earliest efforts seem no longer extant. The Chinese and Tibetan canons were centuries in the making as different groups translated materials of interests, different translations methods were used, and the collecting and editing of the whole slowly took place over time. We do have records of some of the activities involved in these efforts. For example, the Chinese were very keen on trying to make sure "teachings" were authentic and not apocryphal. The Tibetans too were interested in this but far less so than the Chinese. Since there is no central authority in Buddhism each school made determinations according their own needs and dynamics. And even when one group decided that a text was dubious another group may include it in its collection. This explains why most Buddhist schools today accept the *Mahayana Sutras* and yet one school rejects them. The creation of the Christian canon was by council through debate. We all know that there was much left out some of which has been know from early centuries and some has been found in the last century or so. It was at the Council of Trent that the Bible took its shape. Before that there were lists of scriptures.

Chapter 3

[1] René Latourelle, S.J., *Theology of Revelation* (New York: Alba House, 1966), 21–43.
[2] Etiological narratives are accounts offering constructed as historical narratives in order to explain contemporary phenomena.
[3] Norman Perrin, *What is Redaction Criticism?* (Philadelphia: Fortress Press, 1969).
[4] See Michael Duggan, *The Consuming Fire: A Christian Guide to the Old Testament* (Huntington: Our Sunday Visitor Publishing, 2010), 81–116.
[5] Terence E. Fretheim, *Deuteronomic History* (Nashville: Abingdon Press, 1983), 15–27.
[6] Much of the Bible is written in the form of narrative and communicates its meanings through plot devices, characters, stylistic use of time and historical motifs, along with the voice of narrators. See Shimon Bar-Efrat, *Narrative Art in the Bible* (Sheffield: Sheffield Academic Press, 1997); Yoram Hazony, *The Philosophy of Hebrew Scripture* (Cambridge University Press, 2012), 140–160.
[7] Edwin M. Yamauchi, *Persia and the Bible* (Grand Rapids: Baker Books, 1996).
[8] Walter Brueggemann, *The Prophetic Imagination* (Minneapolis: Fortress Press, 2001).
[9] David M. Carr and Colleen M. Conway, *An Introduction to the Bible: Sacred Texts and Imperial Contexts* (Malden, MA: Wiley-Blackwell, 2010), 225–287; E.A. Judge, "Rank and Status in the World of the Caesars and St Paul," *Social Distinctives of the Christians in the First Century: Pivotal Essays by E.A. Judge* David M. Scholer, ed. (Peabody: Hendrickson Publishers, 2008), 137–156.
[10] See Charles B. Cousar, *The Letters of Paul* (Nashville: Abingdon Press, 1996).
[11] See Burton L. Mack, *The Lost Gospel: The Book of Q and Christian Origins* (San Francisco: Harper Collins, 1993).
[12] Christopher A. Richardson, *Pioneer and Perfecter of Faith: Jesus' Faith as the Climax of Israel's History in the Epistle to the Hebrews* (Tübingen: Mohr Siebeck, 2012).
[13] For an excellent scholarly introduction, see Richard Bauckham, *The Theology of the Book of Revelation* (Cambridge: Cambridge University Press, 1993).
[14] On this possibility, see Nicholas Wolterstorff, *Divine Discourse: Philosophical Reflections on the Claim that God Speaks* (Cambridge: Cambridge University Press, 1995).
[15] J. Merrick and Stephen M. Garrett eds., *Five Views On Biblical Inerrancy* (Grand Rapids: Zondervan Academic, 2013).
[16] Second Vatican Council, *Dei Verbum*, 10.
[17] Hirakawa, *ibid.* 32-35.

[18] A different cousin than the one who wanted to be named head after the Buddha's passing.
[19] Zenno Ishigami, *Disciples of the Buddha*. (Tokyo: Kosai Publishing Co. 1989), 45 *ff.*
[20] *Ibid.* 37 *ff.*
[21] John S. Strong. *The Experience of Buddhism Sources and Interpretations.* (3rd ed.) (Belmont: Thomson Wadsworth, 2008), 98-99.
[22] U Ko Lay. *Guide to Tipitaka.* (Selangor: Selangori Buddhist Vipassana Meditation Society, 2000), 16 *ff.*
[23] *Ibid.* 1 *ff.*
[24] *Ibid.* 136 *ff.*
[25] Hirakawa, *ibid.* 131-132.
[26] Ronald M. Davidson. "An Introduction to the Standards of Scriptural Authenticity in Indian Buddhism," Robert E. Buswell. *Chinese Buddhist Apocrypha.* (Honolulu: University of Hawaii press, 1990), 291 *ff.*
[27] Daisaku Ikeda. (trans. Burton Watson) *The Flower of Chinese Buddhism.* (Santa Monica: Middleway Press, 2009), 29.
[28] I.e., *The Diamond Sutra* part of the Mahayana *Perfection of Wisdom* genre. See: Joseph Needham, ed. *Science and Civilisation in China* vol. 5 (Taipei: Caves Books. Ltd. 1986), 151.
[29] Aurel Stein, Sir *On Ancient Central-Asian Tracks.* (Taipei: Southern Materials Center, Inc., 1982).
[30] A.W. Barber, ed. *The Tibetan Tripitaka: Taipei Edition.* (Taipei: Southern Materials Center Inc., 1991).
[31] Gregory Schopen. *Bones, Stones, and Buddhist Monks.* (Honolulu: University of Hawai'i Press, 1997), 1 *ff.*

Chapter 4
Sin and Karma

Sin

As the Protestant theologian, Ian McFarland states, when Christians talk about sin they speak of the "twin convictions that things are not right in the world, and that human beings are deeply implicated in what has gone wrong."[1] Christian teachings on sin tend to indicate one of two primary aspects of this doctrine. First, Christians speak of what has traditionally been called original sin. Original sin speaks of the state humanity finds itself in when Christians speak of the need for redemption. At its core, the doctrine of original sin articulates the Christian understanding that the world is in a troubled state and in need of redemption. The experience of hardship, violence, betrayal, wrongdoing, and harm reflect something about the current problematic nature of human existence. In other words, the condition of human frailty and fault is inveterate and impossible to entirely avoid. Second, Christians speak of committing sins, or of sinning as a way to classify and characterize individual actions of wrongdoing. Because sin is the Christian way of referring to the human need for redemption, it is not comprehendible unless it is located in connection within broader discussions of God, Christ, or salvation (what theologians call soteriology).

While there are many biblical passages which address the nature and role of sin, the classic passage to open the discussion is the narrative found in the third chapter of Genesis recounting the fall of Adam and Eve. In this narrative, which is the J-Yahwist's account of creation and differs from the Priestly account in the first chapter of Genesis, the first humans are located within a garden and are charged by the creator to tend the garden, care for the other animal creatures, and to live in a community which is to grow, be fruitful, and multiply. Despite the living situation of these humans being, at first glance, seemingly idyllic, they are cajoled by a crafty serpent into partaking of fruit from the one tree the creator forbade. The result of this act of rebellion was the illumination of one's vulnerability and shame, expressed in the realization of nakedness, and God issuing a series of pronouncements detailing the increased difficulty each party in the sin would have in life. The serpent must be denigrated and slither on its belly. It will live in enmity with human offspring. The woman experiences increased pangs and difficulty in childbearing while the man experiences increased pangs and difficulty in tending the land. The earth itself appears to not be immune as it brings forth thistles and thorns which provide difficulty for human life and agriculture.

Often times, this narrative is read as an origins story for sin in the world and used to illustrate both the causal beginnings of original sin and an emblematic example of the commission of particular sins. The results outlined in the divine pronouncement illustrate the negative results and effects of human folly in having sin enter the created order. Such readings find common assent in Christian communities due to the use Saint Paul makes of these figures and narrative in his epistle to the Church in Rome found in the Greek scriptures of the New Testament. Writing in the second half of the first century (ca. 58 CE) the apostle Paul draws a correspondence between the intrusion of sin through the acts of the first humans (expressed as "the first Adam") and the redemption Christians understand to come through Jesus Christ (expressed as "the second Adam"). However, this is a later interpretation given to this passage centuries after it was written and compiled. When viewing the texts on their own historical terms the narrative does not as easily fit into a causal account of sin.

First, within the texts themselves there is ambiguity over the state of the first humans prior to partaking of the forbidden fruit. While after the divine curses are given human labour and relationships are deemed more difficult, there are indications that the narrative views labour as endemic to creation. For instance, while in the Priestly text found in Genesis 1 God creates by merely speaking, in the Yahwist account, God creates the garden by planting it and tending it as a gardener. It is a visceral image that portrays God dirtying the divine hands in the soil to plant a garden and using the soil to construct the first human as a sculptor does a clay pot.[2] If God needed to be a farmer to initiate a living space for the first humans, then there is no reason to assume the first humans would be exempt from such work. Indeed, the texts state that God placed the first human in the garden to till and keep it. Moreover, the J text depicts the first human naming, and thus exercising a form of authority over, other animals that were also made from the soil (Gen. 2:19). This seems to indicate the need to settle and tame a rather unruly creation at the outset and prior to the incursion of sin through the acts of the first human pair. This is echoed in the later Priestly text found in Genesis 1 where the first humans are instructed by God to subdue the earth and to exercise dominion in tending and caring for creation (Gen. 1:28).

Second, the understanding of human development, growth, and evolution offered by modern science has rendered attempts to view these texts as literal descriptions of a historically existent couple who provided parentage for the whole of humanity as untenable. Therefore, it is equally untenable for the Christian understanding of sin and humanity's need for redemption as resulting from a finite historical act by two persons who were ill-equipped, due to lack of knowledge and experience, to either understand the ramifications of their choice or the nature of their original predicament. The texts exhibit the mythical character of the genre often employed by writers in the Ancient Near East and show knowledge of a wide array of myths, at times borrowing from them while at other times engaging in disputes with them.[3] In addition to these historical problems there is also the issue raised in the relationship between act and nature found in descriptions of original sin. This history of Christianity's teaching on the relationship between original sin, understood as a fallen nature and universal guilt found in humans, and individual sins which are results of disobedient acts of the will have garnered debate amongst historical schools of thought within the Church.

The classical understanding of sin was articulated most influentially by St. Augustine (354–430 CE). Prior to him, the Christian doctrine of sin and the fall was utilized in terms of theodicy. That is, it was employed to offer an historical explanation as to why there is suffering in the world. Augustine continued in this vein but expanded his purview to express not only the origins of sin, but also the congenital effects it had on human existence, when viewed generationally. In viewing the account of Adam and Eve's sin in this way Augustine argued that there was a literal historical point when sin entered the natural order and that this entrée of sin so corrupted humanity that sinning in individual actions is no longer avoidable. Augustine thought that the wrongdoing of the original pair so infected humanity that it altered the essence of what it is to be a human person, including our psychological dispositions and moral abilities. Augustine understood sin as a type of infection that was passed on generationally through the act of sexual procreation. Hence, the concupiscence present in human generational production made it particularly susceptible and a poignant example of the unavoidability of individual sins due to the congenital defects now present in human reproduction.[4] The problematic brought forward in the Augustinian account is the issue of the relationship between

Chapter 4

individual acts and human nature. Can an individual action so change the nature of a person (let alone an entire species) that it can irrevocably alter the nature of that person and that person's progeny? Or is it the case that actions flow from one's nature and therefore human acts of sin were already a nascent possibility prior to the actually of any first sinful act? Moreover, this account raises, for Christians, the question of the nature of God and God's relationship to human fallibility and the justice of the judgment God exercises.

This was the problem that vexed St. Thomas Aquinas in the thirteenth century. He disagreed with Augustine's reading of the role of sexual procreation in the transmission of an infection Christians call sin. Rather, he argued that it was due to an intrinsic human sociality that connects all humanity, both presently and historically, wherein the guilt of original sin is found. For St. Thomas, original sin was not transmitted generationally, but is rather a constitutive aspect of nature itself due to human sociality in an Aristotelian metaphysical sense. Therefore, while the commission of individual sins is the manifestation of a rebellious will, original sin manifests human guilt because in a metaphysical sense, all human could be found within an historical Adam.[5] Modern Catholic theology has expanded upon the Thomistic insights to argue that human life an action is always informed by a context and these relationships are constitutive of human life, virtue, and guilt. Therefore, if the historical, biological, societal, and relational components that comprise human life are flawed prior to the existence of a particular human, then any individual human being will share in that reality, even in his or her freedom. In such a way, modern Catholic thought can account for the evolutionary realities of human emergence in dialogue with science and understand the social realities expressed in the doctrine of original sin.[6]

These issues, which bring forward important questions for any Christian account of sin, were expressed forcefully by the Protestant theologian, Friedrich Schleiermacher. Writing in the first half of the nineteenth century, he stated:

> [It is not] possible to suppose that such an alteration of nature should have resulted from an act of the alleged individual as such, since the individual can act only in accordance with the nature of his species, but never can act upon that nature....And indeed it is glaringly and intrinsically incompatible with all that we can learn of the divine ways, to suppose that to such an extent God should have made the destiny of the whole human race contingent upon a single moment, the fortunes of which rested with two inexperienced individuals, who, moreover, never dreamt of its having any such importance.[7]

What Schleiermacher brings to the fore is the difficulty of the relationship between human nature and action alongside the issue of divine recompense for an act produced by persons ill-equipped to comprehend their role and impact on human progeny. Schleiermacher was keenly aware of the hermeneutical issues surrounding ancient texts, even if he was not privy to the modern scholarship of source and redaction criticism explored in the previous chapter. Schleiermacher engages these narratives as symbolic texts. These are what modern parlance would call mythological narratives. However, these texts, if viewed within a proper interpretive framework are still revealing and informative of how Christians may view the doctrine of sin.

One of the primary recurring motifs arising from the narrative of the fall is that of relationships and their collapse. The first

Chapter 4

human in the narrative of the fall is described in the Hebrew text as a being in relationship. The first human (*adam*) is brought forth from the soil (*adamah*). The primary connection, expressed linguistically, that human beings have in this Hebrew text is to the earth. It is not until afterward, when the second human is made from the first, that sexual differentiation is understood between the male (*ish*) and woman (*ishshah*).[8] Even here, the woman is mythically described as being created from the side of the man and therefore their connection is also emphasized. The first humans are in a profound relationship with the earth, with other creatures that are likewise brought forth from the earth (Gen. 2:19), and with each other. The result of the incursion of sin is expressed in terms of the disruption of each of these relationships. There is enmity between the serpent (as a member of the non-human animal world) and humans, there is hardship in the relationship between humans and the soil, there is tension between the humans themselves, and there is difficulty in seeing one's offspring come to life. Moreover, there is now difficulty in the relationship humanity has with the creator. When God appears after the first pair has eaten the forbidden fruit, the human response is to hide due to a sense of shame. God must seek them out and inquire regarding their situation. The humans' response is to evade their own culpability and to blame those that are around them. This sense of disconnection, enmity, and failed relationship then receives generational expression in the first murder committed by Cain against his brother Abel. These children of Adam and Eve have apparently received the propensity to sin and wrongdoing, and this is manifested in fratricide. Shortly after this, the whole world is portrayed as steeped in violence and in need of purgation (Gen. 6:5–7:24).

Roman Catholics derive their understanding of original sin from Augustine, but also from the tradition as it developed prior to and after the Bishop of Hippo. Notable in this tradition is the theologian of the thirteenth century, Saint Thomas Aquinas. In the *Summa Theologiae*, Thomas writes, "Sin is by definition a withdrawal from the order of things which has God as its purpose" (IaIIae, 79.1). In this definition one can see the primary thrust of Catholic thought on sin. In short, Roman Catholics see sin and evil as a privation, that is, as a lack or deficit of goodness. The *Catechism of the Catholic Church* speaks of sin as a deprivation of original holiness (*CCC*, #405). In using negative categories to describe sin, Roman Catholics affirm that sin and evil do not have an essence, do not exist *per se*, because sin is not a created phenomenon. Evil does not have its origins in God as creator. Sin exists as an accidental quality of a subject. Thomas states that to exist is to be created and therefore is an intrinsic good. However, evil is the contrary of good. Therefore, since good cannot have evil as a part of its essence, or vice versa, evil must not exist in terms of having an essence. Rather, evil exists as something derivative of a subject. It exists as a deficit, or privation, of goodness. In his treatise called *On Evil*, Thomas links this account of existing with the experience of human desire. "[W]e perceive that everything by nature desires to conserve its existing and avoids things destructive of its existing and resists them as far as possible. Therefore, existing itself, insofar as it is desirable, is good. Therefore, evil, which is universally contrary to good, is necessarily also contrary to existing."[9]

The Protestant reformer, John Calvin, had a different view of evil and sin than that of Aquinas. He affirmed what would come to be described by Calvinists as the total depravity of creation as a result of sin.[10] Reformed Protestants in the tradition of Calvin think that total depravity expresses the utter inability of human persons to do anything good or worthy of merit in the divine view. Nature is so thoroughly corrupted by sin that it is incapable of producing good in any measure. Calvin understands our sinful nature in the following way: "For our nature is not only destitute and empty of good, but so fertile and fruitful of every evil that it cannot be idle...whatever is in man [sic], from the understanding to the will, from the soul even to the flesh, has been defiled and crammed with concupiscence...the whole of man [sic] is nothing but concupiscence."[11] Calvin thought the depravity of human nature due to sin was so complete that humans no longer have freedom of choice, and so cannot choose the good, but are bound by sin. Any affirmation of human free will, and hence involvement in coming to know the gospel, usurps God's honor. Calvin argued that the sole solution to the problem of sin was the intervening and deterministic grace of God. God chooses who God will save on the basis of the divine will and grace, which is wholly perfect. This grace alone offers salvation from sin.

Contrary to these strands within Protestant Christianity, Catholics do not believe that human nature has been totally corrupted. Human beings are still created, living, existing entities and, as such, may be described as good. To exist and live and be is a good. However, there is acknowledgement of the great measure to which human failings are a reality. The Catholic Church affirms that human beings are inclined to sin and that original sin creates proclivity to further actions of sin. Sin is defined in the Catechism as "an offense against reason, truth, and right conscience; it is failure in genuine love for God and neighbour..." (*CCC*, #1849). Here one can see the relational emphasis also seen in the biblical myth of Adam and Eve. The disruption of relationship through disordered love results in a privation of goodness for human life. This experience of disordered love fostering disrupted relationships is seen as the experience of human fallibility which is unavoidable and therefore endemic to the human condition. As humans orient themselves to goals and ways of being which detract from their love of God and each other, these can become habit inducing. This is the rationale for the language of sin creating proclivities to sin.

In other words, apart from divine grace, human frailty will lead to ever increasing participation in harmful activities which upset one's relationship with God, community, and the earth.

When Catholics speak of individual acts of sin they are understood as being either mortal or venial. Mortal sin is that which destroys charity and love in a person through a grave violation of God's law. Venial sin offends or wounds charity but allows it to persist. There are three things which are necessary for an act to be considered a mortal sin. First, it must be a grave matter. In other words, it must be of a nature which is disruptive of life with God and community. The Decalogue of Moses, often called the Ten Commandments, provides examples of these. The gravity of the sin must be taken into account. To murder someone is more serious than stealing from someone, although a crime is committed against the person in both instances. Second, for a sin to be mortal it must be done with full knowledge. This criterion means that an act must be committed with the full knowledge that said act is contrary to the divine will and is therefore sinful. Finally, a sin is mortal if it is performed with full consent. Full consent entails the act must be freely chosen, rather than performed under compulsion or duress. Willful or feigned ignorance do not diminish the severity of an act, nor does increased psychological acceptance or callousness due to repeatedly performing a sin or having it become habit. Unintentional ignorance may lessen the severity of sin, but do not remove culpability entirely.

Venial sins are a less serious matter than mortal sins due to the lessened impact on one's life of charity. This is not to say that Christians view venial sins as inconsequential. On the contrary, they are still violations of moral law, though ones which are less grave. A sin may also be venial if it is of a grave matter, though committed without full knowledge or consent of the moral agent. Venial sin is a disordered love for natural objects as their own end rather than being oriented to love of God. These are failures of

Chapter 4

virtue, or minor engagements in vice. It hinders the moral maturation of a person but does not impede participation in friendship with God.

Both mortal and venial have focused on the individual and the personal components of a Christian account of sin. There is another element for a complete account of sin to which one must attend. In recent decades, liberation theologians have reminded Christians what the later Hebrew prophets emphasized in many of their written oracles. They brought once more the reality of structural sin into the consciousness of theologians and lay persons alike. Such theologians have reminded Christians that sin is also a social and historical reality. In other words, if a person may commit sin in violating the integrity, trust, or relationship with another person on an individual level, this may also occur in the manner in which we construct, systematize, and carry out our societies. Social justice is, therefore, seen not merely as a political movement, but rather as the necessary correction to the sin of apathy toward the suffering of our fellow creatures and necessary for a life of virtue. This correction includes working to create the political, economic, and societal structures which aim towards equity and justice because failing to do so is a spiritual act of sin alongside personal transgressions.

The Christian response to sin is contained in the narrative of salvation, which will be addressed in further detail in the next chapter. However, two items merit attention at this point. These are the sacrament of baptism and the sacrament of penance and reconciliation (commonly called confession). Catholics view baptism as a sacrament of the Church given by Christ to the Church in which God is uniquely present and active for the benefit of its recipient. Baptism is often performed on infants, though adults are baptized when received into the Roman Catholic Church if they have not been so previously in a different Christian tradition. Baptism is one of three sacraments of initiation (alongside Confirmation and Eucharist). Baptism is the practice wherein grace is given to the individual to erase the effects of original sin and turn a person toward God. It is a symbol of new life and a gift of grace so that a person's life with God may be borne anew. It also welcomes the person into the communion of the Church and thus relocates them within a wider network of those who acknowledge Jesus Christ as saviour. In both of these, one may see individual and structural elements. A person is personally transformed and socially relocated to participate in virtue and pursue justice and the kingdom of God declared in the teachings of Jesus.

The sacrament of penance and reconciliation responds to those acts of sin which occur through commission and omission. It accompanies an inner penance, which is to say a life daily devoted to humbling oneself and pursuing a life of conversion. In other words, it accompanies a life seeking to become increasingly attuned and attendant upon a life which increasingly exemplifies love of God and neighbour. When someone approaches the sacrament of reconciliation the priest is sacramentally representative of Christ and grace is communicated in this ministerial relationship. The person approaching reconciliation comes with contrition of self, confession of deed, and a willingness to make satisfaction for wrongs done, particularly those which have proven harmful to others. Penance and reconciliation restores the relationship between the person and God through the honesty and contrition of confession. It also restores the person to the rest of the community in the Church by reconstituting them and welcoming them back to right relationship with their fellow Christians. In doing so the reconciled person may exit the confessional to serve others without spiritual hindrance remaining within them.

Chapter 4

Karma

When Buddhist talk about karma they also talk about "twin convictions" and like Christianity one limb is that things are not right in the world but the other limb is that all sentient beings from the highest heaven to the lowest hell including human beings, are responsible for what has gone wrong. The word "karma" seems to have first entered the English language in 1828 according to the *Oxford English Dictionary*.[12] The word originally from Sanskrit has been misunderstood and hence mistranslated from its first usage in England. The *Oxford English Dictionary* states it means "fate" although it does give the accurate translation of "action" which is the original meaning in Sanskrit as it is derived from the "to do" verbal root. "Fate" originally meaning "that which has been spoken by the gods" in classic times was personified and came to mean, "…all events, or some events in particular, are unalterably predetermined from eternity." Various nuanced aspects of the predetermined quality also developed over times.[13] In current parlance people speak of both good and bad karma. This usage may not indicate a notion of predetermination, but it is equally incorrect. I would venture that this usage is akin to good luck and bad luck understanding that one may (and only may) have had a hand in the making of the luck at least. "Good luck/bad luck" generally meaning that some event is favorable/unfavorable to a person's interests. It is akin to good/ill fortune with the later becoming somewhat passé now.

In India, the word in its nontechnical usage can be used as an English speaker would use the word "action" or "to do". On a technical level, "action" came to mean the law of action and reaction. In Buddhism this is called "karma" and its "fruit." However, this law was understood to be operative on the spiritual plane. To say, "good karma" or "bad karma" is really a misnomer and somewhat akin to incorrectly saying "good gravity" or "bad second law of thermodynamics." Buddhist texts in general, do not use the terms "good/bad karma." They speak of wholesome or unwholesome merit or *punya* in Sanskrit. Here the terminology allows for a clearer understanding of the phenomena under consideration. "Merit" is something one is due because of one's actions. It is very personal and requires personal involvement. Equally it is not merely due to the caprice of a god or the gods. So too with the law of karma. The action you engage in will be followed by what you merit. If your action is wholesome then, the law of karma being in effect, it will generate some positive outcome. Reversely, if your action is unwholesome then you will have some negative outcome. Usually, in the English Buddhist materials this is spoken about as being about morality. Although that is a useful way to think about the merit, it needs to be noted that Shakyamuni was speaking about one's spiritual well-being. Therefore, "karma" is not fate as there is no predetermination involved. You alone are making your future just assuredly as if I drop a rock, it will fall down.

It can be argued that in Hinduism because of the presence of the cast system the idea of karma has a stronger connection with determinisms. Yet, here too one is still the origin of the actions. Buddhism rejected the caste system, so this nuanced influence is also lacking. Buddhism holds that although the production of wholesome or unwholesome merit will certainly have its result, there is still free will. The karmic results you generate develop as situations and predispositions. If you are thoughtlessly going through life, then you will just follow your predispositions as you encounter each situation. However, if you are thoughtful, you can decide to not follow your predisposition in any particular situation. Going through life thoughtlessly you will continue to make a mixture of wholesome and unwholesome merit which will generate future results accordingly. Being thoughtful you can decide to take appropriate actions to generate wholesome merit in each situation. Although it is recognized that this may not be easy. It is further recognized that some predispositions may prevent you from having an accurate evaluation of any situation. However, the making of merit is connected with intentionality.[14]

The concept of karma within Buddhism is very complex. There are many different facets that need to be considered and as this concept matured unanswered issues arose. Although it is often claimed that Shakyamuni Buddha understood all aspects of the law of karma, he could not explain it to others because the complexity was too great, and the explanations would be too time consuming. Here I will speak in more general terms. The theory of karma is used in different ways, but two main focuses is to motivate people to undertake wholesome actions and to explain observed incongruences in life. An example of the later would be an immoral man or woman having fame, fortune and never being held accountable for the suffering they cause. According to the law of karma such a person merited the wonderful life because in some past time he/she generated considerable wholesome merit. However, the other side of this is that now that person is creating the conditions for a future onerous life.

To add to the complexity of this topic, Buddhism does not maintain a linear casual theory. As mentioned elsewhere, Buddhism holds that all things in the universe are caused. The notion of causation is like a net or a biosphere and not like a train track. All the elements within the biosphere must be what they are for that sphere to be what it is. Removing one element may have drastic effects on the whole. In addition, since the no-self or no-soul theory is a mainstay in Buddhist doctrine, explanations of how karma is carried over need to be addressed.

It should also be noted that since Buddhas are not gods, they do not issue commandments and therefore, technically one cannot engage in sin in Buddhism. Whether or not a Buddha teaches, the law of karma is in effect for all beings in the realm of rebirth.

Whatever the realm of nirvana is truly like, it is beyond karma. Karma too is used to explain hardship, violence, betrayal, wrongdoing, and harm but for the Buddhist, these can all be avoided by not generating the causes. As the notion of sin requires the notions of God, Christ and salvation, it is incomparable to the notion of karma or more properly unwholesome merit for the gods are still under the law of karma. Lacking a notion of original sin, there is no need for a savior and there is no notion of salvation within Buddhism. Salvation within the religious context means in general the saving of a soul from the outcome of sin. The process of removing oneself from the realm of rebirth is referred to in the Buddhist texts as "liberation." Buddhism has no savior, no soul to be saved, and even the Buddha cannot take you to the goal or open up the goal as a possibility. The Buddhas only point the way, you have to walk the path yourself. There will be more on this below.

The importance of karma within the Buddhist system is beautifully illustrated in the story of the awakening of Shakyamuni. As he sat under the Bodhi tree, deep in meditation, he perceived his many past lives. Indians considered this ability to be common among great yogis. From reviewing these lives, he saw that an action taken in one life had its result experienced at a later time or in a later life. For him karma was no longer a theory but was a living memory. This experience also gives him the wisdom to understand how we continually entrap ourselves in all kinds of situations.[15] Unlike other philosophers of his day who called for people to stop acting and thus stop making new karma, the Buddha's idea was to focus on making wholesome merit and use the resulting fortunate circumstances to hasten one's path to liberation. The viewing of his past lives and the wisdom about karma that he acquired is central to the account of Shakyamuni's awakening. However, scholars have argued that the karma theory may not have been very central in the earliest phases of Buddhism. That is not to say it was dismissed or argued against. On

Chapter 4

the contrary, it was always present but just not as integral. Other scholars have argued the opposite.[16] They hold it is central to understanding early Buddhism although differentiated from both the Hindu theory and the theories held by other philosophers.

Commonly, the Buddhist texts use the metaphor of a seed to discuss karmic merit.[17] You individually have whatever karmic seeds you generated but this would include the development of merited outcomes that only effect you, or that effect you and your family or friends, or that effect you and your community, or that effect you and your country, or that effect you and your planet, or that effect you and the universe. An example of the first would be if I called you a profane name to your face and you punch me in the nose. An example of the second would be if a wife took all the family money and gambled it away and the family does not have the rent. An example of the third would be if your community experienced draught and everyone had to move elsewhere even though you had the foreknowledge to dig a well. An example of the fourth would be if a country decided to allow a second country to be its defence and then at a crucial moment the second country did not act. An example of the last item would be that all beings in the realm of rebirth at the time of the end of the universe, will experience those end days which includes the degeneration of the physical universe as well as much spiritual malaise.

Actions can be dived into those associated with the body, speech or the mind.[18] Thus, one can generate karmic seeds related to any one of these spheres or in any combination of the three. Just like a mixed bag of seeds when broadcast, develop according to the nature of the seed and the circumstances it falls in, so too the karmic seeds. Some actions result in immediate effect. For example, drinking too much alcohol will make you vomit. Some karmic seeds require a long time before they sprout. Some karmic seeds meet needed circumstances quickly and some require the long accumulation of circumstances. Here is an example for the

Buddhist texts about such a long accumulation of circumstances before the karmic seeds could sprout.

The kingdom of the Shakya people was to the north of one of the venerable kingdoms in India called Koshala. Over the centuries Koshala had garnered more and more power and influence so that the smaller kingdoms nearby needed to be diplomatic. King Pasenadi of Koshala who lived one generation before Shakyamuni Buddha, demanded a Shakya princesses for his wife. This is because the Shakya were thought to be decedents of the sun god. Instead, they sent a maid disguised as a princess because they felt that the king of Koshala was too low to warrant a Shakya princesses. Virudhaka was born from this marriage and when he visited the Shakya kingdom it slipped out that his mother was not of noble birth but was low-born. Seeing this as an insult to his father and an irreversible black mark on him, he vowed vengeances. Later he usurped his father's thrown and then led an army to destroy the Shakya.[19] Many Shakyas were killed, the remainder fled in the four directions and the kingdom was absorbed. Virudhaka lived at the same time as the Buddha Shakyamuni.

Because Buddhist view causation as more like a web or a biosphere, then many different points that intersect need to be in place for the whole to hold together. As noted before, a swamp may not be a wonderful place but it can be a healthy biosphere. Mosquitos carrying diseases and generally pesky to humans are an essential member of this sphere. If we spray killing all the mosquitos, then the animals that rely on them are also affected. As the effects accumulate and expand the biosphere changes. With karma, many different conditions sometimes need to be in place for a particular seed to sprout. Thus, one can easily see that discussing a particular action within this web of causes and conditions or trying to speak generically of all possible causes and conditions rapidly become unimaginable. Not only in the generation of unwholesome merit is this complex web of causality

Chapter 4

determinate but also in the maturing of the karmic seed it can bring about mitigations, extenuation, augmentation, *et cetera*.

The karmic seeds are stored in one's mental stream and are carried over from moment to moment or from one life to the next. When they mature meeting the right circumstances, they produce situations and predispositions as mentioned above. If you steal from someone in this lifetime and don't make recompense for your wrongful action, when you meet in a future life you will owe something. That is the circumstance, but it is usually subconscious. An example of a predisposition would be given a confrontational circumstance one person may be predisposed to fight while another would be predisposed to walk away. The karmic seeds you generated in the past is what determines those predispositions. However, having free will, the person who is predisposed to fight can decide to walk away. Usually if he or she fights then more unwholesome merit is made, if he or she walks away wholesome merit is produced.

The generation of minor unwholesome merit usually have their effects in this lifetime like being caught in a lie. Major unwholesome merit can be carried across lifetimes. There is also the possibility that an action may not produce a karmic seed. That is the act is neither wholesome nor unwholesome. Karmic results are spoken about as being fixed or unfixed. That is, certain acts always have the same result at the same time whereas the results generated by other acts will be modified by other karmic seeds or the circumstances encountered. An example of fixed karma would be killing a Buddha or killing one's parents which results in one going directly to hell upon death. In the natural world, seeds that fall close together when they are broadcasted will have an effect on each other. The one that sprout early will overshadow the later ones causing them to be less developed. Or the one that spreads its roots faster may deny important nutrition to the others.

As we can see above, the determining factor to the outcome or fruit in the system is whether or not an action by body, speech or mind is wholesome. Wholesomeness is determined in general on the physical plane (called the realm of desire) by whether the act causes suffering. One conceives of an action usually driven by desire which has as its base a strongly held false notion of a self needing or wanting whatever. If in trying to fulfill that desire, you intentionally cause suffering for other sentient beings than the act is deemed to be unwholesome. This only applies to sentient beings; those who have senses and therefore can experience suffering. Non-sentient things can not suffer and so you cannot create unwholesome merit in relations to them. That is if I hit a rock with a stick there is no karmic seed generated because neither the rock nor the stick has any sense. If, on the other hand, I make intentional suffering for an insect there is unwholesome merit generated. This negative merit falls on a scale. More precisely, killing an insect is not as bad as killing a cow which again is not as bad as killing a person. The creation of these karmic seeds due to one's desires is what keeps the realm of rebirth on going.

The generation of massive amounts of wholesome merit does not get you out of the realm of rebirth but only a better station within it. No matter how much good I may produce in the world, even saving the whole world, will not win me nirvana. It may only produce a better station within this realm. As humans are seen as better off than members of the animal world, acquiring a human life takes considerable wholesome merit. Even within that human life, some are born in wonderful circumstances where there is plenty of food, shelter, and the country is at peace. Such bounty would take even more wholesome merit. Even then some acquire wealth and position easily which requires even more wholesome merit. Compiling a mountain of wholesome merit can get you reborn in heaven as a god. This, however, is really a mixed blessing. Because the gods live a very long time according to human

Chapter 4

reckoning, and because whatever they desire magically appears according to them thinking about it, they have little impetus to practice Buddhism allowing them to gain liberation. Although this is not always the case and the Buddhist texts do mention some of the gods and in particular Indra (i.e., Jupiter) as attending the Buddha's teachings. Human life being a mix of "fortune" and "misfortune," is more suitable to providing an appropriate situation to motivate one to practice both the making of wholesome merit and Buddhist teachings to gain liberation.

The opposite of heavenly birth is also true and even the gods are not free from the effects of the karmic seeds they have generated. Although the gods live incredibly long periods of time compared to humans eventually the wholesome merit that generated the god life is exhausted and the god will be reborn into another life according to whatever karmic seeds mature at that time. This often means being born in a lower station. From lowest to highest the stations are: hell beings, ghosts, animals, humans, titans (*asuras*) and gods. Regardless of what station one is born into, none of them are permanent and so you will eventually be born out of one station and into another. There is no idea of spiritual evolution in Buddhism. There are no learnt lessons of which the accumulated wisdom guarantees a better rebirth. It is simply a cause and effect scheme. Liberation from the realm of rebirth is produced from insight. Although there is an indirect relationship between insight and karma, there are cases of individuals who had amassed a significant amount of unwholesome merit becoming liberated. Evolutionary reincarnation was first conceived in the declining years of the nineteenth century and is not part of Buddhist doctrine.[20]

Liberation from this endless cycle is only had with the gaining of nirvana. Karma is not part of the nirvana realm because there is no longer the false sense of a self or soul. This false idea of a self or soul is a prerequisite for there to be some phenomena wherein the karmic seeds can be stored. However, since one who is free of a sense of self cannot act selfishly, then all of his or her actions are wholesome. This accounts for the Buddhas' activities while still among us. Having a human life, a comfortable and safe environment, adequate free time, and other benefits allows one to pursue spiritual activities leading to liberation. Some of these may be wholesome merit making such as aiding the poor, some may be out of compassion disregarding the merit, but some may be geared to gaining wisdom from direct insight such as meditation.

One could argue that in the early development of the idea of karma within Buddhism the notion was simpler and more literal as well as mechanical. Killing is bad so any killing is the creation of unwholesome merit. Maintaining malicious thoughts towards another is bad so any malicious thoughts creates unwholesome merit. Early writings place more emphasis on the desire that drives our actions. As time passed and Buddhist thinkers explored these ideas, they determined that because the mind underlies all actions of body, speech and mind, then it is really one's intention that comes to the fore and not just the desire or the simple act. We can easily understand that although I have no malevolent intention in mind and may even try to be kind, sometimes an act can produce unforeseen negative consequences. How could it be justified to suffer negative karmic results when one tried to do something good? Thus, by putting the emphasis on intentions the model of actions being divided into the three spheres of body, speech and mind is maintained but the force of the intention takes on a significant role in the production of merit instead of the desire or the mere activity.

Another way to look at this is that any particular action is not in itself good or bad; that is produces wholesome or unwholesome merit. It is the circumstances and one's mind set that makes it thus. Even killing is not always bad. Killing for selfish reasons is bad but killing for selfless reasons is good. For example, in

Buddhism suicide is unacceptable in general. However, a brave soldier throwing his body on a grenade to save his friends even though it is suicide and thus killing, it is wholesome because it was done for selfless reasons. The intent is what makes the difference.

Once the Buddha, in a life before he became a Buddha, while still training, was leader of 500 merchants returning home by sea. A robber onboard planned to kill all of them and steal their merchandise. Learning of the intent of the robber and with no other way, the leader killed him.[21] This not only saved the 500 merchants, but it also saved the robber from the negative karmic seeds generated from killing so many people. One can suppose this or that and make arguments regarding the appropriateness of this action. The tradition holds it up as an example of compassionate killing. It is not difficult to imagine that circumstances can arise where compassionate killing is a possibility. The tradition however is not clear on the type of merit such an act generates. Some texts are inclined in the direction that the one in training must be willing to take on the unwholesome merit and thus willing suffer the pangs of hell (although hell is temporary). Other texts seem to present the idea that having good intentions and since one generated wholesome merit by saving the 500 merchants and even prevented the robber from creating so much unwholesome merit, the merit accrued to the one in training on balance would be wholesome. This conflict in interpretations is never resolved.

A major philosophical problem arises when viewing the concept of karma in connection with the concept of no-self or no-soul. Since there is no soul, what caries the karmic seeds over time. Elsewhere in the volume, I spoke about Angulimala. This is the serial killer who wanted to kill the Buddha but coming into his presence he became a disciple. Eventually, Angulimala became a Worthy one (Arhat) and gained awakening but his life as a monk was difficult because of the unwholesome merit he had generated. For example, when he went to beg for food as all monks did in those days, the common people would throw rocks at him.

This is explained within the tradition in this way. Nirvana has two phases referred to as "with remainder" and "without remainder." The first is when your mind is liberated by insight, but you are still living in the world and thus still have the karma associated with your living. So, like all people, you still need to eat, drink, and find shelter. Whatever personal merit you generated may also have its effects. Upon your death or "nirvana without remainder" the karma associated with your body, speech and/or mind is exhausted. While Angulimala was still living even though he personally had gain insight and was liberated, he still had to suffer the negative merit he generated although much mitigated. Upon his death, he was never reborn slipping from the sphere of rebirth.

Also as already mentioned, Buddhism does not accept the idea of a self or a soul, but it does talk about a mind stream. This mind stream is a changing phenomenon although some aspects of it can last over multiple lives. Because of this, it can be the store of the karmic seeds. Of course, as already indicated above, much of this is transpiring at a subconscious level. There are stories of a rare individual who can remember his or her past life or lives, but for most of us the rebirth process moves the memory of the previous life or lives into the subconscious. Advance abilities of meditation are supposed to free up these memories just as it did with Shakyamuni Buddha.

Various humanist and free thinkers hold that it is possible to have a viable morality without God. In a limited sense Buddhist can be said to agree with this position. It seems to me however, that this would be overstating the Buddhist position and placing it within the wrong company. For Buddhist, the universe has an ever present "moral" aspect for those who are still bound be

Chapter 4

rebirth within it. This would include all beings in any of the realms of possible rebirth from the lowest hell to the highest heaven. I put quotations around "moral" to indicate that within Buddhism this is understood as spiritual good health and not either a secular ethical system or a belief about right or wrong behavior based on commandments. Given this caveat, we can speak of Buddhist morality. At a higher level of analysis, both Buddhist and Christians agree that morality is based on a transcendent reality. For Christians that reality is God and for Buddhist it is the universe itself.

At the highest level of reality, Buddhist hold that all is one (technically called "not-two"). Therefore, differentiating morality from anything else would be to make a bifurcation and hence negate the enterprise. However, for all those within the realm of rebirth, which is the reality that all except the awakened are dealing with, morality is imminent. It is similar to when we think of the physical universe gravity is imminent. It is gravity that keeps us earth bound, keeps the earth spinning around the Sun, and keeps our solar system within the Milky Way. In a sense of speaking, it is that the universe itself has as a spiritual function–morality. That is according to Buddhist understanding, after being reborn countless times one comes to the thought that while in the realm of rebirth one suffers. As noted, the Buddha once asked his attendant which is greater the waters in all of the seas or the tears you have cried in all of your lives? Since it is natural for all sentient beings to not want to suffer, then one conceives of the idea of becoming free from suffering. This in turn leads one to realize that spiritual health (i.e., morality) is important. Although Buddhist will concede that morality has a large gray zone, upon final analysis, it is not much different than Christian morality. Killing, lying, stealing, disrespecting one's parents and overindulging in sense pleasures are in general understood as producing negative consequences. Desiring (coveting) is heavily condemned. Bearing false witness is discussed under lying. Adultery is part of overindulging in sense pleasures. There may be a rare occasion where killing or other unmoral activities are in fact moral, for the most part and for most people this is not the case.

One of the major problems in understanding Buddhism in the West is considering it to be atheistic. I am not aware of one example in the thousands of Buddhist scriptures where it states that the gods do not exist conventionally. In fact, the gods are often mentioned. Some gods are mentioned frequently such as Indra (i.e., Jupiter) and Yama (i.e., Pluto) and some very infrequently. They are however, often mentioned. Therefore, one cannot say that Buddhism is atheistic. Further, the sense of the spiritual is placed very differently in the Buddhist conceptualization of the universe than how it is placed in the western way of thinking. Yet, it is not absent. Because of these factors, "morality" as explained above, is not secular. Although not based on God's commandments it is spiritual and perhaps even more demanding that Christian morality. How is this? Immoral Christians may be saved from the consequences of their sins through the agency of Christ. Buddhist can only hope to mitigate the negative merit they have generated through generating wholesome merit. As stated, there is no savior in Buddhism. The positive side of this thought is that it ought to drive Buddhist to the highest levels of moral behavior.

Conclusion

The notions of sin and karma within Christianity and Buddhism, respectively, are not equivalents, though they both reflect twin convictions. The first of these convictions they hold in common: that all is not right with the world. The second of these differ in their scope. Whereas Christianity locates the culpability for wrongdoing, suffering, and evil in the world within the responsibility of human agents, Buddhism takes a broader view in stating that all sentient beings have a role in what has gone wrong. Sin and Karma also differ in their definition and point of reference. For Christians, sin is first of all understood as a violation of what God has desired for human life. This was expressed mythically in the narrative of the fall of the first humans in the Garden of Eden. Having been instructed to not eat the fruit of the tree of knowledge of good and evil, the first humans did so, and in violating the divine command became aware of their finitude and vulnerability expressed in the shame of nakedness. On the other hand, karma is simply expressed as action and is understood to be a law operative on the spiritual plane. It is neither good nor bad, but rather is the merit which is due in accordance with one's actions.

These differences can be understood in light of the discussions on original sin and the nature of karma. Augustine argued that original sin was both congenital and inveterate. Additionally, it was passed along generationally through the act of sexual procreation thus affecting the entirety of humanity. Thomas Aquinas differed in his understanding, giving original sin a social interpretation rather than a genetic one. The latter of these was more able to adapt to modern, scientific understandings of the emergence of humanity in the light of evolution. With this the relational aspect of sin were emphasized in order to illustrate how the early Hebrew myths understand the divine curses impacting various human relationships: with each other, with other species, with the soil, and with God.

In articulating the role of karma with the metaphor of a biosphere the relational capacities in the effects of karma are also emphasized. Here actions' merited outcomes can affect the agent, the agent's close family and friends, the whole community or country, and even the planet and universe. However, these actions are not only negative. The metaphor of planting seeds is a helpful and prominent way of understanding this. A person might "plant" both wholesome seeds and unwholesome seeds. The outcomes of these actions are the fruit of the seeds that are planted. Some seeds have immediate effect and are within a narrower frame of influence while other seeds require a long accumulation of circumstances and time before the fruit may sprout. Some of these seeds may influence across lifetimes whilst others are seen within one's present life experience. The determining factor in whether one's karma result in positive or negative fruit is whether one's action in body, speech, or mind is wholesome or unwholesome.

Within Christianity, the remedy for sin is redemption, which is the work of God upon human lives, history, and relationships. This is the work of God and is experienced prior to the resurrection in the sacraments of baptism and reconciliation. Whereas baptism is the gift of Jesus Christ to the Church to heal a person of the effects of original sin, reconciliation is the sacrament of confession and making amends for the grave commissions of mortal sins and the less severe, though still serious venial sins. These sacraments are communications of divine grace and presence to those within the Christian community, though ultimate redemption within God's salvific work is a broader affair.

Different from this is the Buddhist notion of liberation. While karma is formed by the wholesome or unwholesome merit which is the fruit of the seeds one planted in one's lifetime, an awakening to the fortunate or unfortunate circumstances these create indicates a path toward liberation from the karmic cycle. Illustrative of this is the story of the awakening of Shakyamuni, who in perceiving his past lives saw karma more as a living memory rather than only a theory. This offered Shakyamuni the wisdom to understand how the seeds of one's actions implant within the biosphere of life present and can potentially impact future lives. The insight and wisdom that arises from the awakening is liberation from the realm of rebirth. Nirvana is gaining liberation from this endless cycle.

Both Christianity and Buddhism understand that there is harm, fault, and negativity present in the world, and both see how humanity has a role in these. Whereas Christianity sees sin as more congenital and unavoidable, Buddhism's sense of karma allows for both wholesome and unwholesome merit to result from human actions depending on the fruit of the actions. Christians affirm that redemption by God's action is needed to solve the problem of sin whereas Buddhism reflects on the insight gained in understanding karma to the eventual liberation from the endless cycle of rebirth.

---

[1] Ian A. McFarland, *In Adam's Fall: A Meditation on the Christian Doctrine of Original Sin* (Oxford: Wiley Blackwell, 2010), 3.

[2] Claus Westermann, *Genesis 1–11: A Continental Commentary* trans. John J. Scullion S.J. (Minneapolis: Fortress Press, 1994), 178–275.

[3] E.A. Speiser, *Genesis* (New York: Doubleday & Company, Inc., 1987).

[4] See his personal accounts in Saint Augustine, *The Confessions* trans. Maria Boulding, O.S.B. (New York: Vintage Books, 1997).

[5] Rudi A. te Velde, "Evil, Sin, and Death: Thomas Aquinas on Original Sin" *The Theology of Thomas Aquinas* Rik Van Nieuwenhove and Joseph Wawrykow eds. (Notre Dame: University of Notre Dame Press, 2005), 143–166.

[6] See Karl Rahner, *Foundations of Christian Faith: An Introduction to The Idea of Christianity* trans. William V. Dych (New York: The Seabury Press, 1978), 106–115; Karl Rahner, "Christology Within an Evolutionary View of the World" *Theological Investigations Volume 5* trans. Karl-H. Kruger (Baltimore: Helicon Press, 1966), 157–192.

[7] Friedrich Schleiermacher, *The Christian Faith* eds. H.R. Mackintosh and J.S. Stewart (Edinburgh: T & T Clark, 1999), §72.3, 4.

[8] For a helpful discussion on this, see Carol Meyers, *Discovering Eve: Ancient Israelite Women in Context* (New York: Oxford University Press, 1988).

[9] Thomas Aquinas, *On Evil* trans. Richard Regan (New York: Oxford University Press, 2003), 55–62 [*De Malo*, 1.1].

[10] See John Calvin, *The Bondage and Liberation of the Will* trans. G.I. Davies (Grand Rapids: Baker Books, 2002).

[11] John Calvin, *Institutes of the Christian Religion*, trans. John T. McNeill (Philadelphia: The Westminster Press, 1960), 252. [Vol. 1, Book II Ch. 1]
[12] *The Compact Edition of the Oxford English Dictionary* (Oxford: Oxford University Press, 1971), 658.
[13] All quotations from *ibid.*
[14] Vasubandhu. *Karmasiddhiprakarana The Treatise on Action by Vasubandhu* trans. Fr. Étienne Lamotte /trans. Eng. Leo M. Pruden (Berkeley: Asian Humanities Press, 1988), 15.
[15] A.K. Wader, *Indian Buddhism* (Delhi: Motilal Banarsidass, 1980), 48.
[16] Johannes Bronkhorst. "Did the Buddha Believe in Karma and Rebirth," *Journal of the International Association of Buddhist Studies,* vol. 21, no. 1, (1998), 1-20.
[17] See Vasubandu *op cit.*, 30.
[18] *Ibid.* 16.
[19] Akira Hirakawa, *A History of Indian Buddhism From Sakyamuni to Early Mahayana* trans. Paul Groner (Delhi: Motilal Banarsidass, 1993), 36.
[20] This theory is first developed within the writings of the Theosophists.
[21] Garma C.C. Chang, ed. *A Treasury of Mahayana Sutras* (University Park: The Pennsylvania State University Press, 1983), 456.

Chapter 5
Salvation and Liberation

Salvation

Christians view the history recounted in the Hebrew and Greek scriptures, along with the perception of God's ongoing action within the life of the Church, as expressing God's saving humanity and all of creation from the pernicious effects of sin. The fulcrum of this history is the life, death, and resurrection of Jesus of Nazareth, who is affirmed to be the incarnated, second person of the divine Trinity. While Christians offer near universal affirmation of these fundamental points, there are particular questions remaining which complicate one's understanding of salvation. For example, in what manner is a historically contingent event, or series of events, efficacious for a trans-generational and ongoing phenomenon such as universal humanity? Why must salvation come about from the death of a single representative? What role does affirmation of the resurrection have in the Christian articulation of salvation? These questions have proven to have perennial relevance and have been the source of much controversy in the history of Christianity. In what follows, a brief sketch will be given that addresses some of these issues.

First, the centrality of the historical crucifixion of Jesus in the first century has always been paramount.[1] In the first century, St. Paul declared in his letter to the Christians in Corinth, "but we proclaim Christ crucified." Later in the same letter, he emphasized that he knew nothing among the Corinthian cohort "except Jesus Christ, and him crucified." However, interpretations as to how the death of Jesus was made efficacious for human salvation have varied and been the source of disputations. Prominent among the interpretations is the Satisfaction model, which was definitively articulated by St. Anselm of Canterbury in the eleventh century. Anselm argued this view in his book entitled *Cur Deus Homo* (Why God Man?).[2] In doing so, Anselm links the satisfaction theory with the rationale for the incarnation. The satisfaction theory states that, with its rebellion, humanity had brought dishonor to God, much in the way a disobedient and obstinate serf would to a lord in feudal society. However, no one human is able to repay the debt since that human, too, has sinned. The requirement needed to restore the debt of humanity is beyond any one human being's capacity. In taking on humanity, the second person of the Trinity fulfilled humanity's obligation of perfect obedience and paid the debt owed to God. Therefore, the humble willingness to die on behalf of humanity was a perfect surplus of obedience and thus restored God's honor. In substituting himself for humanity, Jesus Christ offered and completed what sinful humanity was unable to do, thus restoring humanity's relationship with God.

Akin to the satisfaction model, though not identical with it, is the Penal substitution view.[3] This interpretation maintains that with human rebellion and sin, the necessity of God's punishment and wrath was incurred. The requirement of justice for wronging God must be maintained for God to be true to himself,[4] and so God was either unwilling or unable to simply forgive without balancing the scales of justice through some form of recompense. However, to incur the just wrath of God would necessitate humanity's eternal separation from God and therefore be an affront to God's love. On this reading, to offend the God of eternity is an infraction understood qualitatively, rather than merely quantitatively in terms of temporal succession, and therefore requires eternal recompense. The solution was that the second person of the Trinity, in the person of Christ, would bear the weight of divine wrath as a substitutionary sacrifice on behalf of humanity. In doing so, the mandates of both divine justice and divine love are satisfied. Penal substitution was given expression most poignantly by the early Protestant Reformers in the sixteenth century and has been a common feature of Protestant Christianity to this day. Versions of this theory appeared in Martin Luther, Ulrich Zwingli, and Philip Melanchthon. It was argued that by incurring the totality of God's wrath, Christ did away with the need for central features in Catholic piety such as good works, confession, and the doctrine of purgatory (purification of a person prior to entrance in heaven). While Satisfaction and Penal theories are typically found in Catholicism and Protestantism respectively, variants of these are shared and found across Christianity's spectrum.

Third, there is an ancient interpretation of Christ's work to accomplish salvation called the Ransom theory. The Ransom theory holds that in sinning humanity came under the power and dominion of Satan. Since humanity was sold over to the devil, they had to be purchased back from evil to enter into a blissful relationship with God. The notion of a ransom needing to be paid to Satan has been widely criticized despite its ancient lineage. Lutheran scholar, Gustav Aulén augmented the theory in terms of *Christus Victor*.[5] In the framework of *Christus Victor*, the crucifixion and resurrection were not a ransom to be paid, but rather a victory over fallenness, sin, and ultimately death. In this setting, ransom is not to be seen as a transaction as it is a liberating event rescuing humanity from its negative condition.

Each of these accounts has focused on the crucifixion of Jesus Christ and has attempted to explain its soteriological efficacy (how it was effective for salvation). These theories are not the only ones which have been proposed in the history of the Church, but they have occupied a place of prominence. Despite this, each leaves open questions regarding the manner in which other aspects of Christ's life impact salvation.[6] For example, if the cross is the central soteriological event, then what is the specific role of the resurrection? To quote St. Paul's letter to Corinth once more, "If Christ has not been raised, your faith is futile, and you are still in your sins." Moreover, what salvific place does the life, ministry, miracles, and relationships of Christ have within Christian thought and practice? In addition to these important questions, the above theories still leave open the issue of how Christ's work for salvation is appropriated by people historically removed from the event in the first century CE.

The ancient doctor of the Church, St. Gregory of Nazianzus (c.325–389 CE) famously stated, "That which was not assumed is not healed; but that which is united to God is saved."[7] In saying this, St. Gregory was highlighting the importance of the incarnation to salvation. It was not only that the second person of the Trinity died, but that this person died as a human being. This was highlighted in the above theories, but it also expands upon the theme. As Jesus encountered the world, he did so as a creature and thus united the created world with God. Roman Catholic Christians highlight this making present divinity in the created order as sacrament. St. Thomas Aquinas in the thirteenth century wrote that God's presence in the particular sacraments of the Church was made possible by the incarnation making the created order open to the sacramental divine presence of God.[8] Therefore, as we read the Gospels' descriptions of Jesus in relationship with people from all walks of life, see him interact with nature (Mark 5:35–41) and animals (Mark 1:13), raise the dead (John 11:38–44), forgive sins (Matthew 9:1), or when he commissions and breathes the Spirit onto people (John 20:21–22) we see the salvific, sacramental presence of God at work. This presence is seen to be that which produces changes in people and the wider world, bringing them into fuller communion with God, and therefore saving in nature.

Chapter 5

The question of how this presence and the overcoming of sin and death in the events of crucifixion and resurrection become efficaciously present for those historically removed from personal encounters with those realities is given articulation in the doctrine of pneumatology; that is, the Christian affirmations of the Holy Spirit. In the fourth gospel, just prior to Jesus' arrest, he speaks to his disciples of his leaving them, but also that he would send a comforter. This comforter is the Holy Spirit, whose coming and transforming presence was instrumental in the institution of the Church in the New Testament book of Acts. While Jesus founded the Church upon Peter as the rock, to whom he gave the keys of authority, the Spirit's presence in the Church made the historically contingent work of Christ in his life, death, and resurrection, efficacious to a people whose trans-historical continuity would be ensured through the passage of space and time. This is most notable in the sacraments of the Church.[9] Christ's presence in the sacraments is operative through the presence of the Spirit to the glory of God. Therefore, the sacraments operate for the ongoing work of salvation throughout the life of the Church and the world.

For Catholic Christians, conversion to Christ is not a singular event, but is rather an ongoing process of continually being changed and saved with the divine aids of the sacraments, prayer, community, and learning. The personal reality seen in each is the existential expression of the historical work of salvation experienced in the continuity of the Spirit's presence in the Church, in history, and in making Christ present in the sacraments.[10] As such, human life and history become sacramental realities as the continuity and constancy of God's presence through the Spirit aids human life in its various modes of life. This, too, expresses the implications of the phrase of St. Gregory quoted above. Christ took on all of the vicissitudes and contingencies of human life and so each of these receive the benefits of salvation. Some Christians, particular Protestant evangelical Christians, often view conversion to salvation as a particular moment expressed in a decision to assent to the reality of Christ's work and to believe in it. The remainder of Christian life is expressed in terms of increasing fidelity to Christ's call to holiness, that is, sanctification. While Catholic Christians certainly resonate with the call to holiness, there is a sense that such a stark polarization in the "before" and "after" of conversion bifurcates human life in a manner not consistent with the human experience of continuity or the Christian testimony to God's constant, faithful presence, regardless of human awareness or acknowledgment. It also seems to pair itself too closely with the historical European Enlightenment[11] necessity of intellectual assent, rather than the biblical testimony of faithfulness and love.

Simultaneously, the Protestant evangelical notion of salvation leaves open the question as to the efficacy of Christ's work as his alone. While evangelicals certainly believe that the death and resurrection of Christ's work is the source of salvation, there is a clear affirmation among these Christians that without assenting to this reality, in other words, without belief in this reality, a person is not saved. In framing the manner in such a way, evangelical Christians place an addendum of sorts upon the reception of salvation: belief. This addendum creates a tension in that the objectivity of Christ's work is not applied insofar as it is not subjectively appropriated through personal and intellectual assent. Therefore, salvation is made possible by Christ's life, crucifixion, and resurrection, but is not efficacious without belief. It is true that the biblical testimony does attest to sin's universality (Romans 3:23) and that sin is connected with death (Romans 6:23) and the biblical testimony links faith to peace with God. However, evangelicals posit this connection as a causal one and thus inserts human works (coming to believe by intellectual assent) as the actual mechanism of salvation (i.e., you become saved *by* believing in Jesus' death and resurrection). Thus, it can

Chapter 5

appear, in some ways of understanding evangelical doctrines of salvation, that human beings make a substantial contribution to their own salvation. In such theologies, death becomes the line of demarcation in terms of one's ability to appropriate this salvation. If one dies without the requisite intellectual assent, then such a person goes to hell. This is because in popular evangelical piety the objective and subjective aspects of salvation are elided.

Contemporary Catholic theologians differentiate between the objective and subjective dimensions of salvation. The objective dimension is the act of God in Jesus to accomplish salvation once and for all. The subjective dimension is the reception of that in a person's life and the lifelong pursuit of a life lived with God in fidelity to the Gospel.[12] This distinction is important because while the subjective appropriation of God's work is essential, human salvation is entirely reliant upon the objective dimension of Christ actions. The objective dimension is Christ's merits outside of our own action while the subjective dimension is the humble acknowledgment and acceptance of these merits within our experience. This is important because the subjective dimension does not speak to the scope of salvation, but only the manner of its participation in the earthly life of faith. The objective dimension of Christ's work provides the logic for understanding of the scope of salvation in history. Therefore, it is important to now address the scope of salvation in terms of the language of heaven, hell, resurrection, and the new creation.

Christians have long thought of heaven in multiple ways. Most importantly, heaven is described as being in eternal bliss having communion with God. Heaven is described metaphorically in scripture as fullness of life, a wedding feast, a kingdom, a heavenly city, paradise, and the experience of peace. Because of God's transcendence a person cannot experience unfettered access to the divine presence apart from God's making this possible. This is what Christ's resurrection accomplished in overcoming the power of death. As such, heaven is described by Catholics in terms of the beatific vision. The beatific vision is the hope Christians have for full communion with God. It is expressed in aesthetic language as it reflects the biblical claim that "we shall be like him, for we shall see him as he is" (1 John 3:2). Coinciding with this image is the importance of noting that this hope remains within the language of resurrection. Christians do not hope for salvation of souls, but rather the resurrection of the body. As such, salvation is an embodied reality even as Christ's own resurrection was such.

The emphasis on the resurrection of the body was prominent from the Church's outset (1 Corinthians 15) and is combined with metaphors of a transformed created order. This is expressed in the symbols of a new heaven and a new earth. Many symbolic descriptions of a redeemed world include peaceable living with animals and with the earth. In St. Paul's letter to the Romans, he speaks of the earth and created order itself longing for salvation. The famous prologue to the Gospel of John states that the Word took on flesh. Many contemporary theologians note that the more limited understanding of Christ taking on humanity limits his solidarity in ways that language of flesh can expand. Such scholars note that it is not an essential human nature that Christ took upon himself, but rather an embodied existence we share with other creatures. Such language may then cast new light upon St. Gregory's maxim: "That which was not assumed is not healed; but that which is united to God is saved." It was not only humanity that Christ assumed, but the more expansive category of flesh. This emphasis upon the physical can easily coincide with both the emphasis on the physical resurrection and the cosmic scope of Christ's significance, which St. Paul highlights in his letter to the Colossians.

This expansive view of salvation has not only received greater emphasis in contemporary theologies of creation. In contemporary Catholic theology it is also impacted ideas on the related topic of hell. Roman Catholics, along with all Christian traditions, teach the reality of hell. However, there has been tension throughout the history of the Church in reconciling a loving and powerful God who makes salvation possible and a God who condemns people to suffer for eternity. Additionally, the necessary humility recognizing the deficit of human knowledge of what occurs after death is important to accept. As early as the third century, the theologian Origen (ca. 184–254) put forward a form of apocatastasis. Apocatastasis is the doctrine that all will be saved, even the devil and his minions. This view was condemned at the Second Council of Constantinople (553 CE). However, it is debatable that Origen actually held the view ascribed to him. It is more likely that Origen advocated that all free willing beings would be saved provided they survived the purification of all that was sinful. This view is also echoed by St. Gregory of Nyssa (335–395 CE) who also calls the eternity of punishment into question and thereby opens the question of an expansive view of salvation for the majority. These themes have been echoed in contemporary Catholic thought, most notably in the work of Hans Urs von Balthasar. Balthasar carefully argues that universal salvation is a hope for the Christian, but it is not a doctrine.[13] Pope John Paul II reflected similarly when he wrote that one cannot even make a claim as to the final destiny of Judas Iscariot who betrayed Christ to death.[14] Similar trends can also be found in Protestant theology in emphasizing the objective dimension of Christ's work in salvation in the thought of Karl Barth, Jürgen Moltmann, and others.

In the light of these views the Catholic doctrine of purgatory may truly be seen as a doctrine of hope. Roman Catholics believe that because God will not have sin before him, and because people are not entirely without sin at the time of their death, additional purgation is required. Therefore, purgatory is a doctrine of hope because it points to one's end being eternal bliss. Moreover, purgatory speaks to God's faithfulness to complete the work of salvation begun with Christ and made efficacious through the Holy Spirit. God's continuous desire is to be in communion with creatures and because of the resurrection death is not a barrier to this loving pursuit. Therefore, purgatory is conceived as a space of purification. The recent teaching of the Church, rooted in its historical tradition and insight, is that there is reason to hope that this will result in an inclusive account of salvation.

Liberation

Although readers will find the word "salvation" and the more technical term "soteriology" used in many books on Buddhism, there is actually no comparable idea or technical term within the Buddhist tradition. In particular, "soteriology" is a misnomer in Buddhism. The goal of Buddhism is liberation from the cycle of samsara or rebirth and all that it implies. As already stated in the chapter "Sin and Karma," there is no concept of sin in Buddhism. Any single Buddha or all the Buddhas together are not savior figures and therefore do not save one from the burdens of sins. However, the Buddha does appear in a grouping of three. History may be exemplary but not causally connected with liberation. The fact that Siddhartha Gautama Shakya became the Buddha Shakyamuni and the act of his teaching the *Dharma* (Buddhism) in India more than 2,500 years ago is not a single significant in one's individual realization of liberation but may be an aid. Shakyamuni's birth and death are also not causally significant in the liberation process. Affirming that Siddhartha Gautama Shakya was indeed the Buddha is not even mentioned in the texts.

Buddhist understand that the current teachings are articulations by Shakyamuni but that they are expressions of universal truths as explained in the chapter "Sacred Texts." Those truths were not hidden and thus requiring revelation and they were not created by Shakyamuni. Each Buddha, including Shakyamuni whose expression we are still living with, provides teachings that help the beings in a certain place and during a certain time gain liberation. They cannot "save" one up to the goal of liberation also called nirvana. The Buddhas point the way and they assist just as any good teacher would help a student. Just as the student must learn for himself or herself, so too a disciple has to do the "work" of liberation on their own.

The Buddhist understanding of "history" is unique. In one text where the Buddha Shakyamuni lays out the differences between himself as a teacher and other teachers of his day, he is very critical of those who spend time on the materials of history.[15] That is things such as the stories of kings, war, society, etc. are from his point of view a waste of time. The reason being these do not promote one spiritually but only lead one astray. Therefore, in the earliest period, Buddhism did not have an over-arching historic narrative. It did have accounts of episodes in the life of the Buddha and some of the most famous disciples. It also had accounts of the first councils, and it began keeping track of the ordination lineage as the tradition grew and spread across India as a means of authentication. Yet, even though it had these elements it was not until a few centuries after the complete nirvana (*parinirvana*/ death) of Shakyamuni that the information was woven into a history. The purpose of this narrative was not the accurate recording of events nor to understand the past but was for pedagogic reasons. That is the tales of Shakyamuni, the famous disciples and great masters, were used to instill Buddhist virtues, to elucidate practices and to inspire later disciples. We can say that Buddhist history is instructive and not reconstructive. In this sense, the facts of the accounts are not as crucial as is the "moral" of the story. This orientation in the materials provides significant challenges for modern historians of Buddhism because the facts may not be altogether absent from the accounts.

Sitting in a heaven called Tushita, the Bodhisattva who would become Siddhartha Gautama gave his final instructions to the gods. In Buddhism a viable human life begins with the sperm, egg and mind stream (i.e., that which will be reborn) come together at the very moment of conception. The night of his conception, Siddhartha's mother dreamt she saw the Bodhisattva's mind stream had entered her womb. According to legend, the custom in the Shakya kingdom was that the expecting mother return to her parents' home to give birth. Shakyamuni's mother was the queen and in a royal procession was returning to her parents' home when about halfway, she gave birth in the beautiful Lumbini grove. The grove is still there. Indra (Jupiter) and the gods came down and bathed the infant. Various miraculous signs were manifested. Later, his mother dies and his aunt became his primary care giver.[16] In East Asia, this account is reenacted on the celebration of the Buddha Shakyamuni's birth. Usually a smaller statue of the baby Siddhartha Gautama Shakya standing in a basin will have tea ladled over it. Offerings are presented and there is usually an accompanying chant.

The "facts" of the future Buddha's birth are no different in nature from the "facts" of any person's birth. We all begin with the coming together of the mind stream, sperm and egg. Thus, Siddhartha Gautama was fully human. He was spiritually advanced, and this is indicated by the various miracles, but then each of us are at different stages in our spiritual progression. The historical event of the birth of a Buddha is significant but not necessarily causally connected with liberation. There are basically two types of Buddhas: the Complete Perfect Buddha and the private Buddha. According to most accounts, only one Complete Perfect Buddha can appear and live in the same locale during the

Chapter 5

same time frame. However, some texts grant that a private Buddha may appear when other Buddhas are already present.

One of the main responsibilities of a Complete Perfect Buddha is to reintroduce the teachings after the dispensation of a previous Complete Perfect Buddha has disappeared. This is why the universal truth of the teachings takes on specific expressions. Each Buddha being wise and understanding the needs and modes of his times, tailors the teachings to those people in those times. About 2,500 years ago in northern India/ southern Nepal, the Buddha Shakyamuni, who was a Complete Perfect Buddha, endlessly travelled from kingdom to kingdom teaching. Those teachings were especially efficacious for humans during several eons, in one of which we are currently living. However, if one were living at that time and met Shakyamuni, it was far easier to reach liberation than it is now. The Buddha could provide you with a specific teaching determined to exactly deal with your mind explains why it would be easier. Whereas now, we have to pick our way through many distractions, and multiple theories, and practices making things more difficult. This is comparable to taking a highway to one's destination or taking a winding road. Since a Buddha cannot "save" you even if you met him, you still must make the journey.

From earliest times, it has been held that a Buddha has more than one "body." The first way to look at this was that he had two "bodies." The "form body" i.e., his physical form and a "*Dharma* body."[17] This later is understood perhaps in two connected ways. That is, it is the body of the universal teachings embodied within a particular form body, or a particular form body as a manifestation of the teachings. Both of these two connotations can be summarized as the "body of the absolute." As time moved forward, a third body was added to the theory.

Some early schools of Buddhism held that once a person reaches liberation and enters complete nirvana that awakened one is cut off from this world. However, Shakyamuni actually never stated this. In fact, he left the explanation of the liberated state (nirvana) very open and vague on purpose. Mostly, we find negative statements about what liberation is not. Words like unborn, deathless, unconditioned, extinction of negative mentalities, abound in the descriptions provided by the texts. Positive statements on what the nature of the liberated state is, are rare. Perhaps the best example of this is "peace."[18] Some Buddhist in the past thought the idea of the Buddha Shakyamuni being cut off from the world was going beyond the very teaching he had provided, and they understood the Buddha as still being compassionate in the world even though he was liberated from it. This eventually leads to the development of an addition to the two body of a Buddha theory. The third body called "enjoyment body" is to account for the manifestation of compassion of a Buddha in our realm. This enjoyment body is akin to but not the same as western theories of an astral body. However, the enjoyment body is situated between the form body and the *Dharma* body. Further, it is not of subtle material. Although this three bodies of a Buddha theory has a long tradition of commentary within the Buddhist world, it is at its fundamental level based on experience.

The form body is a given and I shall not dwell on it here. The "enjoyment body" is experienced within visions of those who have a talent for certain types of meditations. Because of several doctrines within Buddhism "visions" are not understood as delusions or hallucinations necessarily (although these are clearly known) but as having a sense of reality. Just as our dream seems real as long as we are fully immersed in the dream our normal daily consciousness seems real as long as we are in samsara. With these types of arguments "reality" becomes relativized in Buddhism. Thus "visions" can be understood as just as "real" as the "reality" of being conscious. It may be analogous to a vision of the Madonna or other Christian figure although, I would want to be very careful with this comparison. The *Dharma* body as the absolute can also be experienced in deep levels of meditation and for the awakened, at all times.

There is a wonderful story about oneself doing the work necessary for liberation from Tibet. There once was a great yogi named Milarepa. He was very earnest in learning the teachings that would liberate him from the cycle of rebirth. He went to a famous teacher and requested the teachings. The teacher said to him, "My teachings are so great if you meditate on them in the night, that very night you will be liberated and if you meditate on them in the day that very day you will be liberated." He taught Milarepa the meditation and put him into a cell during the evening. After a couple of days the teacher went to see the disciple. Right away the master knew Milarepa was not liberated. He asked him what the cause was. Milarepa said that he had not done the work as he thought he would do it later. The master advised him to seek another famous teacher who would help purify his wrong thinking.[19]

That a Buddha is born is important as this occurrence will produce a fresh articulation of the teachings suitable for the place and time, but the birth does not make liberation possible. It also means that more people can be liberated as the path and the aids on the path are already prescribed. So, each person does not have to find their own way completely. Be this as it may, there are no sacraments for one to receive or participate in that mark one's life as a Buddhist. One's life as a Buddhist is only marked by the applications of the teachings to whichever extent possible by that each individual. The concept of sacrament is foreign to Buddhism. Birth, puberty and marriage, ceremonies are neither sacraments nor universally found in the traditions. Even becoming a monk or nun is not understood within the framework of sacerdotalism.

Christian-Buddhist Conversations

There is one school of Buddhism where the word "salvation" is often used in the English literature more than in discussing any other school. This school is called Pure Land Buddhism. It is the most popular form of Buddhism in China and Japan. It is based on texts that originate in India and teach about a Buddha named Amitabha. The primary texts to this tradition make it clear that by establishing a karmic connection with Amitabha one can be reborn in his Buddha field wherein attaining liberation is far easier than here in our world.[20] Also, by meditating on this Buddha (as with meditating on other Buddhas) one can obtain liberation. It is this rebirth into Amitabha's Pure Land that has too frequently been called "salvation." As the tradition developed in East Asia, it came to be understood that simply repeating the Buddha's name in a formula "I pay respect to the Buddha Amitabha" (Ch. *Namo Amito Fo*/ Jp. *Namu Amida Butsu*) mindfully, was sufficient to obtain rebirth in his realm. This is made possible because the individual who became the Buddha Amitabha spent countless lifetimes building up an immense store of positive merit which aids in establishing people on the path.

In the nineteeth century when Japan was modernizing two important events transpired that had an impact on how the Pure Land teachings were presented to the West. The first was the redefining of the Japanese concept "religion" to mean something based on belief instead of on ritual. This change in definition allowed for a dialogue in Japan to resemble western dialogues even though it was not truly representative. The second was Japanese scholars who had studied in Europe borrowed some Protestant ideology to try to explain Buddhism to fellow Japanese in a more "modern" manner. Interestingly enough, they even redesigned Pure Land priests' robes to resemble Protestant robes which was considered a more modern look. As the Japanese Buddhist were often the first Asians to bring the Buddhist intellectual tradition to the West, they used Protestant ideology and even technical terms in attempts to make something so very different understandable. This was particularly the case among the immigrant population in places like Canada and the United States of America. Although, the priests may well have understood the differences between their tradition and Protestant thought this attempt produced a number of problems.

One problem is that the Japanese living outside of Japan began seeing their own Pure Land thought in Protestant terms and many could no longer distinguish between their original tradition and the Protestantized Buddhism. This is to be expected as the world they were living in was a Protestant Christian world at the time. The second was that westerners became confused as the Pure Land form of Buddhism seemed in conflict with the forms they were coming to know from Indian and later Tibetan sources. Perhaps for the first two-thirds of the twentieth century the majority of western language publications on Pure Land Buddhism were produced by Japanese or from Japanese sources. This Protestantized Pure Land teaching style was also used by Chinese and others explaining Pure Land thought. It was not until the last part of the twentieth century that authors began changing the style and terminology used in discussion. Thus, for almost a century we have publications that misrepresent the Pure Land thought in western languages. It is in these publications that one will find the word "salvation" used in a Buddhist context more than in any other. This is simply a poor choice of terminology. There is no Buddhist technical term that comes close to "salvation."

Amitabha is a Buddha who most consider as being an enjoyment body manifestation without a form body here on earth. His Pure Land realm is understood as not being on the same level of reality as the earth. One could say it exists on the astral plan but there would be caveats as to the meaning of such a statement. He is not the only such Buddha and texts record the names of hundreds of these types of Buddhas. However, there are a few who garner more attention than others. Akshobhya Buddha although not historic was probably the most popular after Shakyamuni in India. Vairocana Buddha was popular in India but gained perhaps greater popularity in East Asia for a few centuries. The incredibly beautiful giant Buddha housed in the cleverly constructed Todai ji Temple in Nara, Japan is Vairocana.

In addition, there are many Bodhisattvas that are said to manifest on this same level. The most popular is Avalokiteshvara the Bodhisattva of compassion. This Bodhisattva in a female East Asian form appears similar to the Madonna although the image predates the introduction of Christianity. Manjushri the Bodhisattva of wisdom is another. Without a doubt, the most popular geographically is the Bodhisattva Maitreya who is considered to be the future Buddha on earth. He sometimes appears in many of these astral realms but also appears in heaven to teach the gods.

The Three Jewels is a technical term referring to the grouping of the Buddha, the Teachings, and the Community. It bears no similarity to the Christian concept of trinity. A Buddha or all of the Buddhas, are teachers, aids, spiritual doctors, guides and their lives are exemplary. The texts of the tradition and in general the monks, nuns, priests, and gurus within the tradition understand that a Buddha is distinct from the gods. Although in some folk traditions this distinction seems blurred. A Buddha can be seen as a father figure but throughout Asia one's teacher is usually seen as a second father; stern but loving in dispatching his responsibilities to his charges. Monks and nuns are sometimes referred to as Buddha's sons or daughters, but this is clearly understood as metaphoric language and there is no direct family relationship as exists between God and his son Jesus.

The Teachings are understood in both a limited and an expended sense. The first book ever printed was in China and was a Buddhist text called *The Diamond Sutra*. Printing allowed for the economic production of all the Buddhist teachings to be held

Chapter 5

in collections. Before, handwritten copies existed but to make a complete set was laborious. By tradition the Buddha Shakyamuni taught thousands of texts compiled into three collections: the *Sutras* (teachings on various topics), the *Vinaya* (encoded culture & rules for monastics) and the *Abhidharma* (systematic doctrine). In addition to these collections, the works of various great masters are also added to the entire canon. As noted in the chapter "Sacred Texts," there were debates as to particular texts being considered canonical. Thus, in a limited sense, only the teachings of the Buddha as found in the *Sutras*, *Vinaya*, and *Abhidharma* constitute the teachings. In the expanded sense, the teachings of the great masters would be added. This, however, does not mean that the teachings are limited to printed texts. Many schools within Buddhism maintain a living oral tradition and current master's explanations are also considered part of the Teachings.

The Community can be understood in the limited sense as the monks and nuns. However, in the Three Jewels formulation, it is the expended sense that is often used. In this case it includes: all Buddhas, Bodhisattvas, Arhats (Worthy ones), monks, nuns, lay men and lay women. Among the last four groups would be counted all the great masters both male and female. Some gods can also be included if that particular god vowed to protect the Teachings or is known to assist Buddhists. The gods of the four directions fall into this group and it is common that in East Asian Buddhist temples a gate house will host statues of the four for this reason.

As mentioned, the Teachings are universal and not constrained by any time factors. As such, whether a Buddha's teachings are active in the world or not, the truth remains the same. Realization of the goal of the Teachings is something within each of us and therefore is accessible although probability of success varies. The Teachings as articulated by any particular Buddha makes it easier to obtain liberation but does not make it accessible. That access is inherent in being. Therefore, there is no direct connection between the historic process and the fact of awakening to liberation. On the other hand, the Teachings of a particular Buddha are a great aid in the process as one does not have to search through the jungle of the cycle of rebirth to cut a path. The path is already cut and there are sufficient signposts and way stations for those who are willing to pilgrimage. This means that the unraveling of history is only secondarily connected with liberation.

Three months before his passing, the Buddha Shakyamuni predicted his upcoming death. He was requested to live longer but used the occasion to teach his disciples that everything must change. As the time approached, he was very ill, and he laid down between two trees in a grove. As the process of death was overtaking him, various marvels manifested like the playing of celestial music. The gods appeared and paid their final respects. The Buddha gave his final teachings and cleared up all the questions the disciples put forth. The king, his nobles, their families, and the commoners hearing that The Buddha was dying all quickly gathered in the grove. The Buddha continued to formally accept disciples right up to the last. When all was completed, the Buddha Shakyamuni entered into deep meditation and from there he exited into complete nirvana. Throughout Asia, one can see statues of the Buddha Shakyamuni laying on his right side in memory of this event.

The death of the Buddha Shakyamuni was much commemorated with music, and offerings, and the building of multiple large monuments. All the realms that he had visited were involved with the massive tribute. Kings, princes, warriors, ministers, great merchants, Brahmans, and a multitude of common people mourned his passing for days. Yet, his passing into complete nirvana in no way changed anyone's access to liberation. Shakyamuni is remembered as the great teacher and the most compassionate of men. Every year his birth and death as well as the day of his awakening are celebrated. This is not because he opened the way but because he provided an abundance of assistance.[21]

Some individuals hold that making the statement "I take refuge in the Buddha, Dharma (Teachings) and Sangha (Community)" is necessary to be a Buddhist. There are, however, people who self-identify as Buddhist who never made this statement. The distinction here may simply be based on a more elitist literary approach to the teachings and a folk approach. The cycle of rebirth from the highest heaven to the lowest hell is like a storm battering one with the winds of karma and the floods of suffering. So "refuge" in this case means a refuge from the storm. One finds shelter and a way out of the terrifying situation howling at the doorstep. In one teaching, the Buddha Shakyamuni said that gods, kings, mountain fastness, etc. are not real refuges because places can be stormed, and those other beings are themselves not liberated so they cannot offer liberation. This formalizing of commitment to Buddhist spirituality should instill in one this understanding that other refuges are not ultimate, that ending suffering is key to the process, and that antithetical teachings and its advocates should not be followed. It also implies that one ought to respect all representations of the Buddhas, the Teachings and the Community. This is a formal statement on one's turning to the Three Jewels as the way for spiritual growth. This also means that a religion such as Christianity does not have to be rejected as it is not antithetical whereas materialism should be because of its tenet that nothing survives death.

One does not have to affirm that Shakyamuni or Amitabha or any other Buddha is in fact the Buddha. Such an affirmation finds no textual expression and would make no difference. Shakyamuni is not a savior so affirming he is a Buddha or not is completely meaningless. There is a famous Zen story wherein the master told the disciple "If you meet a Buddha, kill him." What is meant is that reifying "Buddha" is only a hindrance which must be eliminated.

Liberation as stated above, is the freedom from samsara or the cycle of rebirth. Indians see that near endless cycle of rebirth to be the ultimate spiritual problem facing us. This cycle includes all things that are commonly knowable to humans and more. That is to say, all things from the highest heaven to the lowest hell are found inside this cycle. The problem comes about that nowhere in this cycle is there a place where suffering is not found. This is understood as a statement of fact and not a pessimistic view. To become a god, one must accumulate vast amounts of positive merit. It is this reward for a moral life that allows the gods a life where their thoughts are fulfilled. Even though living thousands of years by human standards, there comes a time when the merit becomes exhausted and the god dies to be reborn elsewhere. So even in heaven suffering is found. In the lowest hell suffering is produced by the negative merit one generated and it is continuous. There is no relief until one dies and is reborn in a better station. This explains the strong desire expressed in Indian thought to be free from the cycle.

In Buddhism, the real problem is understood to be within the mind and not the physical aspect. True, as long as we have a body, we must maintain it in a good state of health, but liberation does not mean freedom from the body. Each of us will be free of this body sooner or later. If we do not free our minds, we will have to acquire another body. That future body may be human or not, may be handsome or not, may be in a wonderful country or not, that all depends on the positive or negative merits we have made for ourselves. If we liberate our minds, then we will not be reborn.

It is needy neurotic energy that fuels the cycle. Buddhism speaks of three negative mentalities in this explanation. These are thirst, aversion and delusion. When one realizes the true nature of the energies of these three alone or in combination one will be

Chapter 5

free from the cycle. Thus, one lives the last life as an embodiment of liberation (i.e., nirvana) and upon death never returns. This give use two different scenarios there is freedom while still living and freedom after death which was discussed in the chapters "Sin and Karma."

The auditor's branch of Buddhism now represented by the Theravada school in Sri Lanka, Thailand and elsewhere, understand this liberation as a synonym for nirvana. It is simply the freedom from the three needy neurotic energies along with the pollutants that evolve from them. Once free, one is out of the cycle. The Mahayana, found from Nepal to Japan, understands two types or levels of nirvana the first being liberation from those neurotic energies and hence liberation from the cycle of rebirth. The second is called non-abiding nirvana. This later refers to the idea that Buddhahood is not constraining, and the Buddha can undertake awakened compassionate activity in this world post-mortem.

The Eight-fold Path is the way out of the cycle. This consists of appropriate: views, intentions, speech, actions, livelihood, effort, mindfulness and concentration. In short you should have the right view and the will to act upon the spiritual path. You should follow a particular code of moral behavior and you should gain a deeply calm mind and wisdom which is produced from concentration within the meditative tradition. The ability to dwell in a deeply calm mind itself comes about from mindfulness. This mindfulness allows the mind to slow down and stay focused. By entering into these deep states of calm, you can be free from the surface energies of the mind. This is akin to laying at the bottom of the ocean where the water is calm as compared to the surface where there is much wave action. Concentration leads to insight into the real nature of things and in particular the lack of any essence behind things and oneself. This is the freedom of wisdom. As the Buddhist tradition progressed more emphasis was placed on the gaining of insight as the primary agent to the wisdom that liberates.

There are a number of ways that liberation has been explained although ultimately no articulation is adequate. Liberation is another name for nirvana, the non-dual, and the unconditioned. Although nirvana and samsara (cycle of rebirth) are ultimately the same, it is often simpler to contrast them for people to understand. The cycle of rebirth can also be called the cycle of death as all things come to an end. Liberation is called the deathless. It is called the realm wherein one does not find wind, earth, fire, water, infinite space, infinite consciousness, nothingness, neither perception nor non-perception, the world, next world, sun, nor moon. Here the texts are not speaking about existence as such (ontology) but experience (epistemology). What is meant here is that our perceptions of things both exterior and interior to us, will no longer have the mental overlays that they now do. Thus, the earth is not the earth. However, this does not negate the statement that nirvana and samsara (cycle of rebirth) are the same. There is a famous Zen story that captures this. The Zen master was asked about his study of Zen. He said that when he began the mountain was the mountain. After studying Zen, the mountain was the mountain no more. Upon awakening the mountain was the mountain again.

This liberation is not some transcendence wherein the consciousness of a person abides disassociated from the world. First, since liberation means cutting through the illusion of a self, ultimately there is no person who can abide. There is also no world existing as other. Second in Buddhism consciousness means conscious of something. Although the experience of liberation can be said to be an awareness it is an awareness that is free of content. It cannot be consciousness as we normally think about it. There is also a being in the "momentness" that is part of the experience of liberation and this implies that the experience is not

Chapter 5

a transcendence because in the moment you are in the world. But you are in the world in a very different way than before. In recent times this has been described as being in the world not of the world. In addition, the experience of liberation is said to also involve bliss which in this case seems generated by the mentality of being free.

Conclusion

Salvation is understood as the saving of humankind from the effects of sin in a process that is documented as both having roots in the past and thus historic and as an ongoing relationship of God with the Church. The crucifixion of Jesus is central to the tradition as borne out by multiple passages in the scriptures. Yet, although this tenet is universally proclaimed, there are a divergence regarding how this single act can be efficacious for human salvation. One model is the satisfaction model originally expounded in St. Anselm of Canterbury's *Cur Deus Homo*. This explanation argues human's rebellion against God was a dishonoring of him. No human could repay this debt because all humans were stained with the sin. By becoming human, the second member of the Trinity was able to pay the debt with perfect obedience. His willingness to die for our sins was a surplus of obedience and this restored honor to God. This in turn, restores the relationship of humankind with God.

Another approach for understanding is the penal substitution model. God necessarily was filled with wrath and enacted punishment with the commission of the sin when human's rebelled. The requirement of justice must be addressed and hence God could not simply forgive. The justice of God's wrath would mean eternal separation from him but that would be an affront of his love. The resolution to this dilemma is found in the second member of the Trinity. Christ takes on the just wrath of God as a substitute for the whole of humanity. This allows the addressing of the injustice and the expression of divine love.

Yet another theory in understanding how the crucifixion can be efficacious, the Ransom theory posits that by their sin, humans entered the dominion of Satan. Thus, Satan had to be paid a ransom for humans to reenter the wholesome relationship with God. Another way to understand this theory is that the ransom is actually a victory over fallenness, sin, and death. Thus, it is a rescuing of humanity from its previous negative condition.

Based on statements in the Bible as well as St. Paul, St. Gregory, and elsewhere, Jesus was not merely taking on humaneness but was the Word becoming flesh. This notion of embodying existence allows for theological connections to be made with resurrection, Christ's cosmic scope and creation. Some modern theologians have been developing ideas along these theoretical lines which even recalls some very ancient topics within the greater tradition.

These four and others have graced the pages of many theological works in an attempt to illuminate the importance and plumb the depth of the most important event in Christianity. Jesus was both the second member of the Trinity and a human. This unique fact is also extremely important in these theories for if he had been only one or the other, the crucifixion in the first century would not have addressed all concerns and thus would not have been efficacious. Be this as it may, the continuing efficaciousness of that single event for present day humanity is explained with the doctrine of pneumatology. Jesus before his execution promised a comforter which is understood as referring to the Holy Spirit. The Holy Spirit's on-going presence in the Church makes the life, death and resurrection of Jesus efficacious in a trans-historical and thus ensured through time and place.

Although Christians can speak of liberation from the negative effects of sin, "liberation" in the Buddhist context has a completely different connotation. In Buddhism, liberation is understood as becoming free from the entire cycle of rebirth including all things from the heavens to the hells. There is neither a technical term meaning salvation nor soteriology in any of the primary canonical languages of Buddhism. Lacking a concept of sin, soul, and savior the entire notion of salvation along Christian lines is missing.

A grand historic narrative was not formulated within Buddhism until several centuries after the *parinirvana* (death) of the Buddha Shakyamuni. The importance of the birth, life, death, and nirvana of the Buddha does not make awakening possible and can only act to assist in one's own quest. This means that in Buddhism, history is pedagogic tool. The Buddha was not divine or the selected one but was born completely human although spiritually advanced. After gaining awakening through his own efforts, he taught and established a community. The Buddha's death was used as occasion to teach that all things change but again not as making awakening possible. After forty-five years of teaching and compassionate activity, the Buddha died, and the event is commemorated until today. In memory of this great teacher small ceremonies, grand monuments and more are dedicated to remembering his compassion.

All Buddhas are considered as having three bodies the form body, the enjoyment body ("astral body") and the Dharma body (=absolute). This teaching in no way resembles the Trinity as these bodies are of one being and appear simultaneously. The Buddha(s), Teachings and Community appear in a formulation representing the three supports (called the Three Jewels) to be adhered to for Buddhist. Many people consider the statement "I take refuge in the Buddha, Teachings, and Community" to be an expression of one's formal commitment to the Buddhist path.

A Buddha's teachings are universal truths, but each Buddha enunciates his own articulation of those truths to fit the times and place of their expression. Currently, we are still living under the teachings of Siddhartha Gautama Shakya (Shakyamuni). At some point in the future, date unknown, the current teachings will no longer be efficacious and "disappear." Then another Bodhisattva will take birth and become a Buddha, reintroducing the teachings but with his own expression.

Liberation in Buddhism means freedom from the cycle of rebirth. This cycle was seen in India as an endless source of suffering for all beings from the gods to the denizen in hell. Freedom from this cycle in Buddhism is understood as being within the sphere of the mind but it has certain physical aspects. Each person's neurotic energies are what fuels this cycle and therefore wisdom into thirsts, aversion, and delusion is needed. Currently, the Theravada school understand that freedom from these three energies is nirvana. The Mahayana branch of Buddhism understands freedom from these three as being freedom from rebirth but that complete nirvana requires freedom of non-abiding as well. That is the non-constrained active compassion in the post-*parinirvana* state. The way to achieve liberation is through the practice of the Eight-fold Path. "Liberation" is another name for nirvana and has many synonyms. Since liberation is a cutting through the delusion of the bifurcation of self and other, it is not a transcendent event. It is "a being in the world and not of the world."

---

[1] Joachim Jeremias, *Jesus and the Message of the New Testament* K.C. Hanson ed. (Minneapolis: Fortress Press, 2002), 1–17.

[2] See Brian Davies and G.R. Evans eds., *Anselm of Canterbury: The Major Works* (Oxford: Oxford University Press, 1998), 260–356.

[3] For a discussion and alternatives, see the nineteenth century Protestant Scottish theologian, J. McLeod Campbell, *The Nature of the Atonement* (Edinburgh: The Handsel Press, 1996).

Chapter 5

[4] Since God is the ground of being, the mandates of justice are commensurate with God's self and therefore God's will. St. Thomas Aquinas refers to God as the perfect unity of being and act.

[5] Gustav Aulén, *Christus Victor: An Historical Study of the Three Main Types of the Idea of the Atonement* trans. A.G. Herbert (London: SPCK Publishing, 1931).

[6] See Jürgen Moltmann, *The Way of Jesus Christ: Christology in Messianic Dimensions* trans. Margaret Kohl (London: SCM Press, 1990).

[7] This statement can be found in his epistle (101) on the Apollinarian Controversy.

[8] St. Thomas Aquinas, *Summa Theologiae* IIIa. q. 60–65.

[9] See Michael A. Fahey, "Church," *Systematic Theology: Roman Catholic Perspectives Second Edition* Francis Schüssler Fiorenza and John P. Galvin eds. (Minneapolis: Fortress Press, 2011), 317–368.

[10] Karl Rahner, "Personal and Sacramental Piety" *Theological Investigations Volume 2* trans. Karl H. Kruger (New York: The Seabury Press, 1975), 109–133; Karl Rahner, "Experience of the Spirit and Existential Commitment" *Theological Investigations Volume 16* David Morland O.S.B. (London: Darton, Longman & Todd, 1979), 24–34.

[11] See Dorinda Outram, *The Enlightenment Second Edition* (New York: Cambridge University Press, 2005).

[12] Hans Küng, *On Being a Christian* trans. Edward Quinn (New York: Doubleday & Company, 1976).

[13] Hans Urs von Balthasar, *Dare We Hope "That All Men Be Saved"?* trans. David Kipp and Lothar Krauth (San Francisco: Ignatius Press, 1988).

[14] John Paul II, *Crossing the Threshold of Hope* (New York: Knopf Doubleday Publishing, 1995).

[15] T.W. Rhys Davids, *Dialogues of the Buddha* (London: The Pali Text Society, 1977).

[16] See: Edouard Foucaux. (trans. Gwendolyn Bay) *The Voice of the Buddha: The Beauty of Compassion*. (Berkeley: Dharma Publishing, 1983).

[17] John J. Makransky. *Buddhahood Embodied*. (Albany: State University of New York Press, 1997), 54 *ff.*

[18] Richard H. Robinson and Willard L. Johnson. *The Buddhist Religion A Historical Introduction.* (4th ed.) (Belmont: Wadsworth Publishing Company, 1997), 13.

[19] W.Y. Evans-Wentz. *Tibet's Greatest Yogi Milarepa*. (London: Oxford University Press, 1971), 85-87.

[20] Luis O. Gomez, *The Land of Bliss The paradise of the Buddha of Measureless Light* (Honolulu: University of Hawai'i Press, 1996).

[21] Foucaux, *ibid.*

Chapter 6
Love and Compassion

Christianity

Love and compassion are inextricably bound together for Christians and both are rooted in the Christian understanding of the being and character of God. Early in the Church's history, God's being was associated with love as an ontological reality. In the New Testament, the author of the first epistle of John writes, "Whoever does not love does not know God, for God is love" (1 John 4:8). For the Greek speaking audience, the use of the equative verb, in saying that God "is" love, would be read as a statement regarding God's essence. It is God's nature to be love. Moreover, this understanding of the divine nature has profound ethical implications for Christians as is reflected in the first half of the biblical statement.[1] The extent to which a person loves others—the consequences of which will be explicated below—is reflective of the extent to which that person knows God. This ethical love is most commonly reflected in terms of compassion and solidarity with those who suffer. The English word "compassion" stems from the Latin terms meaning to "suffer with" someone. This Latin understanding from the medieval era is how Christians came to understand the biblical account of God. God journeys with people, in close proximity to them, and this is a free gift of divine imminence.

Israel's traditions of their national formation from slavery and the grand exodus from Egypt to escape oppressive rule begins with an account of Moses conversing with God through a miraculous burning bush. In this text, the Elohist narrates that God tells

Moses, "I have observed the misery of my people who are in Egypt; I have heard their cry on account of their taskmasters. Indeed, I know their sufferings, and I have come down to deliver them" (Exodus 3:7–8). The Deuteronomic tradition would later locate this liberating act with the divine love. The book of Deuteronomy composes an account of Israel's covenant from the literary viewpoint of Moses' final speech to the people prior to his death. In this text, Moses says, "It was not because you were more numerous than any other people that the LORD set his heart on you and chose you…It was because the LORD loved you and kept the oath that he swore to your ancestors" (Deuteronomy 7:8).

This developing idea of the utter gratuity of divine love being manifest impacted the legal and covenantal relationship of Israel with God. This was intended to be reflected in the ethical life of the people. This is particularly true of the relationship one has to the poor. One poignant example of this can be found in the legal prescriptions regarding the harvest. The legal codes state, "When you reap the harvest of your land, you shall not reap to the very edges of your field, or gather the gleanings of your harvest; you shall leave them for the poor and for the alien: I am the LORD your God" (Leviticus 23:22). There are two important themes in this text. First, the instruction is counter-intuitive to strong senses of personal rights absent of equal consideration of the needs of others. The law stipulates that one cannot be the sole benefactor of one's own work, productivity, and property given the presence of need in the community. A person and their family cannot enjoy the full measure of benefit given the mandate to succor the needs of the poor in their midst. Second, the grounds offered for this law are rooted in the nature and character of God. The rationale given is that Yahweh is their God and, presumably, this entails conformation to a different sort of life in the vein of compassion to those in need.

Chapter 6

Such motifs are prescient of the laws pertaining to the year of Jubilee (Leviticus 25:8–55). Though there is no historical evidence that Israel ever followed this law, the year of Jubilee was to be marked every fifty years as a year set apart to renew land, people, and especially the poor. During this year, property was to be returned to the original owners (or their family) who may have lost it through financial misfortune or other dealings. There was to be no sowing or reaping of agriculture in that year, though the people could eat the natural yield of the land. This was to ensure the land also received its Sabbath rest.[2] If people experienced hardship and had to sell themselves into servitude as a result, they were to be freed unless they chose to stay out of love for the master. Debts were to be forgiven and those in need were thus cared for. This Jubilee also found its rationale in the loving character and compassionate acts of God: "For to me the people of Israel are servants; they are my servants whom I brought out from the land of Egypt: I am the LORD your God" (Leviticus 25:55).

The relationship between covenant, love, and compassion also becomes prominent in the prophetic traditions of both the northern kingdom of Israel and the southern Kingdom of Judah after the national division that occurred following the death of Solomon, with his son Rehoboam and the northern secession under Jeroboam near the close of the tenth century BCE. This can be illustrated with a brief example from each kingdom. Living in a time of chaos in the northern kingdom, likely after the death of Jeroboam II (746 BCE), Hosea offers a starkly critical assessment of Israel's infidelity to the covenant with God. Yet at the end, Hosea proclaims a new exodus for the people and cites the gratuitous love of God. Speaking on God's behalf, the prophet proclaims, "I will heal their disloyalty; I will love them freely, for my anger has turned from them" (Hosea 14:4). The southern kingdom saw many great prophets and the first classical prophet to arise after the renowned Isaiah was Zephaniah, who lived during the reign of King Josiah the reformer. Zephaniah's ministry (ca. 635–630 BCE) indicted Judah for violations of covenant and claimed "the day of the LORD" was coming as a day of judgment. However, Zephaniah also gave a promise for a renewed remnant of the people through divine love and imminent proximity. "The king of Israel, the LORD, is in your midst; you shall fear disaster no more…The LORD, your God, is in your midst…he will rejoice over you with gladness, he will renew you in his love" (Zephaniah 3:15, 17).

The motif of jubilee, in particular, is utilized in the prophetic tradition as seen in the texts attributed to Isaiah. In the later texts of what scholars call "Trito-Isaiah"[3] (ca. 525–500 BCE), the renewal of the people after exile is reminiscent of the language and categories of the Jubilee Year. "The spirit of the Lord GOD is upon me, because the LORD has anointed me; he has sent me to bring good news to the oppressed, to bind up the brokenhearted, to proclaim liberty to the captives, and release to the prisoners; to proclaim the year of the LORD's favor, and the day of vengeance of our God; to comfort all who mourn" (Isaiah 61:1–3a). The early Christian communities understood this passage from Isaiah within the context of their experience of Jesus of Nazareth. The author of the gospel of Luke reports that at the outset of Jesus' public life, he enters a synagogue in Nazareth and reads the above passage from Isaiah, claiming, "Today this scripture has been fulfilled in your hearing" (Luke 4:16–21). The idea that the embodiment of divine love and compassion, which transforms communities and public life, is incarnated in Jesus was prevalent in the early church and came to be most poignantly described in the idea of kenosis.

The theme of kenosis finds its original articulation in the early Christian hymn quoted by the apostle Paul in his letter to the Philippian church. In its simplest terms, kenosis means "self-emptying." The hymn quoted by Paul states, "though he was in the form of God, did not regard equality with God as something to be exploited, but emptied himself, taking the form of a slave, being born in human likeness and being found in human form, he humbled himself" (Philippians 2:6–8). While Christians affirm that Jesus was fully God and fully human, Christ voluntarily emptied himself of the authority and privileges associated with being the divine son. He humbled himself to serve and to take the lowliest place. This is indicated in the manner in which the synoptic tradition conveys Jesus' interactions with others. For example, in one instance Jesus comes ashore to a great crowd and "he had compassion for them, because they were like sheep without a shepherd" (Mark 6:34). The word translated as "compassion" in the gospel text indicates that Jesus was moved to pity in his inward being. He saw the needs of the people and was moved to action and response. Ultimately, this is evident in the Christian tradition of the death of Jesus as the ultimate act of self-emptying. Catholic theologian, Elizabeth Johnson, writes eloquently to summarize these themes.

> The one God who creates is also Wisdom made flesh whose self-emptying incarnation into the vagaries of historical life and death reveals the depths of divine love. Could it not be the case that, rather than being uncharacteristic of God's ways, compassionate self-giving love for the liberation of others is what is most typical of God's ways[?][4]

This kenotic movement from glory to earthly life to death displays the divine desire to live among and journey through life and suffering with humanity.

The first Christian communities, like their earlier Hebrew forebears, understood this kenotic movement revealed in Jesus

Christ to have ethical implications. Returning to the passage in Philippians, the apostle introduces the hymn by saying, "Let the same mind be in you that was in Christ Jesus" (Philippians 2:5). The themes present in the hymn are a surrender of high standing for the adoption of a lower one in solidarity with those in need. It is described that Christ emptied himself and took the lowliest form. This willingness to compassionately live and suffer with others was born of the divine love. Protestant Reformed theologian, Jürgen Moltmann, states that "the more one loves, the more one is open and becomes receptive to happiness and sorrow."[5] This is because compassion entails the rejection of apathy. Compassion, born of love, involves openness to the other and journeying with the other. For Christians, Jesus Christ embodies this not only in the specific relationships witnessed in his ministry but is also enacted in the very journey of the incarnation itself. The apostle Paul understood that as Christians' lives are molded by the communal life in Christ then this would alter the modes of interactions with others.

St. Thomas Aquinas saw the intimate relationship between love of God and love of others. He argued that the true object of love is not only God, but also others with whom we have relationships and share life. In fact, Thomas holds that it is the same act with which we love God and love others and he cites the first epistle of John in support of his claim. For Christians, it is the concrete manifestation of love through solidarity and compassionate action that sets one apart as being transformed by God.[6] This is because the giving of love is not a "zero sum game." Love is not a commodity that once given is now absent from the giver. Love is not a product that must be stored and reserved so as not to deplete one's supply. Rather, the relational nature of love's divine origins shows that it is inexhaustible and fecund. In continuity with Israel's earlier traditions, love is gratuitous.

Chapter 6

Because it is relational and fecund, it transforms both giver and receiver through the relational encounter of mutuality and care.

It is difficult to love someone and remain distant. Love calls forth solidarity and compassion, particularly where there is need. This solidarity and compassion necessitates action which responds to the concrete situations of people in the particularity of their historical location and social context, with cultural sensitivity, and an astute sympathy to the vulnerabilities of others. The ways one responds to others must be contextualized. The lived experiences and situations of others matters when understanding how love brings forth action. Simple recourse to the word of law is unsuitable for Christian love and Christian compassion. This was hinted at in the Levitical codes described above and would be deepened as Christian thought developed. One key example of balancing the contextual response of love and compassion vis-à-vis law can be seen in the medieval doctrine of *epikeia*.[7]

Epikeia can be roughly translated as "reasonableness." This term intends to express the idea that rigid application of law is not always just and, therefore, not to be viewed as a virtue *per se*. Law is meant to give insight into proper action and a single law might be intended to cover a variety of potential actions. However, actions are variable, complex, and require context to allow for fuller understanding. A rigid application of law in any given situation also has the potential to violate the goals of justice, which Thomas Aquinas describes as the societal outworking of love. By way of example, St. Thomas illustrates the necessity of repaying a loan or returning a borrowed item. However, perhaps a madman has leant a person his sword. While loans must be repaid, it could produce potential grave harm to return the sword whilst the individual is in the grip of madness. If law is intended to be for the betterment of all persons, then the principle of *epikeia* follows this intention rather that the letter of law in its rigid application because a law may be framed poorly or may themselves result in injustice. A modern example could be the forgiveness of debt for poor nations in view of colonial histories and their ongoing effects, unjust usury, and the politically subservient positions in which such loans could leave the most vulnerable people. The call for a Jubilee of debt forgiveness at the start of the new millennium by Pope John Paul II embodies this principle. In the papal bull that announced the Jubilee, Pope John Paul II describes the connection between the kenotic movement described in the Philippian hymn and the importance of debt forgiveness as a sign of Christian love (*Incarnationis Mysterium*, 1, 12). For Christians, love becomes the new ultimate law. The gospels record Jesus saying, "I give you a new commandment, that you love one another. Just as I have loved you, you also should love one another" (John 13:34). As such, the particularity of individual prescriptions must conform to this ultimate law. The principle of epikeia ensures that love results in actions and that legalistic approaches to people are eschewed in favor of compassionate solidarity. For Aquinas, this is moral "reasonableness."

Similarly, the Protestant Reformer John Calvin argues that love of God and love of neighbor are integrally related and are the summation of the law. Calvin argues that "no one lives in a worse or more evil manner than he [sic] who lives and strives for himself [sic] alone, and thinks about and seeks only his [sic] own advantage."[8] Calvin argues that despite the natural affinity to those with whom we are most naturally inclined—friends, family, community—our love of others ought to extend to the furthest reaches and, indeed, the whole of humanity. Calvin argues that the love we have for one another mirrors the gratuitous nature of the God's love for humanity. He states clearly that love is not meritorious: "whatever the character of the [person], we must yet love [them] because we love God."[9] This kind of love is the fulfillment of the divine law and, for Calvin, expresses the proper

Chapter 6

human orientation to God's primacy wherein one's dedication to the world might be fulfilled as derivative of that first orientation.

For Christians of all traditions, love and compassion are rooted in the nature and actions of God and preeminently revealed in Jesus Christ. Love is the essence, character, motive, and active presence of God with humanity. The incarnation is the example *par excellence* of God's love in the kenotic self-emptying of privilege, authority, and rights. This is not only a theological statement of God's being for Christians, it is also the supreme ethical principle. It leads Christians to live in solidarity with those in need and to not elevate one's own desires and comfort above that of their neighbor. This has been exemplified in many of the monastic traditions in Christianity, as well as lay life, which is the topic of the next chapter.

Buddhism

> Mind precedes knowables: they are founded on our mind, they are mind made.
> If a man speaks or acts with a malicious thought, pain follows him, as the cartwheel follows the foot of the ox.
>
> Mind precedes knowables: they are founded on our mind, they are mind made.
> If a man speaks or acts with a pure thought, happiness follows him, like his shadow which never leaves.
>
> 'He abused me, he hit me, he vanquished me, he stole from me,'—in harbouring such thoughts hatred will never be appeased.
>
> 'He abused me, he hit me, he vanquished me, he stole from me,'—in not harbouring such thoughts hatred will be appeased. [*Dhammapada*/ Twin verses][10]

In the earliest formulation of Buddhism, loving kindness and compassion are differentiated. Compassion is the sentiment that you would like the suffering of someone or some sentient being to stop. This may include yourself so a thought that your own suffering would stop but the suffering of others is usually emphasized. These others would include all sentient beings from the gods to those residing in the hells. Loving kindness is the sentiment that you would like some being to have a happy life. Although these two are closely connected the tradition across time is to treat them as separate ideas.

Readers may be surprised that in Buddhism the gods suffer. Actually, suffering is one of the most important defining features for each of the states of being that are postulated. That is the amount of suffering you will experience in each of the six states of possible rebirth differs. The greatest suffering is found in the hell realms. Humans are in a realm where they experience both pleasure and suffering in proportion. The gods experience pleasures their entire life but in the last week before they die, they too will experience suffering in that they know they will die and be reborn elsewhere usually in a lower station. Only one who is awakened fully will not suffer and that person we call a Buddha.

The Sanskrit word translated as "compassion" is derived from the root meaning "to pour out" and thus it is an outflow of the sentiment followed by activity to assuage the suffering or to bring about its cessation. Further, the Sanskrit word translated as "loving kindness" could also be translated as "amiability" and is ultimately derived from the word meaning to unite or to pair. In Buddhism, these are far more than simple sentiments that adherents are called on to engender. They have both moral and meditative aspects that need to be understood to reach the full meaning of these terms within the Buddhist setting. It is interesting to point out that the future Buddha is named Maitreya. The name means the "loving one" and is derived from the term

Chapter 6

meaning loving kindness. Why is he called this? Because in the unknown future, human life will become near devoid of acts of love and every other aspect of morality. It is at that time Maitreya will be reborn and reintroduce morality as well as Buddhism. Most readers are familiar with one image of Maitreya. "The Happy Buddha" seen in Chinese restaurants and elsewhere, this is an image of Maitreya, in Chinese call Milo.

The Theravada branch of Buddhism teaches its followers that they should show compassion (freeing from suffering) to all sentient beings and wish them to have a happy life (i.e., loving kindness). These concepts are important and in Sri Lanka or Thailand one can see thousands of acts of compassion on a daily basis. This grows out of an understanding that we are all trapped in this cycle of life and death and so out of sympathy one tries to ease the suffering of others. This may be nothing more than removing an insect from the path by a monk as he walks by or it may be a grand event where the monks gather together to act as relief workers during a disaster. However, in this formulation of compassion and loving kindness it is not foundational but one of many types of doctrinal points leading to actions that fall under the heading of morality in the Eight-fold Path and thus an aspect of the necessities to gain liberation.

Freedom from suffering is understood as calming and if possible eradicating suffering. Suffering at its most foundational level is connected with the impossible attempts by the self or ego to see itself as real and permanent. This self is rather like Pinocchio. It wants to be real and it tells lies in an attempt to propagate that narrative. In addition, on a psychological level, because both self and objects are generated in the mind simultaneously, then one also deeply wishes for the outside world to be filled with permanent or at the very least long enduring objects. Every reader from their basic science courses when students, knows that at the atomic level even in a steel desk the molecules are slowly breaking down and undergoing change. Yet, in our way of conceptualizing the world around us, people looking at the steal desk that supports my computer in January will say it is the same desk when they see it in February. However, it is not the same, yet we keep up the myth in order to make the ego feel comfortable. In the depth of each of our psychologies we are trying to make an unchanging really existing self and objective world. These being impossible because everything changes, then we have an existential type of suffering.

In addition to this existential suffering and based upon it, we suffer from the obvious changes that transpire in our lived experience. Our beloved dog dies after twelve years, a cherished vase is broken, friends depart and are never heard from again or we suffer the breakup of our own family through divorce. All of this and more are experiences we encounter daily. We attempt to hold all of this together. We attempt to make it last, to stop or slow down the change as much as we can. Thus, we have attachment to some things and aversion to other things. However, the cause and conditions that keep whatever in its current state are reaching maturation. When that karma starts to become exhausted then the cherished relationships and objects in our lives must also begin to change and many will simply cease. This type of suffering is not existential, that is it does not necessarily raise questions regarding our existence. It is more superficial but something we grow to know all too well from living life even if unreflectively.

Finally, there is a level of suffering we all experience again established upon the existential suffering but equally and daily encountered, similar to the second type of suffering. That is the suffering of birth, sickness, old age and death. As an unborn baby we are in a near perfect environment. We do not experience hunger, cold, shocking stimulation like loud sounds or harsh lights. When we are born, we are suddenly expelled into a world wherein the first few minutes we will be cold, have bright lights

Chapter 6

hit our eyes and loud sounds assault our ears. Hence, birth is suffering. Sickness we all know. The common cold up to life threatening illness are personally encountered and visited upon our loved one. Old age too is full of problems as we encounter limitations we never had, pains for no reason, a slowing down and a profound tiredness settles upon our bones. It is not simply that we have some illness or some condition although that may be true, but the entire machine of this body is wearing out for no other reason that we have lived past our prime. Death can be for some a very painful experience full of both physical aspects as different systems simply close down and the psychological suffering of leaving the world we know and the people we loved.

For Buddhist in general and particularly for the Theravada branch, this is the suffering that one wishes self and others to be free from. All these experiences can be summed up as existing from birth to death to rebirth. Why so much emphasis on suffering? People have claimed that Buddhism is pessimistic because of this emphasis on suffering. This is not the case. Suffering is the lowest common denominator for all sentient beings. If you poke a one cell ameba with a probe it will move away because the sensation is unpleasant. So, all beings from hell up to the heavens experience suffering but only some experience pleasure. Further, if you think about this, you will come to understand that the anxiety and dread these suffering experiences bring about is a constant source of our unease in life. When enjoying the acclaimed accomplishment of your wife, the look on your son's face when he opens his sixth birthday gifts, the shear enjoyment of your dog chasing a Frisbee we don't experience this anxiety and dread. Yet in quiet moments, when confronting someone else's misery, or perhaps from a news story there, the dread pokes up its head again. Finally, in general meditation can help lessen the attachment and aversion and this decreases suffering.

From the earliest times in Buddhism there is a set of four specific meditations that were recommended to adherents as powerful means for achieving deep states within the mind helping free one for the cycle of birth and death that specifically have a social dimension. These four are equanimity, sympathetic joy, loving kindness and compassion.[11] Equanimity means treating everyone equally and sympathetic joy is being joyful when others perform moral acts. The loving kindness method is calling forth the sentiment of wishing whomever to have a happy life. Focuses his or her whole attention upon it, the meditator undertakes generating this sentiment with reference to different people or animals encountered in one's life beginning with oneself. After meditatively developing the sentiment of wishing a happy life for oneself, next the sentiment is extended to someone respected, a friend, someone neutral to one, and an enemy. Having accomplished this, one can extend loving kindness to all beings. Each of these individuals is successively selected as the object of meditation as one courses through this practice.

As compassion is the sentiment of wishing for the end of suffering, the meditative practice begins with focusing on a person or animal that is experiencing misery. Having generated meditatively compassion for such a being, the meditator next turns attention to a friend, then a neutral person, and then an enemy. Again, as with loving kindness, this sentiment is then extended to all beings.

These four meditations performed separately are said to lead to profound states of concentration and they are termed "Exalted Stations." These are directly associated with the general map of meditative states as found in the systematic presentation of the teachings. Each one of these meditative states is associated with positive qualities and the literature notes the negative qualities that abate. Thus, one way to enter such profound states is through the four Exalted Stations. However as noted in previous chapters,

Chapter 6

these meditative states have a moral dimension as well. Meditation in Buddhism is an ethical act and just like accumulating vast amounts of positive merit will produce rebirth in one heaven or another, so too will mastering the ability to enter and dwell in these meditative states. Hence one can readily understand how they are linked. It is held that if one can master the compassionate meditation for example, then one's rebirth in heaven is guaranteed. This is because the various meditative states are associated with particular heavens in an ascending order and thus form part of the Buddhist cosmology.

Be this as it may, the Theravada tradition does not see compassion or loving kindness as central to the nirvana project. This branch of Buddhism places its emphasis on insight that liberates. There basic philosophical position is that by focusing on gaining insight the fundamental form of suffering, the existential suffering, will be eliminated when you realize there is no self and the whole edifice is merely a construct. When the existential suffering is utterly dissolved, then all the other types of suffering which are based upon it, will also dissolve.

Therefore, for the Theravada, compassion and loving kindness are both a means of engaging in advance levels of spiritual cultivation leading to profound states of meditation and they from part of ethical behavior that adherents are called on to enact for the sake of their own development as well as to the benefit of others. In Buddhism, many activities are seen as being a benefit to the other party as well as to oneself as the direct goal is the assistance given to others, but this generates positive merit for oneself. This positive merit will produce future circumstances that will support one's cultivation of the Dharma (Buddha's teachings). Further, by engaging in actions to alleviate the suffering of others, they will better be in a position to cultivate moral behavior and possibly even progress on the path to liberation.

With the Mahayana, the configuration of compassion within the overall framework of the doctrinal formulation as well as in the realms of practice takes on a different dimension from that previously explained regarding the Theravada. The Mahayana branch of Buddhism has twin cornerstones wisdom and compassion. Their understanding of wisdom includes the Theravada wisdom and surpasses it. Their inclusion of compassion at the very foundation of their tradition is both an inspiration within and a criticism of the Theravada's tendency to be disengaged from the life of the common people. In fact, the Mahayana texts proclaim that gods and men will honor one who generates the Mahayana compassion for all beings and that negative merit formulated by one's own actions will be voided.

Over time, a rather large collection of stories of the Buddha Shakyamuni lives before his last wherein he became a Buddha were compiled. Accepted by both branches of Buddhism, these stories often called *Jataka*, always present the future Buddha as acting compassionately or applying his wisdom to different concerns. The future Buddha appears in a number of lives that are overwhelmingly human or animal. The animal lives when read remind one of *Aesop's Fables*. There are hundreds of these *Jataka* tales, and the tradition accepted these as stories about the same being going from one life to the next until reaching the last life where he became the Buddha Shakyamuni. This can be seen within the Mahayana as the gaining of initial insight into the Buddhist truth and the enacting of compassion to assist others while refining one's own insight. Thus, compassion is the activity of insight and not a completely separate sentiment. This justifies the central position Mahayana gives this concept in its doctrinal formulation.

In general, Mahayana Buddhists are also following the Eightfold Path to gain awakening. However, in addition to those eight or in cooperation with them, adherents of the Mahayana also must

Chapter 6

develop the set of Six Perfections. These are: Giving, Morality, Patience, Energy, Meditation and Wisdom.[12] These virtues were also mentioned in the Theravada literature, but they come to have a more central status in the Mahayana. As one can readily see, there are crossovers with the Eight-fold Path. Morality, Energy and Meditation in particular are understood as being the same with a Mahayana overlay doctrinally. Giving in this context comes to represent all acts of compassion. As mentioned in the previous chapter, the first book printed in human history was the Buddhist text entitled *The Diamond Sutra*. This shorter text is about the Mahayana way to approach giving and thus compassion in general. However, in its explanation of giving, it also instructs one in Mahayana wisdom. *The Diamond Sutra* and the other texts forming the Perfections class of literature have two main thrusts to their teachings.

The Diamond Sutra teaches that compassionate activity like giving should be undertaken within the framework of a particular orientation or vision of the world. First, the Buddha Shakyamuni teaches his disciples that all things are not exactly as they seem to be. That is everything is constantly changing but we, having limited abilities, do not see the change and impute on thing a permanence or duration. The implication of this aspect of the teaching is to not only see things as impermanent but to not cling to anything as it is fleeting. Second, the compassionate activity as symbolized in giving is undertaken without the view of a permanent self (one too is ever changing) who gives, a real recipient, and without an idea of the reality of the object given.[13] Therefore, an act of giving or any compassionate activity that maintains a different view from that just outlined, still has an ego involved. Giving because it makes one feel good, giving because one may be rewarded with positive merit, giving when one expects reputation, or giving wherein one expects a benefit is denigrated in Buddhism as an act for oneself and not primarily for the other and thus not true giving. However, even if it is selfish giving, it is still seen as better than no giving at all. Third, the *Sutra* also teaches that even clinging to the idea of awakening, Buddhahood, or nirvana must be abandoned. Clinging to the goal actually prevents one from achieving it.

This can also be approached from a different angle. The Mahayana branch of Buddhism also understands that all there really is—is the non-dual. This non-dual admits no separation. The separation of things is ultimately an illusion although it proceeds in a regular fashion which we term cause and effect.[14] This position is based on meditational experience. In certain profound states of meditation one can experience a vivid awareness that is nonreferential. Although while in such a state one cannot have a thought, "I am in the non-dual," this experience can be known reflectively after leaving that state. As one moves from the non-dual state into duality, the moving from the pure awareness first produces a recognition of a self and other. For example, a thought like, "I am conscious of X." Once one has moved from the state of nonreferential vivid awareness into the unawareness associated with self and other, then in a casual sequence the world as we know it comes about as an experience for that individual. This is not an ontological statement but an epistemic one.

The energy of the non-dual is that very compassion. In fact, to even label it in this way betrays what it is. The non-dual and compassion are one and the same. One is not an aspect of the other, it is not based on the other, and it does not maintain connections and associations the other does not have. We must speak of it in the manner above because of the very limits of what our language can present and because of the limits of our own intellects to be able to articulate something so mysterious as to defy differentiations. Therefore, the realization of the goal according to Mahayana, is compassion. When the Buddha Shakyamuni was alive, he did not simply beg so as to maintain his life but to allow

Chapter 6

others to accumulate vast amounts of merit for their own benefit. Because the Buddha was fully awakened his own survival was not a concern. He did not provide teachings to his disciples because he desired to be a famous teacher or get remuneration for teaching. He spent his career teaching so as to help free others from there suffering. He did not lay down restrictions on the monks and nuns in order to be the controller of their lives similar to a cult leader, but to provide a moral environment where spiritual pursuits can come to the van guard. Thus, all his actions were for others because as the living embodiment of the non-dual, all actions were compassion. In this frame, compassion and loving kindness are not something we need to add to who we already are; it is at the core of our being. In fact, it is at the core of our being before "our being." This means that from the meditative experience wherein we naturally rest in the pure awareness vivid and nonreferential, that very state, which is ours already, beneath all the mental overlays, is one and the same as compassion. As we begin to move into unawareness we first generate being (self and other). Thus, the core of our being is compassion before there is being.

This deeply grounded other oriented activity in conjunction with the wisdom of the Mahayana as explained above and in other chapters, needs to be made manifest guided by skillfulness. Although compassion united in meditation has moral force in the world, in general compassion, if it is nothing more than a sentiment held in one's heart, may be beneficial to oneself but is impotent in the world. As compassion and loving kindness are "social" in orientation then it must be active and lived in the world. It is not sufficient to feel sorry for others, one must do something about it in the Mahayana understanding and meditation may be one venue but taking action is another.

Years ago, while I was living in Nepal, this was brought home in a wonderful example. I was walking with a Tibetan monk when a herder came along the same road with a sheep all tied up. The monk asked the man what he was doing with the sheep. The man said he was taking it to the butcher to sell it. The monk then offered to buy it from the herder, and they negotiated a price. The animal would then be donated to a monastery with sufficient grounds for pasture. The monks would sell the wool but keep the animal for its natural life.

This is not only an example of compassion, but it is an example of skillfulness. The monk did not organize a protest against the herder trying to force social opinion or perhaps the government to enact a proscription against sheep herding. The herder received what he needed, the sheep received a pardon for its life, and the monastery will make money from the wool. Mahayana Buddhist recognize that sometimes providing money and nothing more is important to enacting changes in the world to bring about better living situations for all sentient beings. In particular, they are called on to be personally engaged. As I have often explained to my students, it is great to donate money to the local soup kitchen but then you should also go there and serve the soup.

This approach to compassion is the very foundation of the Mahayana path. In the first instance, an individual comes to realize that every being is like oneself in that we all suffer. Further, just like with oneself, every being wants to be free from suffering. This generates within one a strong wish to tread upon the path to becoming a Buddha. Not just to free oneself from the suffering of samsara but to free all being from there suffering as well. When such a though matures into a willingness to vow to pursue the extremely difficult road to Buddhahood for the sake of others as well as oneself it is called the "thought of awakening." And this is where the actual path of the Mahayana begins.[15] Why do adherents of the Mahayana undertake for multiple lifetimes the troubles and tribulations that each life may entail? It is for the sake of gaining Buddhahood for others as well as oneself. Thus, the reader can readily see that compassion is a corner stone in the Mahayana.

However, in the Mahayana there are other meditational practices focusing on compassion beyond the Four Exalted Stations mentioned above. Although those four still play a role in this branch. A Mahayana text entitled the *White Lotus of Compassion Sutra*,[16] provides short *Jatakas* for a number of Buddhas and Bodhisattvas. In this *Sutra*, it states that the person who became Avalokitishvara (the Bodhisattva of compassion) was one of the major disciples of a past Buddha. It was at that time he made vows to stay in samsara until all beings were liberated. The famous text entitled *The Basket's Display*,[17] tells of the Pure Land of this Bodhisattva. It is a fabulous mountain home. Most importantly this *Sutra* provides the famous mantra OM MANI PADME HUM. Texts enumerated various forms of Avalokiteshvara emphasizing different aspects of compassion. The central Buddhist temple in Kathmandu which is dedicated to Avalokiteshvara displays 108 different forms around the walls of the court in charming paintings on plaster.

One of the most important practices associated with both the concept of compassion and the Bodhisattva Avalokiteshvara is called the "Great Compassion Dharani." *Dharani* is a Buddhist term meaning a mnemonic device. They are usually strings of phrases encapsulating important Buddhist ideas for practice and doctrine. They are meant to be chanted. The Great Compassion Dharani is associated with the Eleven-headed (faced) Avalokiteshvara who has 1,000 hands. Ichno-graphically the heads represent both the seeing of suffering and the hands the different manifestations of methods of relieving it. The *dharani* is several hundred syllables long listing various attributes of the Bodhisattva and requesting him to help one end suffering and gain awakening. This *dharani* is extremely popular in Chinese Buddhism. Other shorter mantras of compassion also exist.

Significantly, the most chanted Buddhist text entitled the *Heart of the Perfection of Wisdom Sutra*[18] is a teaching given by Avalokiteshvara to a disciple of the Buddha Shakyamuni with his blessing. This one-page text contains a summary of the teachings of Mahayana wisdom based on the concept of emptiness. It also contains a short mantra but here the mantra is connected with wisdom. Therefore, one ought not to think that the Bodhisattva of compassion is devoid of wisdom. Or the Bodhisattva of wisdom, Manjushri, is devoid of compassion. They simply emphasize one or the other aspects.

This idea of practicing and mastering the Mahayana teachings is reiterated at the end of each formal Mahayana practice. Either as an extension or as a separate tract, there are benedictions that state the wishes of the practitioner to the effect that the merit gained by the practice be offered for the benefit of the awakening of others as well as oneself. Because of positing the theory of the possibility of merit transfer, this benediction is seen as an actual way of help others and as a means to repeatedly imbue Mahayana foundational motivation in the person dedicating.

Strengthened with the armor of the Bodhisattva vow coalescing the synergy of compassion and wisdom, the individual willingly accepts multiple rebirths as he/she maturates Giving, Morality, Energy, Patients, Mediation and Wisdom to the level of a perfection. As implied in the *Diamond Sutra*, the wisdom of compassion is the compassion of wisdom.

Conclusion

Whereas love and compassion together are seen by Christians as the being and character of God, in Buddhist loving kindness and compassion are two different sentiments to be cultivated through meditation and enacted in life. Buddhist and Christians

Chapter 6

support their individual understandings of love and compassion based on their canonical scriptures as well as a long tradition of post-canonical writings.

For the Jews, God chose them out of his divine love and therefore freed them from enslavement. The covenantal relationship between God and his people is enacted daily through the ethical behavior of the people and their treatment of the poor. Such a relationship is also reflected in some of the sayings of the prophets. Early Christians believed that the fulfillment of Jewish prophesy is testified to in Luke (4:16–21) wherein Jesus of Nazareth proclaimed it to be so. Thus, the divine love and compassion was made flesh. Jesus was full human and fully God but humbled himself though being the Son of God he drew close to the needs of people. For Christians, the love of God is reflected in the love shown others. Love is openness, solidarity, sympathy calling for compassionate action. This position on love and compassion within Christianity even influenced early legal thought in the western tradition. Upon conclusion God's love is manifest in the incarnation of Jesus whose compassionate ministry is the model for Christian behavior.

In Buddhism, compassion, meaning the wish that others suffering ends, and loving kindness, meaning the wish that others have a happy life, are both focal points in specific meditations and a call to action. Upon final analysis, suffering is the product of the conflict between our ego needs and reality. One of the methods for reaching advanced meditational states is by first focusing on compassion or loving kindness with the emphasis on the suffering of a familiar person or animal. Then, through a series of stages come to expand that sentiment meditationally to all sentient beings including one's enemies. Gaining these advanced states is understood as not only meditative abilities helpful on the path to nirvana but as an ethical act that can lead to rebirth in one or other of the heavens.

Further, a Buddhist is called on to enact compassion and loving kindness in their daily lives whether in small acts like removing an insect from the path so that it is not stepped on or in large operations like flood relief. The Buddha no longer have self-interest, always acted out of compassion and loving kindness. For Buddhist compassion and loving kindness should be like the sun shining on others indiscriminately. Yet wisdom in the exercise of compassion and loving kindness is important so that a positive outcome is reached and contributing to negative outcomes is avoided. This is the Theravada branch of Buddhism's understanding.

The other branch of Buddhism, Mahayana, place compassion on equal footing with wisdom. For this branch, compassion is the activity of insight. In addition to following the Eight-fold Path, Mahayana followers also must practice the Six Perfections of: Giving, Morality, Patients, Energy, Meditation and Wisdom. This is enacted in compassionate activities that are without a notion of self, other, and object given. Without this framework then any act of compassion would still have a sense of ego involved. Although even selfish giving is better than no giving.

The Mahayana also presents the idea that nirvana is the non-dual and the activity of the non-dual is compassion. Thus, in this understanding, the goal or nirvana, is compassion. The Buddha every act was compassionate because he realized the non-dual. This helps explain the fact, according to the Mahayana, that compassion and loving kindness are not something we need to add to our composure but are fundamental to it. However, cultivation may be necessary to realize this point.

In addition to the meditations on the Exalted States of compassion or loving kindness, Within the Mahayana there are other meditations and practices that focus on these sentiments. One of these is the meditation on the Bodhisattva Avalokiteshvara, the Bodhisattva of compassion and another is the reciting the Great

Chapter 6

Compassion Dharani. All of these practices lead one to willingly take on multiple rebirths in order to affect the liberation of others from cycle of suffering.

---

[1] On the relationship between Greek patristic conceptions of the Trinity and human interactions in Orthodox Christianity, see John D. Zizioulas, *Being As Communion: Studies in Personhood and the Church* (New York: St. Vladamir's Seminary Press, 2002).

[2] On the role of land as gift and sign of divine love, see Walter Brueggemann, *The Land: Place as Gift, Promise, and Challenge in Biblical Faith Second Edition* (Minneapolis: Fortress Press, 2002).

[3] This is due to the scholarly understanding that the latter texts in the book of Isaiah exhibit linguistic features and reflect a historical location much later than the earlier portions of the book which are thought to be the product of the historical Isaiah. They are likely the result of a prophetic school in the tradition of Isaiah.

[4] Elizabeth Johnson, *Ask The Beasts: Darwin and the God of Love* (London: Bloomsbury Publishing, 2014), 158.

[5] Jürgen Moltmann, *The Crucified God* trans. R.A. Wilson and John Bowden (Minneapolis: Fortress Press, 1993), 253.

[6] St. Thomas Aquinas, Summa Theologiae, IIaIIae q. 23–25.

[7] St. Thomas Aquinas, *Summa Theologiae* IIaIIae q. 120. See also Daniel Westberg, "The Relation Between Positive and Natural Law in Aquinas" *Journal of Law and Religion* 11.1 (1994–1995): 1–22.

[8] John Calvin, *Institutes of the Christian Religion* trans. John T. McNeill (Philadelphia: The Westminster Press, 1960), 417 [Vol. I Book II Ch. VIII].

[9] Calvin, *Institutes of the Christian Religion*, 419 [Vol. I Book II Ch. VIII].

[10] Narada Thera, *The Dhammapada Pali Text and Translation with Stories in Brief and Notes* (Taipei: The Corporate Body of the Buddha Educational Foundation, 1993), English translation my own.

[11] Bhadantacariva Buddhaghosa, *The Path of Purification* trans. Bhikkhu Nyanamoli (Colombo: A. Semage Publishing, 1964?), 321 *ff.*

[12] Har Dayal, *The Bodhisattva Doctrine in Buddhist Sanskrit Literature* (Delhi: Motilal Banarsidass, 1970), 165 *ff.*

[13] Edward Conze, *The Short Prajnaparamita Texts* (London: Luzac and Co., 1973), 122–141.

[14] (n.f.) *The Seekers Glossary of Buddhism*. (New York: Sutra Translation Committee of the United States and Canada, 1998), 404-405.

[15] Dayal, *ibid.* 50 *ff.*

[16] *The Karuna Pundarika Sutra*. Only partial translations into English available, see below.

[17] Alan Roberta, *The Karandavyuha Sutra.* http://www.pacificbuddha.org/wp-content/uploads/2014/02/Karandavyuha-Sutra.pdf
[18] Conze, *ibid.* 140 *ff.*

Chapter 7
Monasticism

Christianity

Early monasticism arose as spiritual practice in Christianity in response to a series of events that came about as a result of both socio-political changes in the Greco-Roman world and the personal charisms and insights of exceptional individuals. The former deals with how Christians understood devotion to the crucified Christ as Christianity grew in prominence and gained stability under Emperors Constantine and Theodosius. The latter understands the distinctive contributions and particular devotion of individuals attempting to achieve spiritual maturity and purity. These are two sides of the same historical coin. Some individuals respond to their surroundings and changes in spiritual and social life by enacting a new way of expressing one's piety. This is no less true of early monasticism as it came to fruition in the desert fathers and mothers of Egypt in the second half of the third century.[1]

The first generation after the death and resurrection of Jesus Christ worked out its devotion to Christ in terms connected to apostolicity. Most notably, this can be seen in the writings of Paul where he states, "We are afflicted in every way, but not crushed; perplexed, but not driven to despair…always carrying in the body the death of Jesus, so that the life of Jesus may also be made visible in our bodies…So death is at work in us, but life in you" (2 Corinthians 4:8–12). This was similar to the principle of apostolicity found in the canonization of the New Testament scriptures. In being connected to an apostle, one is connected to

Christ in his sufferings. The goal is to "imitate" the apostle as the apostle exemplifies the imitation of Christ in his own body (1 Corinthians 11:1). As the early generation of apostles was coming to an end, Christians needed new exemplars of faith and devotion to Christ, particularly Christ in his sufferings. Such exemplars were made possible as the fruit of sporadic persecutions throughout the Roman Empire, which resulted in martyrs.

Once the generation of the apostles had passed, along with their eyewitness accounts of Christ, those who were seen to be closest to the sufferings of Jesus were the early martyrs. If an apostle could say that "in my flesh I am completing what is lacking in Christ's afflictions for the sake of his body, that is, the church" (Colossians 1:24), then the martyrs of the second generation were viewed as the heirs of that legacy. In their persecution, martyrs did not only follow Christ in imitation, they also mystically participated in the sufferings of Christ. In other words, they did not only suffer for Christ, but also with him. As such, the martyrs were viewed as having a special connection to Christ that went beyond that of faithful witness. They were understood to be joined with Christ's sufferings, in a unique way, through their own flesh.

After Emperor Constantine issued the Edict of Milan (313 CE), giving Christianity the status of being a legally practiced religion, the sporadic and at times violent persecutions of Christians by the Roman state (such as those under Nero [64 CE], Decius [249–252 CE] and Diocletian [284–305 CE]) came to a close. In the decades prior to Constantine's edict, the persecutions had already begun to recede, and Christians began wrestling with the increasingly stable and affluent status that their faith and practice was attaining in significant urban centers throughout the Empire. The increased size and numbers of the Christian churches in these areas had the result that many members of these communities were less fervent in their observance of Christian practice. Such persons might partake in the religious life of the community but not necessarily adhere to the strict devotion or adherence of the sacramental life with uniform regularity. Coincidental to this, the loss of the profound witness of those martyrs, and the secure place they achieved in the afterlife due to their imitation of Christ's sacrifice was an opportunity lost for those whose fervent devotion must now seek other means of demonstration. This piety, coupled with anxiety over one's sins in a prolonged life not quickly culminated in martyrdom, led individuals to seek other paths of discipleship and consecration. Monasticism arose, in part, in response to this need.[2]

The person most often identified as the originator of monasticism was St. Anthony (251–356 CE), whose biography was written by the great theologian of the fourth century and archbishop of Alexandria, St. Athanasius.[3] St. Anthony originally lived on the outer edges of the Roman Empire, in the great metropolitan and intellectual city of Alexandria in northern Egypt. Alexandria was renowned for being a diverse, cosmopolitan center that boasted one of the largest and most important libraries in the ancient world. Born of well-to-do Egyptian parents, Anthony's life would change irrevocably after entering a Church one day and hearing a homily in which the words of Jesus to a wealthy young man were recounted: "If you wish to be perfect, go, sell your possessions, and give the money to the poor…then come, follow me" (Matthew 19:21). Anthony interpreted this as a call he was meant to respond to in a literal way. He fulfilled the threefold commandment and sojourned out to the desert (271 CE) where he would withdraw from people into the wilderness to seek solitude and the ascetic life. Anthony embraced asceticism, which is a rejection of luxury and an embrace of self-mastery through abstention from regular comforts through fasting, chastity, hardship, and spiritual discipline. Anthony's retreat from urban life to the desert resonated with Christians already grappling with the desire to exemplify the devotion of the martyrs in a time of relative comfort. Anthony was the most famous exemplar in a broader movement of Christians to become holy. This way of life attracted others to seek his counsel and wisdom; a distinction he repeatedly sought to avoid.

Athanasius records the solitary life of Anthony as one full of challenges in an effort to purify himself and live up to the unattainable ideal of the martyr. He saw the mandate to expunge thoughts such as lust or desire for things of this world above eternal life as the pathway to such purification. In doing so, hours of prayer to tame the mind and abstention from food and home comforts were a part of his asceticism in an effort to draw near to God. Anthony is said to have done battles with Satan by overcoming temptations, but also was said to have received beatings at the hands of the devil. Such imagery connects Anthony with the trials and beatings of the martyr in the coliseum, but also with Christ who, according to the synoptic gospels, spent time in the wilderness to contend with the temptations of Satan prior to entering public ministry. Anthony's purification through such experiences, along with his spiritual discipline of fasting, prayer, and partaking of the Eucharist drew many to imitate his hermit lifestyle. Some journeyed to seek advice or wisdom while others only desired to be in physical proximity to the saint. The latter example mirrors the early Christian pilgrims who would journey to be close to a relic of a martyr, be it the martyr's grave or part of the martyr's body or clothing. Athanasius records that Anthony retreated ever further into the desert to avoid public life and eventually made an abandoned fortress his monastic cell. He would spend twenty years there while followers would come and go awaiting his reemergence from seclusion. When he emerged the throngs of people were amazed to see a man in good health, seemingly unaged, and is described in ways reminiscent of the resurrected body of Christ in the gospels. The hermit's ascetic life is intended to be viewed in this text in terms both reminiscent of the pure martyr and in terms of the eschatological fulfillment available for people through Christ's resurrection.

Anthony's monasticism was followed by others in the Egyptian desert, notably Pachomius (286–346 CE). While Pachomius would gather monks together in early orders, there were those who followed Anthony's hermit life more closely. These monks would gather periodically into hermitages and for work, meditation, and the Eucharist. However, they would then retreat to their own desert caves, or other monastic cells, for quiet meditation and purgation. The way of life exemplified in such desert fathers came to be known as eremitic monasticism. Eremitic monks maintain a solitary life that would be consumed with work and meditation. At times such monks would have disciples and exercise authority over postulants, but this was more of an authority achieved through wisdom or charismatic personality rather than an organized structure or hierarchy. Asceticism was a central feature and, at times, led to extreme behavior and even self-abuse by some of the desert monks. Such examples include St. Simeon the Stylite (ca. 388–459), who reportedly lived atop an eight-foot pole to achieve solitude from admiring pilgrims and to achieve quiet meditation and communion with Christ. There were others who engaged in self-flagellation (striking oneself with a whip), or even self-castration (in an all too literal interpretation of Matthew 19:12) in order to mortify the flesh in an effort to stave off temptation, particularly sexual temptation. The Council of Nicaea (325 CE) would condemn self-castration as a means of achieving holiness, though the practice was occasionally advocated by individuals such as Peter Damian (1007–1072 CE) as late as the eleventh century. Such extreme behavior was not indicative of Eremitic monasticism as a whole. The legacy of the desert mothers and fathers, particularly their wisdom, quiet meditation, and piety, continues to inspire Christians to this day.[4]

While the eremitic monks were some of the earliest examples of Christian monasticism, it was far more common for groups of people to live in small communities and to develop a structured rule or ordered way of living together. This is called cenobitic monasticism. Pachomius formed one of the earliest groups of cenobitic monks, who lived in monasteries in the desert. Another formative influence in the early development of this tradition of monasticism, and which remains influential to this day, is the Rule of St. Benedict. Benedict was born in Norcia, Italy (ca. 480 CE), seventy years after the sack of Rome. After being sent by his parents to receive an education in Rome, Benedict was dismayed by how easily his young compatriots gave in to vice. As a result, he resolved to leave Rome, selling his possessions to engage a life in pursuit of God. After some time as a priest and other activities, he founded the monastery at Monte Cassino (ca. 520) where he would write his famous rule. The "rule" is intended to provide an authoritative guide for the monks to enable the nurturing of proper character, obedience, daily practice, discipline, and other features of the cenobitic, monastic life.

The life that characterizes the monk in Benedict's rule is one that relies on one's fellow monks in daily life for both spiritual and physical needs. The monastery is headed by an abbot who is both a practical and a spiritual leader for the community. St. Benedict describes the abbot in the following way: "To be worthy of the task of governing a monastery, the abbot must always remember what his title signifies and act as a superior should."[5] The title "abbot" is taken from the biblical word for "father," *abba*. The abbot will bear responsibility before God for not only his conduct, but also the spiritual growth of the monks under him. The abbot should be just, avoid favoritism in dealing with other monks and, in doing so, lead with integrity. The leadership of the abbot in cenobitic monasteries is essential as he guides the community, mentors, and acts as spiritual leader in both devo-

Chapter 7

tional practice and in the practical work of the monks. Such communities will often conduct work in service of the larger society or as members of the broader church and will not necessarily remain cloistered in their cells. Monasticism in this vein sees its vocation fulfilled in conducting works of mercy for the poor, teaching and missionary work within the Church, scholarly endeavors, or more regular priestly ministry in aid of the surrounding area. These monastic communities disavow private ownership for its adherents, but the monasteries support themselves through various means. Monks have a long history of farming, the brewing of beer, or even professional dog breeding in order to support their communal life and their ministry to the surrounding area.

The medieval era saw two prominent monastic traditions arise within Catholicism: Franciscans and Dominicans.[6] These are mendicant orders. Mendicancy refers to the practice of being a beggar and relying on others for the basic necessities of life. In adopting such a practice the mendicant orders were not only disavowing personal property and wealth for the sake of service to God, but were also taking vows of poverty that involved having faith God would provide through the mercy of others. The Franciscans are named for their founder, St. Francis of Assisi (ca. 1181–1226). Born to a serious-minded cloth and spice merchant, the young Francis dreamed of grand military exploits and engaged in frivolous entertainments with young comrades. After spending a year as a prisoner of war, Francis viewed his youthful dreams as insipid and sought to make changes in his life. Francis took a vow of poverty and began tending to the needs of those who were sick. He is particularly known for having a special spiritual connection with nature and penned the renowned *Canticle of the Creatures* wherein he extols "Brother Sun" and "Sister Moon" along with animals and plant-life. He quickly became popular and gathered a following of others who sought to live in accordance with his approach to God and the world. Not being a particularly able administrator, Francis reluctantly consented to founding an official order which was acknowledged as such by Pope Innocent III at the Fourth Lateran Council (1215). It would be largely left to others to draft formal rules for the order and to organize the monasteries that would arise around this movement.

St. Dominic (ca. 1171–1221) founded the order of preachers during the same years that Francis gained a prominent following. Dominic was originally trained in the Augustinian order but developed an order of preachers to communicate effectively the Church's teachings to offset the devotion and fervor of the Cathars and Waldensians, who were zealous sects gaining influence at the time. While the Franciscans developed as a group focused on acts of charity and care, the order of preachers had a more formally ministerial role in teaching, learning, and preaching. The Dominicans were commended for their work by the Fourth Lateran Council, but because of a measure adopted by the council stipulating that there would be no new orders confirmed (the Franciscans were viewed as a previously existing order receiving confirmation of their order), they had to wait until Pope Honorius III officially confirmed to the Order of Friars Preachers in 1217.

In addition to the Franciscans and Dominicans, there are many other monastic traditions within the Catholicism. Among others, one could mention the Basilians (founded ca. 356), the Jesuits, founded by St. Ignatius Loyola during the time of the Protestant Reformation, or the Cistercians (founded in the eleventh century) who nurtured such luminaries as their key founder, Bernard of Clairvaux (1090–1153) and the twentieth century author, Thomas Merton (1915–1968). While the emphases and particularities of the communal life of the different monastic groups vary, there are also broad commonalities in the spiritual practices. There is often a regimented life of work, study, active ministry, and most

Chapter 7

importantly, prayer. The prayer life of such communities follows the Liturgy of the Hours which include set times for the recitation of prayers. These are: matins (during the night, usually midnight), lauds (dawn, sometimes 3:00 am), prime (early morning at 7:00 am), terce (third hour, mid-morning prayer at 9:00 am), sext (sixth hour midday prayer), none (ninth hour or mid-afternoon at 3:00 pm), vespers (evening prayer at 6:00 pm), and compline (night prayer before retiring for the night at 9:00 pm). The liturgy of the hours sets a rhythmic pattern to the life of the monk wherein he is centered in the meditation upon God, and in eucharistic practice, so as to infuse the more mundane work of the monastery with a sense of divine presence, influence, and camaraderie among the members of the community.

While the rhythmic patterns of the liturgical and work life of a monk are central to the communal formation of those comprising a monastery, monastic traditions speak also of contemplative prayer as a pinnacle of the spiritual life. The Cistercian monk, Thomas Merton, begins his book-length reflection on contemplation in the following way:

> Contemplation is the highest expression of [humanity's] intellectual and spiritual life. It is that life itself, fully awake, fully active, fully aware that it is alive. It is spiritual wonder. It is spontaneous awe at the sacredness of life, of being. It is gratitude for life, for awareness and for being. It is a vivid realization of the fact that life and being in us proceed from an invisible, transcendent and infinitely abundant Source.[7]

Contemplative prayer is not the prayer of liturgy, with its use of words, scripture, or other rites. It is a growth in the awareness of being and one's connection to it. As such, it is not a rejection of the physical world since the Christian cannot reject what God has created and declared good. At the same time, it is not an assertion of the ego of Western philosophy without it becoming a dissolution of the autonomous self at the same time. It is the recognition and enablement of a self-in-relation with and dependency upon the divine. In this guise, contemplation is not didactic reasoning for exegetical or philosophical truths. Neither is it an ecstatic experience with the loss of self or emotively based enthusiasm. It is an awakening to the transforming presence of divine love in all that is and thus is best expressed as a peaceful communion between the individual, God, and the world where the meeting occurs. Contemplation, therefore, is the experience of connectedness to the source of all things in the experience of transcendent love. This tradition, among others of social justice, scholarship, and teaching, are some of the core contributions of monasticism to the Christian tradition.

Buddhism

The Indian Vedic religion like its cousins the Roman and Greek religions, was a sacrificial tradition and not a devotional one. Along with sharing gods and cosmology in the main, the Vedic ritual of *soma* ingestion stands out. This seems to have been a now unknown psychotropic plant that required processing after which ingesting, one saw the gods. The knowledge of the specific plant was lost. Scholars postulate that it was probably a plant found in Central Asia as the Aryans moved from their homeland in the Caucuses to the subcontinent. However, one which did not grow in the jungles of India. Regardless, the ideal based on visiting an altered state has continued to inspire Indian spirituality and may have significantly influenced the development of meditations as an alternative to *soma*.

Chapter 7

If we identify yogic activity with asceticism, then when asceticism entered Indian religion is unknown. There is a Harappan (ancient city on the Indus River) seal showing a figure in a yogic posture which is more than three thousand years old.[8] As the Harappan script is undeciphered, anything authoritative about Harappan religion or even the seal's image is unestablished. By the ninth century BCE, asceticism was well established in emerging Hinduism and in the alternative systems that were being founded shortly thereafter. Two of these alternative systems were Buddhism and Jainism. There were others but these did not endure. At the core of Jainism is asceticism coupled with mendicancy. Even today one of the sects renounces their clothing and the monks walk through India begging naked. Some of the extinct groups aspired to very severe ascetic practices even onto forceful religious suicide. The Jains did accept fasting onto death in certain cases.

Shakyamuni before his awakening, trained with two of the most famous ascetics of his day. These men were Alara Kalama and Uddaka Ramaputta. He mastered their teachings and their meditational techniques, but these did not lead to the end of samsara (cycle of rebirth) and so he departed from each. He next entered into severe ascetic practices such as fasting for lengthy periods and holding his breath until experiencing the bends. He was so ardent about this that people thought he was a walking skeleton. These also did not lead to liberation from samsara and so he gave them up.[9] After his awakening, he founded a mendicant order that adheres to the middle way of neither indulgence nor severe asceticism. Thus, from the beginning Buddhism had an order of monks. However, men who wanted to become monks were not his first disciples. Laymen were the first disciples. In time, he established what is called the Four-fold Community: monks, nuns, laymen and laywomen. The creation of a nun's order was very controversial in India at the time and the Buddha may have been the first master to formally establish one. Others would follow.

For the first couple hundred years, the Buddhist monks and nuns were living as mendicants with no permanent dwellings. They wondered from town to town begging for their food and slept where they found themselves. There was one exception and that was during the monsoon season. The rains being near over whelming and the roads impassable, the monks and nuns would find shelter where they could for a few months. There were a few buildings on land donated to the monks or nuns, but they also often stayed in people's guest rooms or even mangers. Eventually, the monks and nuns acquired sufficient buildings. They generally stayed in these facilities for the monsoons and abandoned them as the weather improved. Over the centuries some stopped wandering and stayed in permanent establishments. They may have still went begging each day or they may have stored food donated by the faithful. As time passes, they became major landowners.

The body of literature that is most relevant to the monastic tradition is called the *Vinaya*. I term it the encoded Buddhist culture but much of it is the rules for the monks and nuns along with explanations. There are hundreds of rules for monks and nuns many of which are minor and deal with issues arising from groups living together. The more important rules deal with morality and ecclesiastic acts. The first of the most important rules is that a monk or nun is not allowed to have any sexual activity. The explanations go into great detail on how this is to be understood. For example, if a monk is raped it does not count as breaking the vow of celibacy. Both the rules and the explanations are thought to have been originally enunciated by the Buddha Shakyamuni. The *modus operandi* of the text is that each explanation is connected with a story of someone who violated the vow in specific ways and the case is placed before the Buddha for adjudication. Because it is considered Buddha speech, it has a sanctity that other writings do not even when such a text is by a great master. Throughout this literature there is no claim that simply by living as a monk or nun one would gain liberation. In some circles, the claim is that this is the most conducive mode of life for liberation.

Modern scholarship sees this body of literature as having developed over centuries. In fact, the development of the *Vinaya* seems to have consumed the most energy in the early centuries. From internal evidence we can see that there was movement in the rules from the wandering stage to the semi settle stage to the completely settled stage. We also know that the books composing the whole of the collection underwent editing and these changes were debated. Finally, we also find there were changes to the minor rules that were allowed due to local customs and settings. For example, originally monks and nuns were not allowed shoes, but these were allowed later as monasteries were established in the mountains where it snowed during part of the year. Another example is the case about money. Originally monks and nuns were not allowed to accept money only goods. However, as India's economics changed from a complete barter system to a moneyed system the question arose as to what should monks or nuns do? The resolution was that a trusted layperson would accept the money for the monks or nuns and so they would never touch it. Interestingly enough, in later centuries the monasteries acted like banks loaning and making profits on the interest but usually with the help of the laity. The updating and editing of the *Vinaya* concludes with the formulations of five major *Vinaya* traditions and several minor ones.[10] There is agreement on the most important rules, and it is in the minor aspects that there is differentiation between these five groups of texts.

In general, all the necessary teachings for liberation from samsara were provided to the monks, nuns, laymen and laywomen. It was first held that it was extremely difficult for the laity to gain awakening although possible, so the monastic life was the optimum. Over time, the laity was devalued as too were the nuns and extra-canonical explanations were formulated that justified the monks' special status. This movement also paralleled a change in the administrative structure of the monasteries. The change in the administrative structure took as its norm the new political reality in India.

Shakyamuni Buddha was born into a kingdom that was a democracy based upon a republic model. In this way it was very similar to Athens. The more important families selected a representative (usually an elder) to sit on the senate and decide the business of the kingdom. Each person in the senate had one vote. This was the model for the monasteries originally. Each fully ordained monk or nun (they had separate establishments) was allowed to sit in the assembly and each regardless of seniority or accomplishments had one vote. The democratic republics of India were conquered by true monarchies and their very existence was long forgotten. In the monasteries emphasis shifted from the one-man-one-vote decision making to the senior monk being the head and having most of the power to decide the monasteries business. This model becomes the dominant approach to organizing all Buddhism monasteries. Although we think of the land called India as a single country, in ancient times it was more like Italy, being composed of many different kingdoms that were frequently at war with each other until unified by an emperor. This unity, fortunately or not, was never enduring in the Indian setting. This non-centralized world acted as support for the decentralized orientation to the monastic community that was originally established by the Buddha Shakyamuni. Each monastery even within a single *Vinaya* tradition had considerable autonomy. This is well attested by documentation and accounts by foreigners in ancient times that went on pilgrimage to the holy land of Buddhist India.[11]

Unlike in Christianity, wherein doctrine became the driving force behind the division of sects and denominations, in Buddhism it was the differences in the *Vinaya* that acted as the underlying factor. As far as we know, no monastery in India had individuals who followed different *Vinayas*. All the inhabitants followed the same one. This seems logical as the *Vinaya* determines much of monastic life including times to eat and so on. The division into different *Vinayas* became standardized, garnered much debate but also efforts at reconciliation.[12]

One of the major reasons that the monks came to have a more exalted status was the fact of their education. For the first four or five hundred years, the Buddha teachings were not written down. The writing of religious texts was considered unacceptable and the *Vedas*, the works associated with the *Vedas*, and so much more were never written. This meant that years had to be spent in memorizing the texts. The Buddha Shakyamuni provided humanity with thousands of teachings. Some of these are very short but some are indeed long. In the canon the texts are grouped in part by length and the part of the collection of texts that are grouped as "long" would equal several Bibles in length. Yet, that is only one part of the canon. This of course, provides considerable challenges for any individual to memorize. It would take years for someone to memorize an entire division and most monks never did. A few rare and talented individuals could memorize the whole of the canon constituted by several thousand texts. Most monks memorized the *Vinaya* rules and liturgical texts needed and perhaps a few chosen *Sutras*. Most nuns seem not to have participated in the grand memorization exercise but like the average monk memorized what was needed and perhaps some well-liked texts. Both monks and nuns were required to recite a delineation of the monastic rules of their order each fortnight in addition to monastic ritual services. The educated monks were called on by other monks and nuns as well as the laity including kings and officials to teach. Teaching was by invitation and we do not hear of monks knocking on someone's door wanting to preach.

Other activities of the monks and nuns was administering to the laity. India is and was a gender segregated society. Nuns were allowed to administer only to women although monks could administer to both sexes however, if administering to women there were a number of rules that had to be closely followed as the tradition saw this as inherently dangerous for the monks. Indian is well known for having multiple genders and not just male and female. How non-male/female gendered people were treated by the early Buddhist community seems to run the gamut of possibilities and no single position emerges until late. In addition, monks and nuns would teach Buddhist principles and morality to the general public. They would also advise the upper echelon of society particularly the kings and ministers. As noted, they offered financial services to merchants, they sometimes kept grain stock for the farmers and the monasteries could act as hotels for travelers. Some would eventually evolve into major educational institutions similar to Oxford or Harvard. Perhaps most importantly they were to be a field of merit generation so that the laity could make donations and gain positive merit to a better life in the future with the hopes that one could also become a monk or nun.

Monasteries were built both in villages and in remote areas. Many of the surviving ruins of monasteries are noted as being founded by some king, queen, or minister. In addition to monasteries and universities there is also a tradition of establishing forest hermitages for those who wanted to be more secluded even from numbers of their fellow monastics. Temples and shrines were also common, and these may have monasteries or even a single cell for a monk associated with them. Monasteries were established in cave complexes and the layout followed the land formation. Monasteries in the open often were square in shape with an inner courtyard containing a raised platform (for teaching and rituals) and the well. Cells surrounded the court as too did the functional rooms. Each cell often had an elevated bed and a niche in the wall for a statue or other object. Monks and nuns were supposed to spend their time cultivating the teachings. This may include considerable periods of each day spent meditating, but also study, self-study, ritual acts and the drudgery of daily existence in ancient India (even when washing cloths one can gain insights).

China received all but one collection of the monastic literature. However, the tradition itself has an interesting history. Having nothing native approaching such an organized form of life and because only partial information was available early in the transmission, the Chinese began by developing tendencies within the Buddhist monastic tradition that were not found in India. Even after the whole of several traditions were transmitted, these tendencies make themselves felt. A couple of examples should suffice.

The classical Chinese social hierarchy was unique in the world. Scholar-officials, farmers, craftsmen, and merchants constitute the four divisions. It had high regard for farmers (i.e., the major work force at the time) and no position for holy men. Religion in ancient China was a family concern and the father was the "priest." It also had very low regard for beggars because they were seen as being non-productive and hence a drain on society. Enter an institution of organized men and women who begged and as an institution, initially did not achieve status for the doctrinal and ritual knowledge housed there. The outcome of the paradigm clash was that donations became sufficient to allow the inhabitants to not beg. Second, from prehistoric times the Chinese held that the male son had to perform the ritual offering to the departed family members. If these were not enacted, the departed became ghosts—an unwanted state. Therefore, it became the duty of the males to produce a male offspring, the more the better to guaranteed that the deceased would receive offerings. The first rule for monks is no sexual activity. Thus, men wishing to become monks at an early age were violating the most important duty to their families. Although various movements in this dynamic are noted in history, the conflict was never resolved, and Buddhist in China often faced criticism for being anti-family.

Regardless of these difficulties, the monasteries flourished and were supported by the underclass as well as the emperors. A group of monasteries were officially supported by the government to perform rituals for the emperors' long life and good health as well as for the empire in general and often for the war dead. Although the government controlled who officially ordained there were large populations of unofficial members of the monastic order over the centuries. From the beginning many monasteries did not need governmental approval so monasteries large and small, recognized or not was the norm. As Buddhism became a major force in Chinese society, whole villages would dedicate themselves to the teachings and created communities of laypeople who lived like monks and nuns, maintained their own temples but were not officially ordained. Various alternatives to the strict Indian model developed and so one reads about married monks.

The relationship with the imperial government was always fraught with problems. At times the emperors were great supportters of the monastic institutions and at times some persecuted them. Although monks and nuns had to bow to the emperor (in contrast to the Indian tradition) monks were given positions in the government and bestowed high honors. Nuns were often the advisors and confidants of the impresses and acted on their behalf. An exam system was established for the monks and in some centuries highly educated monks were seen as the equals of the literati. At other times, monks were chastised as having secret wives and not the field of merit they claimed, as being anti-family and foreign. Most importantly the vast wealth accumulated over centuries in land, jewels and precious metals, was looked upon with covetous eyes when emperors and high officials had missmanaged the country. The confiscation of metals from the monasteries although not frequent, led to the decrease in the production of metal statues and the increase of wood, plaster, and stone as a major artistic medium.

In addition to this sometimes elevated and sometimes persecuted situation in the Buddhist intuitional relation with the government, some emperors took Buddhism to heart and were deeply involved. For example, Emperor Wu of the Liang dynasty was so leaned in Buddhist doctrine; he would give lectures attended by large numbers of the monastic elite as well as foreign visitors. He also composed ritual texts, banned animals sacrifice, and much more. These activates garnered for him the epithet "Bodhisattva Emperor." Another early emperor thinking that having different *Vinayas* created problems, ordered that all monks and nuns be ordained in one *Vinaya* alone. The others could be studied but not lived. Thus, in East Asia, only one *Vinaya* continued to today. It is different from the one followed in Thailand and Sri Lanka but equally valid from a historic perspective.

The *Vinaya* is essentially based on an auditor or *shravaka* orientation which conflicts with the Mahayana doctrine in a number of ways. The *shravaka* orientation is focused on becoming an Arhat, renunciation, and personal liberation. Mahayana is focused on being a Bodhisattva (considered superior to Arhats), skillful living and universal liberation. India used to have many different schools based on the *shravaka* orientation. Today, only the Theravada still exist. Some *Vinayas* are more conducive to Mahayana ideas than others. Both Mahayana and the *shravaka* schools were transmitted to China, but the Mahayana schools became favored. The *Vinaya* selected by the emperor as the only one to thrive in China is one of these that is compatible. In addition, based on Mahayana texts another ordination tradition came about unknown in India although the notion of its base may be traced there. This is termed the transmission of Mahayana vows. These type of vows can be held by either monastics or lay people. It incorporates a number of monastic ideas but codifies the Mahayana emphasis on compassion. If adhered to, one becomes a person living a life somewhere between the strict monasticism of the *shravaka* type and secular life.

Korea, Vietnam, and Japan all follow the *Vinaya* and Bodhisattva code as developed in China, but we see differences emerging. Vietnam bordering on countries where the Theravada school is dominant (i.e., a *shravaka* based school) in the mid-centuries of the current era began having both Theravada *Vinaya* tradition and the one stemming from China along with its Mahayana ordination. Japan was the most innovative.

Buddhism in Japan was originally imported from Korea and China. Japanese culture being different from Chinese culture, Buddhism was supported and became a dominant force with a completely different dynamic than we see either in China or in Korea. Originally, all Buddhism monks had to take ordination in the ancient capital of Nara. When the new capital was built in Kyoto, the Emperor also began supporting the two new schools to arrive on Japanese shores. These two schools were imported by two outstanding monks who both joined the ranks of the most influential men in Japanese history. Saicho was the Japanese founder of the Tendai school in Japan. He was favored by the emperor and an intellectual power of his day. He argued in an address to the emperor that Mahayana followers should not have to take *shravaka* based ordination because it is not in keeping with Mahayana sentiments. This was accepted by the emperor. The outcome is that in a short period of time, the *shravaka* based ordination died out in Japan and only the Mahayana ordination survived. Most Japanese schools active today can trace their ordination through Tendai back to the original texts used in East Asian Mahayana transmission. The major exception is the Exoteric school started at the same time as Tendai by the other leading intellect of his day, Kukai. This school traces its ordination to exoteric texts.

Tibetan Buddhism has a very different history than East Asian Buddhist history. Tibet received Buddhism beginning around the seventh century. About seven hundred years after China which sparked the East Asian traditions in multiple countries. Although Buddhism entered Tibet from both India and China, it was Indian Buddhism that had the most enduring presence. In particular, the Tibetans only received a sub-tradition of one of the major *Vinaya* systems. The complete monk tradition was transmitted but at least according to some research only the novice nun tradition was transmitted. Full nun ordination may never have reached Tibet. In addition, Tibet too had the Bodhisattva code but this "ordination" was based on different texts than the one used in East Asia.

Perhaps one of the reasons for the incomplete nun transmission is the same reason why Tibet had an extremely high percentage of their male population ordained as monks. At the top of the world, life is difficult. Much of Tibet is above the tree line leaving limited areas in high alpine valleys as the living space. The land is rocky and so farming is indeed difficult, and the growing season is not long. Hailstorms are frequent in the warmer months so what you grow may be destroyed. Women died usually by the time they were forty-five due to poor health or complications from childbirth. Men usually lived longer. Women of childbearing age were at a premium. Having them enter the nunnery was removing a very valuable social resource. On the other hand, have large numbers of men in the monasteries help reduced the competition for the women. Tibet was one of the few cultures that socially sanctioned women have more than one husband probably to ensure continued pregnancy and support for the children.

Currently, there are only three *Vinaya* traditions alive in the world. All *Vinayas* are based on the *shravaka* orientation. The Theravada *Vinaya* is practiced in Sri Lanka and in South-East Asia and has been exported to many countries in the West. It is not conducive of Mahayana ideas or practices. The Tibetan and Chinese (/Korean/Vietnamese) *Vinayas* as found in those countries have also been exported to many countries in the West. These two *Vinayas* are conducive to the Mahayana. However, the larger Buddhist monastic communities established in the West tend to be populated by and supported by natives from the home country who now live in the West. For example, the rather expansive complex just outside of Los Angeles named Hsi Lai Tsu has a large number of Chinese monastics living within and is greatly supported by the Taiwanese and Chinese immigrants settled in that area. Monastic Buddhism among those of European or African decent in the West is still in a fledging state. This is probably due to various cultural factors and perhaps to the fact that Mahayana Buddhism is the most popular and this does not require ordination into a *Vinaya* although in some traditions it is much preferred.

Given the precipitous decline in Western Europeans and North Americans who are ordaining in the Catholic Church from just a century ago, I personally do not think there will be a popularization of Buddhist *Vinaya* ordination in the near future. There is a cultural dynamic well in place that removes serious consideration of the monastic career from devout followers and equally infringes upon the fortitude of the few who do decide to ordain as Catholic monks/ priests and nuns. This same cultural dynamic is also working in the Buddhist community. I have known a small number of Westerners who have ordained in a Buddhist *Vinaya* tradition and although some have made it a lasting life choice, most have defrocked. Just as with the sacrament of marriage in the Catholic Church the societal supports for the monastic life are now long absent regardless of being Buddhist or Catholic/Christian.

Conclusion

The developmental history between the Christian monastic tradition and the Buddhist tradition share some similarities but in the main is a mirror image of each other. In Christianity, monasticism fills a need within the community only after the apostles' and the martyrs' days had passed and a new grounding for the religion was needed. This was brought to the forefront with the legalization of Christianity at the time of Emperor Constantine. Buddhism was accepted by the Indian society and supported by kings from the onset. Monasticism was a cornerstone from the beginning. Although in India at that time, there were many who followed severe ascetic practices, the Buddha chose a middle way with moderate asceticism and moderate comfort. Life was in no way luxurious for monks and nuns, but it was also not overly austere. It did include self-mastery, chastity, discipline, partial fasting and hardships. Whereas monastic authority in early Christianity was based on charisma and wisdom, in Buddhism it was assigned by the texts from the beginning. However, personal authority was through the station of teacher and preceptor while institutional authority was a democratic mechanism.

Both Christian and Buddhist institutions upheld traditions of self-cultivation, contemplation, scholarship, being a spiritual refuge and service to the larger community. Why these activities originated in each religion is different as too is the need that was addressed in their formative period. However, in both leading a life that is outside of the mainstream of society's norms is well understood. The dedication and the fortitude that is required for such a lifestyle choice is well shared by both Christians and Buddhist.

The glories and the power of these long traditions in both religions allowing us to touch in this life and with this very body the ancient world from whence they grew, is having to face new challenges in the twenty-first century. However, as they say in psychology, "history is the best predictor of future behavior" in the history of these monastic traditions they have faced many challenges as the centuries rolled by. Certainly, they will adjust and continue well into the future.

---

[1] David Grumett and Rachel Muers, *Theology On The Menu: Asceticism, Meat and Christian Diet* (New York: Routledge, 2010), 1–35.

[2] Jürgen Moltmann, *The Crucified God* trans. R.A. Wilson and John Bowden (Minneapolis: Fortress Press, 1993), 53–65.

[3] St. Athanasius, *The Life of St. Anthony* (New York: Newman Press, 1950).

[4] Williston Walker, Richard A. Norris, David W. Lotz, Robert T. Handy, *A History of the Christian Church Fourth Edition* (New York: Scribner, 1985), 153–158.

[5] Benedict of Norcia, *The Rule of St. Benedict: In Latin and English with Notes* ed. Timothy Fry, O.S.B. (Collegeville: The Liturgical Press, 1981), 170–173.

[6] For what follows, see Malcolm Barber, *The Two Cities: Medieval Europe 1050–1320 Second Edition* (New York: Routledge, 2007), 131–154.

[7] Thomas Merton, *New Seeds of Contemplation* (New York: New Directions Books, 1972).

[8] A.L. Basham, *The Wonder that was India* (Allahabad: Rupa Co. 1991), 23–24.

[9] Robinson and Johnson, *ibid.* 13-14.

[10] E. Frauwallner. *The Earliest Vinaya and the Beginnings of Buddhist Literature.* (Roma: Istitute Italiano Per Il Medio Ed Estreme Oriente, 1956), 1 *ff.*

[11] See: James Legge, *A Record of Buddhist Kingdoms* (New York: Paragon Book Reprint Corp and Dover Publications, Inc. 1965?) and see: Samuel Beal, *Si-Yu-Ki Buddhist Records of the Western World* (Delhi: Motilal Banarsidass. 1981).

[12] See: Charles S. Prebish. *A Survey of Vinaya Literature.* (Taipei: Jin Luen Publishing House, 1994).

Chapter 8
The Place of the Human Being in the World and Cosmos

Christianity

In varying historical, cultural, and religious contexts humanity has sought to understand and make sense of its location in the world and the cosmos. Christianity has done so starting with the rich inheritance of the ancient Hebrew myths of creation and a developing doctrine that has, at times, rejected expansion in Western scientific knowledge, but which has come to accept modern science whilst still affirming its core theological and spiritual tenets. It has sought to provide sensibility to the question, "What does it mean to be human?" by responding through scientific, philosophical, and theological ideas. Most recently, Pope Francis has helped move the conversation forward with his encyclical on the environment, *Laudato Si*. In this text he brings together history, science, and theology to offer a robust Christian understanding of the natural world and the significance of human beings within it. Humanity's relationship with nature, our identities as creatures of God, and the central idea that human beings are made in God's image are all essential to grasping the Christian understanding of humanity.

The ancient Hebrew scriptures offer two accounts of creation and, therefore, two unique views of the place of human beings in the world. The second of these in the biblical book of Genesis (Genesis chapters 2–3) is the more ancient of the two. In this myth, the Yahwist writes of God using the imagery of common trades in ancient Mesopotamia. Here God appears as both a gardener and a potter who works with clay. In this ancient text, the author has God form the first human from the soil and breathes the breath of life into the lungs of this person (Genesis 2:7). The imagery is stark and signals a repeated theme in the Yahwist's material throughout the Pentateuch; humans are connected with the earth. It signals humanity's finitude and limits, but in the context of the ancient world it also elevates us as the creation of humans was often portrayed as the fruit of violence or associated with acts of evil.[1] This imagery of being made from the soil and receiving the breath of life also places humanity in connection with other living animals. This creation narrative also states that other animals are likewise made from the soil (Genesis 2:19) and were to be companions for the first human, although ultimately inadequate as full partners. Likewise, in the myth of the great deluge, the flood, the Yahwist states that "all flesh," in other words all living things such as humans and animals, have the breath of life (Genesis 6:17). This places humans in connection with the living world of nature and agriculture. For an ancient people, this was their most immediate surroundings and can be difficult for modern, urban humans to appreciate fully. However, for ancient Israelites, the world was the sphere of God's creation and humans were within it as but one member. Nature was not something "out there" or separate from human life. The texts of the Yahwist illustrate that humans and the earth are entangled with one another and always interrelated.

As these Hebrew texts were adopted and interpreted by early Christians, the relationship between humans and the earth became reinterpreted, while natural knowledge of the world remained important. In Augustine's commentary on Genesis, he acknowledges the potential for a plurality of interpretations of the biblical texts in what they convey about humans' location in the world. For example, when he discusses the meaning of the seven days of creation in the later, priestly Hebrew myth, Augustine states that people of various faiths know much of the natural world. Therefore, Christians have a mandate to speak intelligibly. He says, with some exasperation, that Christians, "presumably giving the meaning of Holy Scripture, talking nonsense" about nature and the place of the human within it "embarrass" Christian faith when they speaking ignorantly regarding either.[2] With this affirmation Augustine admonishes Christians that great care and diligence is needed when interpreting scripture alongside the contemporary understandings of the cosmos and that the interpreter of scripture ought to be aware of developments in human understanding of the world as this will aid in more faithful exegesis in the light of natural knowledge.

Augustine understood that the place of the first humans being above other animals in the biblical phrase of having "dominion" indicates our rational superiority. The fourth century theologian argues this dominion is indicative of humans being made in the divine image. This interpretation of the nature and role of humanity in the natural world became dominant in Christian interpretation and would subsequently become connected with rationality being described as a uniquely human trait. However, modern scholarship calls this into question on two fronts: (1) recent Hebrew scholarship has offered new insights into what it means for humans to have dominion, and (2) scientific and philosophical investigations into animal rationality have broadened our understanding of the cognitive and rational capacities of other species. Thus, the ancient Hebrew understanding of dominion has grown to offer new insights into the relational care entailed in that affirmation of human beings' role in the world. This will be discussed again below.

As Christianity reached the medieval era, theologians found a great resource in the newly rediscovered works of Aristotle that helped them reframe how they understood the location of the human in the cosmos. Aristotle's work in metaphysics and the soul, among others, helped the medieval thinkers reconceive the role of natural knowledge in Christianity and aided in reshaping how they understood the human person in relation to the rest of the created order. Thomas Aquinas was a leader in this Aristotelian movement and was instrumental in this reconceptualization. Following Avicenna and Averroes,[3] Thomas posited that while everything that exists has being (*esse*) there are gradations of being indicative of a thing's nature. For example, living things are ranked on a higher gradation of being than non-living things, but both have the being of existence. Higher levels of being contain all of the properties of lower levels of being while also having the properties unique to the thing's particular gradation. For example, rocks are made of matter and are solid. Plants are also made of matter and are solid but are living as well and therefore on a higher gradation while retaining the properties of lower gradations. These gradations of being are essential in understanding how the medieval thinkers understood humanity's location in the created order and can be illustrated in the various understandings of the soul.

Thomas understood all living things to have a soul. "The soul, according to Aquinas, is the one organizing principle of the internal structure of living things through which their health and activity are both regulated and maintained."[4] Along with other medieval Christians he argued that there were three types of souls: nutritive, sensitive, and rational. The nutritive soul is the power of growth and the ability to gain nutrition from one's surroundings as plants do with moisture, nutrients from the soil, and from sunlight. The sensitive soul is exemplified in the power of movement and the ability of a living being to respond to the senses and act within one's environment. Animals have this and engage the world through the senses, move within their environment, and therefore have some measure of knowledge as they interact with their surroundings. The rational soul enables the capacity of a living organism to engage in complex systems of thought, to deliberate over problems, and produce reasoned choices. It is the capacity to comprehend abstractions and perceive oneself and others and organize these in systems of thought. Humans have this capacity and, according to the medieval, unique among earthly creatures in having a rational soul. Thomas defines a person as an "individual substance with a rational nature."[5]

While Thomas believes that humans are the highest of earthly beings, he does not affirm that humanity is the highest order of creatures *per se*. Recalling his gradations of being, to be a material substance without any living qualities was beneath being a material substance with life and to be a living material substance was beneath a living material substance with sense reason and so on. Therefore, to be a material substance with a rational nature (humans) is to be beneath a creature of pure intellect (angels). Angels are a part of the created order and so beneath God, who is being-itself. However, Thomas conceived of angels as a single substance (pure intellect) and so are located above humans who are an admixture of matter and intellect. Because of this, it would be a misunderstanding to argue that Thomas believed humans to be the pinnacle of the created order. Because he thought humans were an admixture of substances, he believes humans to be on a lower rung of the ladder of being than angels, who are also created beings. However, humans do stand as a transition point between heavenly and earthly creatures because of our ability to live materially and intellectually. The resulting view of humanity elevates our standing in the world and makes humans the logical vehicle for the incarnation of the divine Word. These soteriological implications nurtured a view where Earth was the center of the universe and humans the pinnacle of earthly life. This would be called into question with the advent of scientific cosmologies forcing Christianity to rethink its beliefs regarding the place of humans in the cosmos.

When Nicolaus Copernicus (1473–1543) published *The Revolutions of the Heavenly Bodies* he revolutionized both Astronomy and how European Christianity thought of humanity with his advocacy of a heliocentric universe. His work decentered the Earth, and humanity with it, removing both from its central place in the universe. This notion was intensely contentious and so Copernicus waited to publish his work until days before his death as he did not want to be the subject of controversy. As such, the book escaped condemnation until the work of Galileo Galilei (1546–1642). Galileo constructed a telescope that allowed him to observe the satellites of Jupiter, the rings of Saturn, the phases of Venus, and the moon's craters. Seeing the movement and observing the changes in course of astronomical objects confirmed Copernicus's theory and refuted the Aristotelian cosmology that change occurred only on Earth while the perfect heavens were eternal and unaltered.[6]

The Catholic Church did not respond positively to Galileo's findings. Despite Galileo being a devout Catholic who sought to reconcile the new science with the ancient faith, the religious authorities wanted him silenced. As a result, Galileo was summoned before the Inquisition and his book was condemned. Under threat of punishment he was forced to recant his theory on his knees. The ecclesiastical authorities then placed him under house arrest in Florence, Italy, where he remained until his death. The challenge to humanity's secure place atop an earthly hierarchy of being affirmed by the medieval Church would again arise in the nineteenth century. What Copernicus and Galileo changed in the view of humanity's place from the standpoint of astronomy, Darwin would do from the standpoint of biology. Darwin's theory of evolution through random mutation and speciation became widely accepted by the scientific community, though there was initial debate. In this instance the response of the Catholic Church was more varied, though initial negativity remained.[7]

Pope Pius IX was a conservative pope who responded negatively to all modernizing tendencies after the wave of radical revolution in Italy that saw the assassination of his prime minister and the Pope was forced to flee the Vatican. This led the pope to reject the Enlightenment and modernity, and this became crystallized in his infamous *Syllabus of Modern Errors*. The concern over Darwin's theory was, once more, that it decentered humanity from its place in the cosmos. This could have several implications. First, it was thought to threaten the incarnation of Christ and the role of salvation that humanity would have. Second, it called into question particular readings to the biblical account of creation and the entrance of sin as the product of the wrongful choice of an original couple. Third, it appeared to bring humanity in closer relationship with other species, highlighting the randomness of mutation which was viewed to threaten divine providence. All of these resulted in the perception that the theory of evolution was thought to call into question the place of humanity in God's providential design of salvation.

However, not all Church leaders thought this. Blessed John Henry Newman[8] was Cardinal at the time of the publication of Darwin's work. He wrote in a letter dated May 22, 1868 that he saw no reason to be overly critical of evolution. He wrote, "Mr. Darwin's theory need not then to be atheistical, be it true or not; it may simply be suggesting a larger idea of Divine Prescience and Skill."[9] The openness and insight of Newman would become the dominant position of the Catholic Church. The Catholic Church now has an open view to the theory of evolution, with its implications for reconfiguring how humanity's role on the Earth and in the cosmos is perceived. For example, in the year 1950 Pope Pius XII advocated evolution being a theory worthy of study while Pope John Paul II stated in 1996 that the theory of evolution is more than a hypothesis. This synthesis of science and religion in Christian theology reflects much more closely the original insights of Thomas Aquinas, who brought together the very best understandings of the natural world in the Aristotelianism of twelfth century Europe with fresh interpretations and understandings of religious thought and life.

Modern Protestant theology has responded in varying ways to the development of scientific knowledge and its impact on how Christianity locates the human within the world. One approach modern Protestant thinkers have taken to the topic is to examine the role of biological evolution in terms of theodicy: the question of divinity in the face of suffering. Such an approach highlights the suffering, superfluity, and redundancies found within evolution. On this reading the primary question of evolution to Christianity is not the goodness of humanity after a fall into sin, but rather the goodness of God in light of death and suffering as a constitutive necessity for the evolution of life.[10] The response is to highlight the cruciform nature of God's participation with the world. This is to say, this account highlights the role of solidarity in suffering expressed in the crucifixion of Christ as revelatory of God's solidarity with suffering creation. The task of the human is then to embody the redemptive features of the kingdom of God expressed through ethical engagement.

A more robustly theological account from the standpoint of Protestant theology is expressed in the animal theology and ethics of David Clough.[11] Rather than taking biological evolution as the starting point for religious inquiry, this approach expounds Christian doctrines to reconceive of the relationship between humans and other animals from a theological perspective. Without disputing the reality of evolution, this approach nonetheless is less concerned with squeezing Christian belief into scientific discourse than it is noting the Christological and redemptive features within Christian belief that locate humans alongside other animals in life-affirming relationship. God's identity as creator of all things inversely entails that all things are loved by God and have equal standing before God, since God's love is the reference point rather than the differentiated capacities of varying species. The incarnation of Christ has particular resonance with the biblical affirmation that Christ took on "flesh" not only humanity. Thus, the incarnation entails Christ sharing in all of creation, rather than only that which is distinctively human. In the words of David Clough, "if we judge it illegitimate to discriminate between Jews and Gentiles or women and men on the basis of the kind of creature in whom God became incarnate, it seems that we should also consider it illegitimate to discriminate between humans and other animals on this basis."[12] Similarly, understanding the continuity and connectedness humans have with the other species and the natural world through Christ has led to fresh spiritual insights, exemplified in Catholicism by Pope Francis's encyclical, *Laudato Si*.

Pope Francis continually emphasizes the relational realities that comprise human life. He advocates and embodies connecting with people, especially those in need, and realizes that we are in profound relationships with our fellows. He continually asserts that we do not live isolated or in an intrinsically hierarchical relationship with other persons, where some have claim to greater moral consideration over others by virtue of wealth, prestige, or intellect. In his encyclical letter on the environment, Pope Francis broadens the scope of these relationships to the non-human world. Francis was not the first to speak of this. Pope Benedict XVI wrote of the moral and practical responsibility humanity has toward the natural environment in our economic endeavors.[13] However, in bringing together considerations from the natural sciences and moral questions from theological and pastoral concerns, Francis highlights the relational quality of human connectedness with other creatures. In *Laudato Si*, he notes that non-human animal species and other living beings such as plants are not mere resources for human use and extraction. Rather, they have their own dignity, relationship with the Creator, and role in the natural workings of the Earth.[14] The recognition of our integral relationship to others in the created order sets humanity in loving communion with the natural world. This relationship "entails a loving awareness that we are not disconnected from the rest of creatures, but joined in a splendid universal communion."[15] This reconfigured under-standing of the place of the human in the natural world is developed from the key moral insights of the Christian tradition beginning with God as intrinsically relational within the Trinitarian life *in se* and is then reflected in human life as image bearers of God.

The priestly creation account states, "So God created humankind in his image, in the image of God he created them; male and female he created them" (Genesis 1:27). While this assertion has been integral to Christian anthropology, its cryptic nature has resulted in millennia of debate over its meaning. However, theologians have noted that humans are a synthesis of the individual and the relational just as Christians affirm the one God is Triune and relational. Thus, there is not only an analogy of being (*analogia entis*) between humans and God, but also a relational analogy (*analogia relationis*). Thus, if humans have a priestly vocation to the world and model this after Christ's priestly vocation, then a Christian understanding of the divine image has a Trinitarian grounding and a Christology focus. In other words, humans are constituted in their essence by the Triune God and participate in the relational reality of that being through Christ's participation in the incarnation and vocation of love. In this way, the divine image can be understood to have a passive and an active component. The passive component exemplifies the gratuitous gift of life and being. The active component exemplifies the vocation humanity has to the world in relationship with it. This active relationship is how Christians are intended to understand the "dominion" over creation described in the Hebrew accounts. It is not an authoritarian dominion, but rather a mandate to care as a loving shepherd cares for the sheep or as a parent loves a child.

Buddhism

In the Indian context, Buddhism initiated a position on humanness that was unique in its foundation if conforming to the general expectations of the spiritual dialogue in general. It is well documented that based on the *Vedas,* Hinduism held that seeds which could be germinated were sentient. Even such phenomena as wind and fire had a divine aspect. Of course, animals and those of the world beyond: gods, denizens, *et cetera*, are also sentient. In Jainism too, plants and seeds were considered sentient. Thus, in these two traditions, humans held a unique position among the group of sentient beings that formed an array including seeds up to the gods. But Buddhism rejected this position.

Buddhism took the position that only those in the world beyond, animals and humans were members of the sentient group. That world beyond included the members of the six stations mentioned before: denizens, ghosts, titans and gods. The general Buddhist position is that the mind stream can be reborn in any of these stations, live out its life, and die to be reborn elsewhere in the system. Thus, in some sense, the basic mind in each class is the same although the abilities of that mind are limited or expanded by the class of rebirth. Gods having the greatest mental powers and lower animals such as amebae having a very limited ability. These mental powers are not directly related to the nirvana project. That is, being a god for example, does not make it easier to gain nirvana. In fact, it is humans who occupy the most beneficial station because their faculties are fully functional (whereas an amoeba's are not) and in general, human life allows for some mixture of pleasure and suffering. The gods, on the other hand, have a life that is overwhelmingly pleasurable, and this distracts from the pursuit of nirvana. A statement based on a pragmatic view that when we are overjoyed, we forget about the suffering and therefore our desire to leave the cycle of rebirth is lessened. We have also seen above that a less popular text although one of considerable significance, states that we started this cycle as a type of light-mind being which underwent a process of devolution. The basis of this devolution is desire and immorality. This process also explains the origin of social organization which for Buddhist has its moral component.

Thus, like Christianity, Buddhism inherited a rich and complex cosmos. In the case of Buddhism, that cosmos closely resembled the Roman and Greek traditions which ultimately came from the same Indo-European source, but the Buddhist understanding is further developed. Unlike Christianity, Buddhism was not hesitant in accepting science but in principle embraced it. No surprise given that both systems have at their core a causation theory. The special status of humans is recognized from the beginning of the Buddhist tradition and remains the primary focus even though a common epithet of the Buddha was "Teacher of Gods and Men." We could also add to this that in the Buddhist mythic stories animals, ghosts, and others may also benefit from the Teachings. The theological underpinnings of Christian ideas on humanity are not found in Buddhism. There is no equivalent to the discussion of being made in the likeness of God and the working out of the implications of this statement are not found. The Buddhist discussion of the special status of humans is grounded in humans' mental capacities and the fact that human life is a mix of pleasure and suffering. There also seems to be no idea of humans having dominion over other creatures. The natural order of humans raising livestock for food and other purposes as

Chapter 8

well as hunting is mentioned. Here too, the texts only speak about the karma generated by various acts performed in relations with these animals.

As noted above, the Buddhist canon contains three major sections (along with various works by great masters in some collections). One of these sections is the *Abhidharma*. This collection consists of a detailed, scholarly, presentation of the teachings and the working out of many implications. So much of what is found in these texts presents sophisticated insightful discussions of the mind, its states, its content, and the implications for liberation that early western scholars referred to it as "psychology." For example, the first text of this class in the Pali language entitled literally, "Compendium of Phenomena/ *Dhamma Sangaṇi*" was given the English title, *The Buddhist Manual of Psychological Ethics*.[16] Although the *Abhidharma* class of literature contains far more than teachings on psychology, this topic is extensively covered.

I know of no Buddhist writings that speak of the divine essence of various phenomena such as that of fire. Nor is there discussion denying this possibility. That there are gods whose function is to control certain natural phenomena is accepted. So, Buddhist do not deny that possibility of a god of fire, or wind, or thunder but the discussion of their essence somehow united with the actual phenomena seems lacking. Initially, Buddhism did not deny followers the possibility to have relationships with the gods. Those relationships were understood as being rather contractual (make a sacrifice and get a boon) and as such were not devotional. However, for Buddhist the gods are also trapped in this cycle of rebirth and therefore cannot help much in liberating one to the shores of nirvana. In fact, they too need to be liberated and that is why it is reported that the gods use to come to listen to the Buddha teach. Remember, a being accumulating a vast amount of positive merit can be reborn as a god but when that reserve of merit is exhausted, they will die out of that god station and be reborn elsewhere.

The relationship between humans and the non-sentient world is expressed in a number of teachings. Plants, plant products, rocks and minerals are not thought to have senses although they can have chemical reactions that respond to their environment. In some commentaries to Buddhist texts composed by great masters of different traditions it clearly states that plants come into existence and go out of existence, but sentient beings are reborn repeatedly. Both in the *Sutra* collection and in the *Vinaya* there are injunctions that one should not be wanton with plants. Buddhist ought not to pollute water with food remnants or excrement. Further, the teachings caution that small creatures live in the water and one should be careful to not injure them. It is known that water was commonly filtered in an attempt to remove these living beings.

Regarding animal life, Buddhist are called on to refrain from killing, from ordering thing to be killed, or to accept meat from an animal that were specifically killed for one's consumption. However, these restrictions were directly connected with the act of killing and not against the consumption of products made from animals. Meats of all types can be consumed as long as the above restrictions are applied. For example, if a farmer had previously killed a chicken for his own consumption and then gave some of the meat to a monk or nun, that meat would be acceptable. In the modern setting, acquiring meat from a market would fulfill all the restrictions and thus rendered acceptable. However, some modern thinkers have argued that there is an indirect connection between the consumer and the industry and that would violate the restriction. The Buddhist texts are silent on this point. Later in India, vegetarianism became popular and this also entered Buddhist thought so many Buddhist are vegetarians. In general, the lay people were not ostracized for killing animals for food, but it was taught that they would have to face the karmic consequences of their actions. In addition, Buddhist are called on to help end the suffering of animals and to save those who would be slaughtered if possible. An excellent example of this is that many Chinese Buddhist monasteries have large ponds where people who have purchased fresh-water fish at a market can release them and the fish will live out their natural lives. Even though the teachings repeatedly state calculating the merit or demerit from an act is only fully understood by a Buddha, it is commonly said that benefiting an animal brings about the merit of one hundred times the act for the benefactor. Further, the inflicting of harm, even onto death, does not all weigh the same. The negative merit garnered from maliciously killing a mosquito is considerably less than from maliciously killing a human. So too with lesser acts. Also unintentionally killing an animal may be under-stood as generating no negative merit although some teachings hold that some minor negative merit is made. Since the negative merit for intentional malicious acts against humans is greater, this attests to the elevated station that humans hold.

In East Asian Buddhism there developed a very refined appreciation of the complex web of interrelationality within nature. This is an outgrowth of the intersection of the Buddhist ideas of casual web theory developing in Indian Buddhism and sensitives in the native culture that find expression in Daoism and Shinto. Expressions of this appreciation can be found in Buddhist poems and art forms such as the Zen garden. Additionally, in order to promote vegetarianism, stories were told on how the animal the farmer is about to kill and eat was his one beloved mother now reborn in an animal form. Considering the veneration East Asians have for the ancestors, this was indeed a powerful tool.

As is know from the other chapters, the corner stone of Buddhism is that there is no soul/self or *atman*. People lack a soul and so do all other sentient beings. The major difference between a soul theory and the Buddhist idea of a mind stream is that the former is or has some aspect that is permanent and unchanging while the Buddhist idea is that change happens even if this may take multiple lifetimes. If the same mind stream can be found in an animal, a human and a god, then what is the difference and how are humans special. The answer to this is not that the mind stream is fundamentally different but that the station it is reborn into allows for the differences.

The human station differs from the animal in providing an admixture of characteristics and properties as noted above. Buddhist texts provide great details on what constitutes these differences. To view some of the more important differences, I will use as my guide the *Abhidharma* writings of Vasubandhu; one of the greatest Buddhist masters who lived in the fourth century CE. Before beginning his understanding of the unique position that humans hold, it is worth noting that he presented in brief a statement on evolution of life first beginning in the sea and ending with some land creatures developing the abilities to fly.[17] Certainly not as sophisticated as Darwin's theory but also not controversial.

To begin with, Vausbandhu informs us that human individuals are only born on the earth's land masses. The daily objects of desire are formed by external factors (to them) but humans have the ability to dispose or destroy these objects. This is contrasted with the gods who merely will things into existence. In our sphere of activity within the universe, only humans born in one of these lands can begin the process of spiritually cultivating. That is the path of nirvana and all that is found on this path must be initiated from the human station. It is possible to cultivate while in other stations either above or below that of human, but the process can only be started from the point of being human. A Bodhisattva might be reborn as an animal in order to enact compassion to assist in spiritually advancing another. In the Jataka tales (the mythic tales of the Buddha Shakyamuni's previous lives) he would sometimes manifest in an animal form. Also, one already fully established on the path to nirvana may be reborn in the heavens. This too could be out of compassion for example the future Buddha Maitreya is teaching in one of the heavens presently. It also could be a rebirth as a god wherein he/she would continue their spiritual cultivation.

Further, generally only in the human station can one plant roots of those qualities required for liberation onto nirvana. Such qualities as non-covetousness or the establishing of the wish to gain awakening for the sake of others. The balanced combination of "disgust" and wisdom appropriate for advancement is not found among the gods or hell beings. It is also in the human station that one can transform one's facilities removing the impure psychological qualities such as delusion, that prevent one from gaining liberation. In general, other stations although sentient do not afford this possibility. Troubled states of mind, including madness are also a possibility for humans although they share this with animals, ghosts, and some of the lower gods (one can recall the stories of the Greco-Roman gods being mad). Additionally, humans can cut off their roots of goodness (the positive merit already acquired) by various means such as developing a false view. This flows as a consequence from a willful act that involves discernment. An animal or denizen lacking the necessary discernment cannot cut off their roots of goodness. However, even in the realm of humans not all have equally developed faculties and those who have lesser developed faculties may not be able to cut off their roots of goodness (e.g., children). There were some who argued that women fall into this group but Vasubandhu strongly argued that unfortunately woman were fully equal in this regard.[18]

Buddhist morality puts forth the idea that there are five "mortal" acts that will bring about immediate retribution upon death whereas the manifestation of what is merited in other cases may take many lifetimes before it develops. These five are: patricide, matricide, killing an Arhat (worthy), injuring a Buddha and creating a schism in the community. These transgressions certainly produce rebirth in hell upon the departure from this life without even the intermediate period. Most Buddhist teachings claim that it is possible to not be reborn in one of the six stations immediately upon departure from this life. There could be a period of up to forty-nine days where the mind is in a dream like state. The determining factor is the karma one has created. However, the five transgressions preclude the possibility of their developing this intermediate period. The gods never engage in these five transgressions while denizen, ghosts, and animals are incapable of committing them. Also, if a human does not have fully functional faculties, they too are not responsible but fully formed male and female humans can generate the negative merit from these acts. Other acts are also counted as transgressions that only humans can engage in such as defiling one's mother or killing a lower level Bodhisattva. However, these will gain one rebirth in hell, but it may not be immediately upon departing from this life.

In addition to these more general characters that the human station allows, there are further, more technical points that distinguish humans from other stations. As such, the discipline that is needed for accomplishment is an important topic in Buddhist literature. This is understood as consisting of worldly morality (not to kill, steal, etc.), trans-worldly morality (arising from profound meditational states) and morality arising from following the path of the Buddha. The first are the basic moral guidelines for a healthy spiritual life and are similar to Christian morality based on some of the Commandments. This approach is understood as being founded on renouncing. The morality arising from the mediational states and from the higher levels of the path are understood as being based on having abandoned the root of immorality. That is for example, one no longer generates the mental state that must preexist before killing a fellow human. Only humans and the gods are able to be disciplined in these three types of morality. Discipline itself is developed from reflection and the vigor of respect and fear. The animals and other lower rebirth stations and humans who lack fully formed faculties also lack the abilities of reflection, respect and fear. The teachings also indicate that if one wishes to destroy morality first remove respect and fear.

In the meditational tradition there are in depth presentations of multiple techniques and the states of mind that can be achieved. These states are increasingly refined as various mental reflections drop off. Another way of understanding these meditational states is as more subtle levels of concentration. According to the *Abhidharma* literature of Vasubandhu,[19] it is only in the station of being human that a person can first produce the "Concentration of Extinction" which leads to the ending of rebirths and the gaining of nirvana. However, simply being able to achieve this concentration is insufficient for gaining nirvana; it must be cultivated repeatedly.

Although there are innumerable concentrations mentioned in the vast collection of Buddhist scriptures and some are based on single-pointedness while others include a range of mental content, there are eight that have greater significance, beginning in the early phase in the development of Buddhism, but maintain their importance through its long history. Four of these are called the "Exalted Dwellings" or the "Immeasurables."[20] In short these are complete states of mind which are concentrated on either compassion, loving kindness, sympathetic joy or equanimity. Only humans can cultivate these dwellings (see Chapter 6).

There is a set of meditations that begins with a rotting human corpse. By meditating on the rotting, being both internal and external, and focused only on the external these two aspects are associated with the disagreeableness of the object and called the two deliverances. When the mind is calmed, and the disagreeableness no longer prevails this is the third deliverance. Further, there is a series of meditations, eight in number, that focus on sense-objects (e.g., sound, odor, etc.) and the mental association with these.[21] This group is called the Dominant Reciprocalities. There is also another set of meditations termed the All-Encompassing Reciprocalities equaling ten that include the four elements: the colors—blue, yellow, red, white; space and consciousness.[22] This group of meditations, the Three Deliverances, the Dominant Reciprocalities and the All-Encompassing Reciprocalities can only be cultivated by humans.

While sitting in a single meditation session moving from one specifically defined concentration to another is possible. In fact, we are informed by the *Nirvana Sutra*[23] that when the Buddha Shakyamuni was about to enter complete nirvana (i.e., death) he transversed eight different specifically defined concentrations. Of course, he was well familiar with each. However, when moving from one to another there is the possibility of losing the concentration and reentering one's normal state of mind. In order to avoid this, there is discussed the possibility of entering a transitional concentration that will allow a bridging from one specifically defined concentration to another. This transitional concentration can only be achieved by humans.[24]

According to Buddhist ideas, the mind-stream can be reborn in any of the six stations from hell up to heaven. The beings in all of these stations are sentient whereas the plants and minerals are not. Thus, the insentient can come into and go out of existence but the sentient beings revolve in the cycle of rebirth until finding release in nirvana.

Of the six stations, humans hold an exclusive position because of the qualities and the possibilities that this station offers to those who are reborn within. With its balance between suffering and pleasure, the fact that all the facilities can be operational, having reason and discipline affords humans the necessary foundation for initiating the path to nirvana. Morality is particularly a determining characteristic along with reflection, respect and fear. Although some qualities may be shared by those born in other stations such as the gods or animals, humans have a specific and unique combination.

In the strikingly detailed meditational literature, there are a number of meditations and meditative states that one can only visit either from or beginning from the human station. Of special note are the Exalted Dwellings which are amply discussed across the centuries of Buddhist root texts and their commentaries. Further meditations like the Three Deliverances, the Dominant Reciprocalities and the All-Encompassing Reciprocalities are also cultivated solely from the human station. Additionally, the development of a transitional concentration when moving between various concentrations can only be generated as a human. Finally, the all-important Concentration of Extinction a necessary step before achieving nirvana has to be first achieved while being a human.

These points and others of less significance help explain the reason that being born on our station is often referred to as "this precious human body." To be able to have these spiritually important qualities, prospects and abilities is understood as requiring a rather large accumulation of positive merit. Furthermore, this opportunity afforded by our station ought not to be wasted on mere mundane enjoyments, the non-cultivation of discipline, and the immoral. Through ardent cultivation in this human life, significant advancement even onto to the shores of nirvana can be achieved. With immeasurably long periods between this human life and another human life possible, what a lost opportunity to not cultivate.

Conclusion

As humans we are driven to understand our world, our place in that world, and for many the world beyond. This insatiable thirst leads us to explore all areas of understanding be they theological, scientific, spiritual, or otherwise in trying to gain wisdom. The religious traditions of Buddhism and Christianity although beginning from very different starting lines and developing along substantially different trajectories, are united in the human desire to know. Orphans are frequently driven to find their birth parents so that they will know their place, their roots and we humans as a collective are equally driven to know our place; so, we explore.

Christianity was particularly taxed to find a path that would allow them to take into account the Hebrew stories of creation, of being in God's image and the unique message of Christ and the soteriological implications. At the same time, they are called on to not fail to consider advancements in human knowledge of the natural world. The later union of Greek philosophy with Christian theology provided considerable depth of insight, demanding methods and exquisitely expressed reasoned arguments but also bolstered the geocentric world view forming a dogma that survived for centuries. With advancements in both technology and new discoveries such as those made from the Campanile of St. Mark's Basilica in Venice by Galileo Galilei with his newly fashioned telescope that had lenses made in Murano, a crises of thought and faith was generated in some Christian spheres as the Renaissance advanced and the age of Enlightenment dawned.

However, not all realms of thought within the Christian tradition saw these discoveries as a direct threat. With time, they could be absorbed and understood within the framework of theology arriving at the current position of Catholics and others that science is furthering our understanding of God's creation, of the position of humans within that creation and to the beneficial relationship that God ordained between humans and nature.

With Buddhism the question of the uniqueness of humans in the greater pictures of things, a picture inherited from and developed upon the Indo-European world view, is not one of God's creation but as that gained by the station on which humans are born. This station allows for those born to have a combination of pleasurable and unpleasurable experiences, to have particular capabilities and prospects both in general and specifically within the capacities to achieve advanced meditational states. This combination and these capabilities are not shared in total with other possible stations of rebirth. In short, one has to be reborn as a human to begin the path to nirvana and to reach that last step before entering nirvana.

Any being reborn in one of the six stations is sentient whereas the plants and minerals as found on earth are not. Killing a plant in and of itself is not karmically harmful but there are teachings on how damaging the environment may be harmful to sentient beings and so producing negative merit. A Buddhist is called on to thoughtfully and conservatively use the environment but only as much as needed and to not be wanton in its destruction. This lead Buddhist in ancient times to even filter the water so as to not harm the unseen creatures living therein.

Being based on causality, having an idea of evolution, and Buddhist masters being actively engaged in advancing knowledge (in mathematics, logic, philosophy, etc., and particularly medicine) the difficulties and conflicts between thought systems as seen in Europe running from the Renaissance through the European Enlightenment were not found in the Buddhist setting.

If we remove for the moment the theological/spiritual considerations, we can see that both systems strove to understand the uniqueness of being human and the relationship and place that humans have with their environment. Further, in both systems they questioned and participated in the development and furthering of human knowledge in its quest to understand one of the most fundamental questions to confront all people in all times.

---

[1] Joseph Ratzinger, *In the Beginning: A Catholic Understanding of the Story of Creation and the Fall* trans. Boniface Ramsey, O.P.(Grand Rapids: Wm. B. Eerdmans, 1995), 42–43.

[2] St. Augustine, *The Literal Meaning of Genesis vol. 1*. trans. John Hammond Taylor S.J. (New York: Newman Press, 1982), 42–43.

[3] Avicenna (ca. 980–1037) and Averroes (1126–1198) were the influential interpreters of Aristotle who were essential to Europe recovering Aristotelian thought. These Islamic philosophers were the primary sources for medieval Christians in understanding Aristotle and their Neoplatonic reading of Plato's student can be seen in Thomas Aquinas's account of the gradations of being central to his locating the human in the created order. See John Marenhon, *Medieval Philosophy: An Historical and Philosophical Introduction* (New York: Routledge, 2007).

[4] Judith Barad, *Aquinas on the Nature and Treatment of Animals* (Maryland: International Scholars Publications, 1995), 27. See also, Celia Deane-Drummond, *The Wisdom Of The Liminal: Evolution and Other Animals in Human Becoming* (Grand Rapids: William B Eerdmans Publishing, 2014).

[5] Thomas Aquinas, *Summa Theologiae*, Ia q. 29 a.1.

[6] William F. Lawhead, *The Voyage of Discovery: A History of Western Philosophy* (Belmont: Wadsworth Publishing Company, 1996), 222–227.

[7] Charles Darwin, *On The Origin of Species* (New York: Bantam Classics, 2008).

[8] John Henry Newman was beatified by Pope Benedict XVI on September 19, 2010.

[9] John Henry Cardinal Newman, *The Letters and Diaries of John Henry Newman*, edited by C.S. Dessain and T. Gornall, vol. XXIV (Oxford: Clarendon Press, 1973), 77–78.

[10] Christopher Southgate, *The Groaning of Creation: God, Evolution, and the Problem of Evil* (Louisville: Westminster John Knox Press, 2008), 13.

[11] See David L. Clough, *On Animals Volume 1: Systematic Theology* (New York: T & T Clark, 2012) and David L. Clough, *On Animals Volume 2: Theological Ethics* (New York: T & T Clark, 2018).

[12] Clough, *On Animals Volume I*, 84.

[13] Pope Benedict XVI, *Caritas in Veritate*, 40.

[14] Pope Francis, *Laudato Si*, 33, 221.

[15] Pope Francis, *Laudato Si*, 220.

[16] Caroline A.F. Rhys Davids, *A Buddhist Manual of Psychological Ethics* (London: The Pali Text Society, 1974).

Chapter 8

---

[17] Sadakata, *ibid.* 54.
[18] Vasubandhu, *Abhidharma Kośa Bhāṣyam* Fr. trans.Fr. Louis De la Vallèe Poussin/trans. Eng. Leo M. Pruden (Berkeley: Asian Humanities Press, 1988), throughout.
[19] *Ibid.*, 1279 *ff.*
[20] *Ibid.*, 1264 *ff.*
[21] *Ibid.*, 1271 *ff.*
[22] *Ibid.*, 1276 *ff.*
[23] T.W. Rhys Davids, *Sacred Books of the Buddhist* (London: The Pali Text Society, 1977), 71 *ff.*
[24] *Op cit.*, 1248 *ff.*

Chapter 9
Public and Political Participation

Christianity

Christianity's historical relationships with political institutions and its participation in the public realm are complex and highly diverse. The early Christian community's connection with Judaism in the Roman era entails that those groups saw that the historical legacy of their national memory under various empires were inextricably connected with their self-understanding of life in the *res publica*. Judaism's perception of its relationship with political groups begins with the legacy of the patriarch Joseph and the narrative recounted in the biblical book of Genesis. Joseph's story is a long and dramatic tale but concludes with his rising to power as second in command under Pharaoh in Egypt. Eventually, his father Jacob's entire clan moves to Egypt during a seven-year famine because Joseph wisely counseled Egypt to store up grains during years of plenitude. When the famine had become severe and the people were without food, Joseph collected the people's money to give them food. When that food ran out and the people came without money, Joseph requested their livestock, thus removing their ability to earn a livelihood. When the famine continued, and the people returned Joseph provided food in exchange for their homes and thus removed their sense of place and their security. Finally, when the people were starving once more Joseph had them sell themselves into slavery before he would feed them (see Genesis 47:13–26). In doing so, the slavery of Israel (among others) would be orchestrated by one of their own people. This experience of slavery and subsequent liberation from Pharaoh's whips generations later through divine intervention would shape the national identity of Israel.

This national myth of origins expresses the complex and often contentious relationship between ancient Judaism and public or political powers. This ongoing dispute continued with ancient Israel's contests between the monarchy and the criticisms of the prophets.[1] The prophetic tradition criticized the collusion of kings with powerful empires such as Assyria and Babylon. They also censured the social, economic, and political oppression of the poor and vulnerable at the hands of the powerful. Ancient Israel was a small and, within its own historical context, insignificant political power in the midst of empires that spanned the Mesopotamian world. As such, the conquering powers and the domination by international empires were viewed with suspicion. This outlook remained dominant in the first century of the Common Era (CE) when the geographic area of Palestine was under the dominating political control of the Roman Empire. The view of Rome held by conquered peoples in the first century CE was unambiguous. The Roman senator and historian, Tacitus (58–117 CE), records the words of a Caledonian chieftain: "[The Romans are] the plunderers of the world…If the enemy is rich, they are rapacious, if poor they lust for dominion. Not East, not West has sated them…They rob, butcher, plunder, and call it 'empire'; and where they make a desolation, they call it 'peace.'"[2] This sentiment was also expressed in Palestine, which was notoriously difficult to control because of repeated, though small and unsuccessful, uprisings.

The Roman authorities installed tetrarchs to govern local areas and this was also true of the geographic region of Palestine. In this setting the local tetrarch appointed high priests in Jerusalem, breaking with the Jewish tradition of the descendants of Aaron, the brother of Moses, fulfilling that role. The appointed priests were chosen on the basis of their complicity with Rome

Chapter 9

along with the accompanying threat of removal and imprisonment for contravening Imperial authorities. These collaborators were given great political, social, and economic power in addition to the religious function they fulfilled. In this complex political situation Jesus was viewed as a disruptor from the economically underprivileged and backwater countryside of Galilee in the north, which did not have any of the social or cultural prestige that could be found in Jerusalem. The inner circle of twelve disciples reflected the complexity of this social situation. Among the disciples, who would become Apostles, were political revolutionaries who sought violent overthrow of Roman authorities through violent means and those who collaborated with the Empire for personal gain. These are reflected in the persons of Simon the Zealot and Matthew the tax collector respectively. These figures symbolize the diverse approaches within Christianity to participation in the public square and even the nature of one's relationship to Empire from a Christian standpoint. In this respect, early Christianity was simultaneously open to multiple ways of living whilst offering critical analyses of these ways.

For the early Christians, these tensions became particularly poignant in the crucifixion of Jesus of Nazareth as a criminal of the state under a dominant Imperial regime. Jesus' status as an executed criminal, in accordance with the laws of the day, set early Christians at times in an oppositional stance to the claims of the Roman powers. Thus, the interaction of Christians in the public realm was strained from two sides. On the one side, early Christians could question the legitimacy of public institutions such as Emperor-worship or the authority of magistrates. On the other side, Christians were viewed with suspicion by those same authorities because of their unwillingness to participate in the public realm where those activities contravened belief or practice. Even with both of these realities, Christianity geographically expanded in the Roman Empire and thus became ethnically and culturally inclusive community.³ However, it was a community of people who had largely been among the conquered of Rome.

For the first three centuries of Christianity these tensions would continue, and Christians would often find themselves in similar circumstances to their Jewish counterparts. The civil religion of the Roman Empire saw devotion to the Roman pantheon as coextensive with political allegiance to the Empire.⁴ This often put Christians at odds with the *res publica* since they would not participate in certain public activities because of the necessity of religious devotion to the gods (as was the case in swearing allegiance to the Emperor or economic participation in trade guilds) or for moral reasons (as was the case in attending the violent entertainment of the coliseum). At times this also led to formal persecution of Christians. It is a common misconception that Christians were universally (or even widely) persecuted in these early centuries. Surely, there was persecution, but these were manifested at the local level and often on an *ad hoc* basis. More often, Christians found themselves as curiosities through misinformation, social exclusion, or rhetorical derision. Christianity was viewed as a mysterious Jewish sect and was often portrayed as a marginal group meriting suspicion.

This was true until Emperor Constantine issued the Edict of Milan in 313 CE, making it legal to practice Christianity. The events of Constantine who, on the eve of battle, saw the sign of the Christian symbol of the cross and then marching out to victory in war under its banner brought a new and uneasy relationship between Christianity and the political realities of Rome. While Christianity would not become the official religion of the empire until the decree, *Cunctos populous*, under Emperor Theodosius in 380 CE, Constantine worked to increase the tolerance of Christianity alongside traditional Roman or "pagan" beliefs. He did so by giving the Christian celebration on Sundays the same privileges as pagan rites and he put the Christian emblem of the cross on a coin along with the Roman symbols of the *Sol Invictus* and the *Mars Conservator*.[5]

The Constantinian heritage is complicated by the ways in which political power was mixed with Christian faith for centuries afterward. It brought together, in an unsettled way, the role that Christianity would have in being either used to sanction, or giving formal approval and divine legitimacy, to the workings of political authorities. The relationship between Christianity and the public square became questioned with the fall of Rome under the Visigoth invasions that led to the sack of the "eternal city" (410 CE). Many throughout the Roman Empire faulted the adoption of Christianity and the forsaking of traditional Roman gods as the reason for the fall of Rome. They argued the Roman deities were angered with the empire in making Christianity the official state religion. St. Augustine responded to these charges by writing *City of God* between 413 and 426 CE.[6] Augustine argues that human societies (what he calls the "city of man") is destined to be incomplete, temporal, and therefore finite and destined to end. By contrast, the "heavenly city" is eternal and founded upon the work of God in redemption. He does allow that these cities are intermingled, and that the heavenly city is also manifest within the human, thereby creating opportunities for public engagement on the part of Christians by those seeking justice in accordance with Christ's gospel. However, in making the distinction even these temporally intermingled realities maintain their distinctive qualities and goals.

This view was appropriated by Reformation Christians in the sixteenth century through Martin Luther's teaching on the two kingdoms.[7] Luther affirmed that the world, in its entirety, belonged to God, but that there were two authorities exercised, each with their own sphere of influence. The spiritual kingdom was the domain of Christianity in its explicitly religious institutions, such as the Christian churches, whereas temporal authority was to be exercised by the king, or public authorities. While divine authority rests over both, each kingdom exercises its own competencies within its jurisdiction. The two ought not to be commingled or confused. Some historians have identified the role this notion had in contributing to the development of the Enlightenment and modernity. In giving the public square its institutional autonomy and separateness, Luther allowed for an intellectual and cultural exploration in order to develop questions pertaining to the natural world (the natural sciences), politics, and philosophy that had its own integrity while being a part of a holistic understanding of the entirety of the world as God's.

Medieval Roman Catholicism took a different approach but still made space for particular institutions to have some independence in the public realm. The development of the papal lands in the eighth century through to the nineteenth century ensured that political power was much more closely aligned with ecclesiastical authority than would become present in the Protestant churches. However, it was the formal development of the medieval university in Bologna (1088) and in Paris (1160) that afforded the opportunity for some creative thinking that was able to span both religious and public spheres.[8] As such, the university was able to speak meaningfully into both realities whilst maintaining its intellectual independence. For example, the University of Paris received independent status from King Philip II in 1200 and later from Pope Innocent III in 1215. While the relationship between the university as an institution of public knowledge and as founded within the Catholic intellectual tradition remained, the view of the Catholic Church was to reaffirm the integral role of the university as an independent body. In 1231, Pope Gregory IX issued the papal bull, *Parens Scientarum*, which upheld and expanded this role for the university. This document maintains a monastic approach to education and learning but affirms that the transformation envisaged for the university was primarily one of learning and intellectual formation rather than solely that of personal piety. This specific point was defended in the nineteenth century by the Blessed John Henry Newman in his work on the university. *Parens Scientarum* also maintains an independent status for the university as an institution in order to protect it from the personal views and proclivities of individual bishops. It made provision that a university (as an institution) could not be excommunicated.

In his classic text on the social teaching of the Church, Ernst Troeltsch describes the rise in Protestantism as a move away from external emphases, with its emphases on institutional developments and actions, toward an inward moment of subjective faith.[9] Troeltsch argues that Luther's reform and emphasis on justification through the faith of the individual believer led to an individualism that result in an inward focus that helped perpetuate some political structures.[10] For example, this led Luther to side with the princes and nobility during the peasant's revolt in 1524–1525, leading Luther to write the text *Against the Murderous, Thieving Hordes of Peasants* (*Wider die Mordischen und Reubischen Rotten der Bawren*). In Protestant Calvinist and Puritan communities, the individual concern for being among God's elect—found within a doctrine of Predestination—led some to work to prove their elect status through diligent labor and thus, financial success. However, due to the Puritan ethic of moderation and humility, such success could not be spent and thus eventually worked to create some measure of wealth, albeit within communities that appeared materially humble. In this manner God's blessing could be displayed and thus the believer could be psychologically relieved whilst the material realities of such persons continued to improve.[11] This emphasis on the individual and the inward turn to subjective realities would continue into the modern era of Europe.

The European Enlightenment grew first in Protestant countries developing from the doctrine of two kingdoms elucidated by Luther. The Enlightenment was typified by a disavowal of mythologies and traditions that could not be defended through rational argument or evidence. In his essay responding to the question, "What is Enlightenment?" Immanuel Kant famously argued that the Enlightenment was humanity's emergence from a self-inflicted immaturity toward an autonomous use of one's own reason that is not governed by an external authority or tradition.[12] This captures the cultural and intellectual themes of the Enlightenment. This distinctly Western and European epoch is characterized by the self-governing, rational person who, through the use of autonomous reason is aiding in the societal and cultural progress of human beings. These ideas spread to traditionally Catholic nations and resulted in change and even social and political upheaval. This was seen in the French Revolution and the uprisings in Italy in the nineteenth century.

The initial response from the Roman Catholic hierarchy was one of rejection and condemnation typified in the *Syllabus of Errors*, published by Pope Pius IX in December 1864. The syllabus contains a series of theses assumed to be perpetuated by modernity that were condemned by Pius IX. The propositions describe the use of independent reason, the political autonomy of secular authorities, among condemnations of certain philosophical and social movements. The document is simply the list of theses followed by citations of longer and complete texts intended to be referenced as more comprehensive teachings and arguments. It is a text of historical interest but carries little dogmatic weight in the Church's official teaching. The reaction to the syllabus was strong and largely negative. Criticisms were provided from bishops, priests, and lay persons, as well as public intellectuals of the day. When taken alone the syllabus misrepresents several of the views it cites, and it provides no response other than condemnation to the entire modern project in what was viewed as an attempt to retain societal influence and political power for the papacy.

The syllabus did not long remain the dominant response of the Catholic Church to the societal and cultural shifts in the nineteenth century. Pope Leo XIII's encyclical letter, promulgated in 1891 (*Rerum Novarum*), would reinvigorate Catholicism's response to the *res publica*, the political realities of the day, and initiate what would become the modern social teaching of the Catholic Church. While the encyclical largely deals with economic matters, if forthrightly affirms the public gathering of individuals in social movements for justice and the benefit of workers. As such, the document explicitly affirms the formation of unions, which has become a staple of Catholic social thought. The course set by Leo XIII would not be without difficulties. At the outset of the twentieth century there was a neo-scholastic resurgence in Catholic thought that sought to adumbrate Thomism as a series of ahistorical principles, rather than viewing Thomas Aquinas within his own historical location and adapting and expanding upon his methods and insights. This led to Catholic teachers and professors being required to take an anti-modernism oath under Pope Benedict XV in 1910. The warp and weft of the Catholic Church's approach to the public square in modernity would reveal the ongoing historical development of doctrine articulated by John Henry Newman and the historicity of Catholic thought and practice. However, the trajectory laid out by *Rerum Novarum* would receive conciliar affirmation at the Second Vatican Council and thus be understood to reveal the Church's understanding of its relationship to the public and political institutions of the world.

The Second Vatican Council was deeply influenced by the so-called Nouvelle Théologie in its attempt to step back from neo-scholastic readings of Thomas Aquinas and the broader intellectual tradition and sought situate these in a genuinely historical account that recognized the historicity of intellectual currents and the historical development of doctrine elucidated by John Henry Newman in the nineteenth century. In this, two key themes came to characterize the ecumenical council exemplified by the French term "ressourcement" and the Italian term "aggiornamento." These terms intended to convey the goal of Pope John XXIII in calling the council, which was to offer a pastoral council that would articulate the Church's teachings in ways that are meaningful for all people and in robust dialogue with the world. Respectively, the terms signify a return to the original sources in their context and an accommodation to culture and the movements of history as the Church comes to understand its teachings in ways that are meaningful to a new era.

Most relevant for the present discussion is the final major document of the council: The Pastoral Constitution on the Church in the Modern World (*Gaudium et Spes*), promulgated in December 1965. *Gaudium et Spes* ("Joys and Hopes") begins with a powerful statement of Christian solidarity with the wider world and those suffering political or economic injustice. "The joys and hopes, the grief and anguish of the people of our time, especially of those who are poor or afflicted, are the joys and hopes, the grief and anguish of the followers of Christ as well" (*Gaudium et Spes*, 1). This opening statement signals the relationship of the Christians to the public square. It soundly places Christians in solidarity with the world and those who suffer political or economic indignity. The pastoral constitution goes on to address several pertinent issues arising in the public realm such as education, poverty, and health. But it also locates these discussions within a Christological context thus signifying that the Savior who was executed by a powerful empire as a criminal of the state entails a particular social and political response on the part of Christians in the public square. With this affirmation, the council was communicating that the response to modernity from

Chapter 9

Pius IX in the syllabus was not validated. In its place was a dialogical engagement with the public sphere through a political engagement that reflects solidarity with those who are most in need. It affirmed the intellectual independence of the university envisaged by Newman, even as the university is intended to bring together the intellectual and social maturation of persons in a holistic way.

Following the trajectory laid out in *Gaudium et Spes*, Liberation theology has become one of the more prominent approaches Christian engagement in political realities in the latter half of the twentieth century. Being rooted within the Latin American context, Liberation theology began with the theological insights of the Latin American Catholic bishops at two conferences: the conference at Medellín (1968) and the conference at Puebla (1979) respectively. These conferences sought to offer a Christian analysis of the social and economic roots of marginalization in ways that were critical of oligarchies of power and plutocracies found in governing bodies. They did so at Puebla by systematizing these themes through the phrase: "the preferential option for the poor." This phrase signifies the consistent biblical notion that the God who liberated slaves from Egypt and the Christ who was executed as a criminal by a powerful empire were partisan on behalf of those who suffer. Following this is the development of a Christian ethic aimed at social justice and liberation for those who suffer in continuity with the conciliar documents and Catholic Social Teaching since the late nineteenth century.[13]

Finally, prominent theologians have identified differing ways of engaging the public square from a Christian standpoint. David Tracy identifies three "publics" in which Christians participate: Church, society, and academy.[14] The Church is the first location in which Christians receive a tradition, a series of texts, and a life of ritual and symbol by which they make sense of the world and interpret their interactions with it. As such the Church is the location through which individuals, as a living and historical community, engage the realities of their particular lives and their world. Society is the broader realm of public engagement and institutional life outside of specifically religious practice. While the relationship between Church and society has, at times, been contentious, it is not an antithetical relationship. Societal institutions aim toward the good of the citizenry and wider world insofar as they work toward equity and justice. Christians participate in these institutions and question them where they engage in violence or injustice to the poor and the marginalized. Finally, the academy (or the university) is a unique place that offers the opportunity to gain the skills necessary for critical engagement with both of the prior two publics, thus ensuring they remain faithful to the mandate endemic to their institutional identities. Moreover, the academy is a place for research and inquiry into the immediate and perennial questions of a given era in an effort to advance knowledge and increase human understanding of society and the world. As educational theorists from varying schools of thought have noted, higher education is an essential public institution to ensure an increasingly just society. Christians participate in this, seeking to understand history, literature, politics, and the natural world according to their own subject matter in an effort to nurture a more knowledgeable faith and a more mature Christianity.

Buddhism

The socio-political environment into which Buddhism was born, was vastly different than that for Christianity in the Mediterranean world. There was no unified empire in India when Shakyamuni was travelling from village to village on the

Chapter 9

Gangetic plane. The first Indian empire was in its formative stage at that time and the different realms that Shakyamuni visited included republics and monarchies. Second, Buddhism is often characterized as "a world denying religion." This, however, is inaccurate. It is true that Buddhism does promote a renunciate lifestyle and that this approach to the nirvana project often was outside of social conventions (monks do not marry, hold property, etc.). The point was not to deny the world as such but to see past the constructs that hinder the realization of nirvana. Freed, one can understand things from a different orientation all together. Thus, in the formative days of Buddhism the Buddha and some of his lead disciples were sought after for advice on very worldly things from economics to war. The interplay of these two dynamics produced a very complex and diverse presence for Buddhism within the Indian socio-political spheres. In addition, as Buddhism spread to different cultures, the manner in which this relationship between the tradition and the prevailing socio-political environment would interact, produced diverse results even though based on the same foundation.

King Bimbisara (c.558–491 BCE) ruled one of the kingdoms on the Gangetic plan called Magadha. The rightful heir of the Haryanka dynasty, he began attacking other kingdoms in the region forming the beginning of the empire. He was also a great supporter of the Buddha Shakyamuni. Shakyamuni and his thousands of followers not only frequented the capital city but one of their favorite places was the Vulture Peak, a low mountain located just outside the capital that has a rock out cropping making the top look like a vulture's head. In fact, the king appreciated the Buddha's council to such an extent that he ordered a road to be constructed out of massive stone slabs so he could take his chariot up Vulture Peak. His son, King Ajatashatru, was also a strong supporter of the Buddha. Many of the other kings in the different realms that the Buddha visited were supporters and sought his advice on numerous topics.[15]

The Indian subcontinent is vast, and the empire created by Bimbisara and Ajatashatru only occupied a portion in the Northeast. The man who unified all but a shard of India, was named Ashoka the Great (d. 232 BCE). Ashoka's grandfather was Chandragupta who began building the Maurya Empire fighting the Greeks in Northwest India. When Ashoka was still a prince only the most southern tip of India and the large kingdom of Kalinga on the East Coast were not yet brought under control. The war with Kalinga had gone on for over ten years. The rest of the empire being pacified, the full extent of imperial forces could be leveled at Kalinga with King Ashoka at its head. One of the greatest battles in Indian history, Ashoka the victor walked through the battlefield where close to maybe 200,000 warriors from both sides lay dead or dying. The sights and sounds made Ashoka question everything and turning to Buddhism, he became an ardent follower.[16] His large-scale promotion of Buddhism from Alexandria to Sri Lanka and his inspired rule became the model for nearly all Buddhist rulers from India to Japan.

We can see from these two examples that Buddhism from its inception had a positive relationship with political powers in India. The Buddha Shakyamuni and many masters after him were frequently consulted in war and peace. An excellent example of this was Shakyamuni's visit to the kingdom of the Vriji. At that time, the realm was a confederation of smaller states and was one of the democratic republics in ancient India. It was located both north of the Ganges River and of Magadha. The area just south of the Ganges River had once been an independent kingdom but now was part of the emerging Magadhan Empire. Once while begging in the Vrijin capital, the Buddha was asked by the senators the best way to preserve their republic. The Buddha told them to follow seven principles: frequently meet to discuss the affairs of state and maintain preparedness; regardless of status in the community to meet in concord and conclude in concord; respect ancient laws, abrogate nothing unduly, abide with propriety and respect; recognized distinctions between male and female, young and old; honor and serve parents and be obedient to teachers; revere their ancestral shrines and maintain their ceremonies; esteem morality, virtue, provide for holy men and serve them.

The Buddha in general was practical in his approach to political affairs. Having been raised in a noble household he well knew the responsibilities of rule and the threat of war. On several occasions he advised Kings against going to war. For example, well after the time when the Buddha had given advice to the Vriji senators, King Ajatashatru wished to attack their kingdom. He sent his minister to Vulture Peak to seek the Buddha's council on going to war. The Buddha told the minister exactly what he had advised the Vriji long before. He also informed the minister that the Vrijin were indeed maintaining these principles. The minister understood the lesson and advised the king that internally, the Vrijin people were strong and now was not the time to attack.[17]

Shakyamuni also counseled monarchs. He advised them to develop ten qualities for good rule: generosity; morality; self-sacrifice for the good of the people; honesty, integrity, sincerity, and fearlessness in discharging his duties; to be gentle, polite and friendly; to be personally austere, self-controlled and disciplined; be free from ill-will, enmity, and not bear grudges; try to be non-violent; be patient, forbearing and tolerant; should not oppose the will of the people, obstruct the interests to their welfare and follow righteousness. However, the Buddha also understood that nations have their karma just as people have and that karma will manifest when the appropriate causes and conditions align. In such cases trying to limit the suffering of the people in the community is paramount.

The Brahman priests were religious technicians who serve the community in a large array of capacities. They had to be highly educated to ply their profession and many were truly devout. They were usually married with family and accumulated land and wealth as do the average people. However, the wandering ascetic, within the Indian context, rejected all worldly engagements. They did not have a steady abode, kept no property or wealth, did not maintain a family. They survived on the offerings of the people and what natural thing came their way (e.g., finding wild fruit). One of these wandering groups were the Buddhist, at least in their formative period. The Buddhist monasteries donated by wealthy individuals, were only used during the monsoon season when travel was made extremely difficult. Over the centuries the monks and nuns began staying in the monasteries year-round. However, the custom of begging for food daily continued. Each morning, a parade of monks or nuns goes from door to door begging food to be placed in their bowls. Donating food generates positive merit for the donor. At times a donor may invite a monk or nun, or a group of them to sit and teach Buddhism. Frequently, the donor may have a specific question.

Most monasteries were located in or near a community of lay people. Of course, there are hermits or "forest dwellers" (small groups of monks/nuns who live apart) but most monastics interacted with the general population on a daily basis. Teaching, talking with, and engaging all sorts of people provided the monastic with news, general information, and a sense of the people's situation. These interactions, however, were limited by design as the monk or nun should be about religious pursuits most of the waking hours. Thus, even though after the formative period, Buddhist monks and nuns were living closer to a community and members were interacting with the community on a daily basis over years, they were still seen as being outside of society.

Chapter 9

The Buddhist lay members still had families, jobs, property, had to pay taxes, had community obligations, etc. and so were still part of society. The expectations placed on these Buddhist were no different than those placed on every member of society. Indian is a segregated society based on caste. Buddhism rejects caste and caste distinctions were not permitted among monks and nuns. However, lay members still in society were not free of caste distinction and the duties and taboos that were placed on Buddhist lay members were no different than the general population. This was particularly true for the warrior caste. Simply because Buddhism generally advocates peace did not remove the feudal responsibility of a warrior caste member from going to war. There was no recognition of conscientious objector status except for monastics who gave up their warrior caste when becoming a monk. One of the outstanding features of ancient Indian society was the tolerance exhibited between religious groups. Through the centuries there are a few incidents of frictions, but this was seen rarely because every social group held that promoting morality (which was generally agreed upon) was good for society so since every religion promoted morality they were all good to one extent or another regardless of doctrinal differences. This was best exemplified by the fact that everyone in society from the king down would donate to all the religions regardless of their one personal leanings.

Further, Buddhism is very individualistic. You and you alone must work out your path to nirvana. The Buddha, great masters, monks and nuns can only aid in the process, but you have to walk the path. Each monastery was hierarchal internally based on seniority and position (e.g., a teacher) in terms of respect and the operation of the monastery. Yet, in terms of general business of the monastery, votes were taken wherein all members were equal and majority ruled. In viewing the pan-Indic situation for monasteries, there was no overarching organization although monasteries were understood as housing inmates of one Buddhist school or another. The division at this level was mostly based on the inmates training in a particular mendicant order. This would make the organizational structure horizontal.

To summarize the general situation in ancient India, the Buddha Shakyamuni provided counsel to both monarchies and republics. He dismissed the notion of the divine right of kings and taught they were selected by the people and then the position became hereditary. There was a social contract between the people and the monarch and a general negative critique of the necessity of a ruler and the institutions of state.[18] He generally advised them to lesson suffering of the people, to show clemency, to hold in high regard one's realms customs, to be righteous and to cooperate with the people governed. Although there are examples of public works undertaken for the kingdom (e.g., bridges, road-side wells) in general liberality was understood in individual terms which fits well with the low taxation rate advocated (one-sixth of an individual's production). It should also be pointed out that the Buddha recommend that people undertake efforts to pay as little tax as possible. Still taxes were to be paid and conscription for various projects was to be meet. The rulers should support the monks and nuns but other than that had little power over these individuals who were outside society.[19] The monastic community being outside of society meant both that the rulers had no power over them, and they had no power over the rulers. In addition to these teachings by Shakyamuni, the Buddhist community supported peace within the country, increase national production by individual acts, the spread of education, to set aside in preparation for calamity. One could argue that the economics supported by the early Buddhist was pre-capitalism with individual accumulation of wealth through one's own efforts accepted. It was also taught that one's wealth should be used for charitable works after supporting one's family.

The implementation of these ideas is well attested to within the Buddhist community. Except for occupations that directly involved killing and the making of weapons, most occupations were considered equally respectful unlike with the caste system. The Buddha had followers who were bankers, ministers, farmers, and even the low caste like a barber. Centuries after Shakyamuni's time, the Buddhist community was supporting large universities such as Nalanda, located in Bihar state. Students from China, Tibet, and South-East Asia came to the Oxford of the Buddhist world. The curriculum included Sanskrit linguistics, mathematics, astrology/astronomy, medicine, ecclesiastic law, Buddhist doctrine, other Indian philosophies, and more.[20] As these universities were essentially very large monasteries, they too were considered outside society and thus had their independents. Being early centers of education not only were monk-students there, but the ruling elite sent their sons for study as well.[21]

The Indian idea of the universal emperor who ruled by the power of his virtue can also be understood as a means of eliminating the situation of multiple kingdoms—constant warfare common place in ancient India. Ashoka, (considered a lesser universal emperor because of early use of warfare) promoted Buddhism as state religion and as part of this, he actively interceded in monastic affairs. In keeping with this, monks became increasing involved in state affairs by promoting universal laws promulgated for internal stability and advocating a powerful army to discourage advances by foreign states. We see this in the developing of the theory of the "two wheels of *Dharma*": the religious wheel of the monastic community and the political wheel of the Buddhist king and Buddhist state as found in the commentarial tradition. This was complex conjoined idea of universal *Dharma* with each sphere focusing on their part but significant theoretical and practical overlapping.[22]

Asoka becomes the model of the best of Buddhist kings both in India in the centuries that follow and beyond. There were many Buddhist kings over the generations in India greater and lesser who attempted to emulate his example. There does not seem to have been any recorded massive political protest that was either exclusively Buddhist or even one wherein Buddhist played a significant role on a large scale. Buddhist masters who were motivated, dealt with issues in a private one-on-one manner. Large scale public displays of a positive nature, however, were frequent.

Rulers and their courts making donations of monasteries, stupas, wealth, and more to the community of monks, nuns or particular masters also followed examples set by Bimbisara and Asoka. It became common for the queen to take particular interest in supporting nunneries. Kings would hold philosophical debates in public awarding fabulous gifts to the victor. These gifts may include an elephant to act as a mount and in one historic case, a string of one hundred and eight meditation beads each made of ruby. Some of the emperors supported massive gatherings of Buddhist to recite scriptures and debate disputes again in compliance of the model set by Asoka.

Buddhist festivals dotted the calendar in ancient times. Because of the rejection of the caste system by Buddhist, the festivals were open to all. From mighty kings to the lowest of the outcaste all would join in. The Buddha Shakyamuni's birthday, his day of awakening, and his death were all commemorated. Monasteries would hold memorial services for their founder or a particularly noteworthy inmate who dwelled there in the past. One of the more interesting festivals was the chariot procession now referred to as Juggernaut. The Lord of the Universe (Sk. Jagannatha), from which the English word is derived, has a massive chariot festival in Puri, India. The origins of this festival are disputed but it is considered a Hindu/Buddhist festival and

Chapter 9

Indians of these two religions (as well as Jains) are permitted to enter the temple of Jagannatha. Non-Indian of both faiths are generally barred. As this most famous example is controversial, a different example is presented below.

In Lalitpur, Nepal there is the famous *Raktalokitesvara Karunamaya* festival dedicated to the Bodhisattva of compassion and instituted by the king in the seventh century. The six-story tall decorated chariot housing a statue of the Bodhisattva is pulled through the city for a month. At the conclusion, a small bejeweled vest "kept by the Bodhisattva" is shown to the public, government officials, and the living goddess Kumari (a young girl believed to be a goddess until puberty by Buddhist/Hindus). This festival is still performed each year.[23] We have accurate records of a yearly ceremony similar to a juggernaut taking place in the Chinese capital circa 618–907 CE wherein the emperor would sprinkle flowers on the Buddha statue as it passed.[24]

Individual monks have protested certain activities but there is no record of large-scale organized political protest within India during these centuries. Nor are there records of individuals protesting wherein one emulates another. There are many examples of large-scale Buddhist public festivals as well as smaller and local events held in public for the celebration on significant dates on the Buddhist calendar in ancient India. In general, India's religious climate was one of considerable tolerance wherein Buddhist, Hindus, Jains and even tribal religions were not persecuted. Kings donated to all major religions but had their own leanings which they promoted. The general populations were happy to celebrate festivals together and we do not see examples where one group openly discriminated against another religion. This tolerance in no way limited the rigorous intellectual tradition where scholars argued one religion claim against another.

This model held true as Buddhism spread to other countries. In some, the monks/nuns maintained the idea of being outside of society and therefore the political authority ability to act upon them was limited and in others, the political authority was directly involved in oversight. Tibet is unique in that the religious establishment became the government. Some governments wished to curtail the political influence that Buddhist held, and others were enthusiastic in promoting it. In China for example, discouraged by generations of continual warfare as one pretender to the throne or another staked their claim, Buddhist developed more interest in millennial movements with many simply withdrawing for the world during a certain phase of history. More common was the example of Uchiyama Gudo (1874–1914) a Zen priest in Japan with socialist's leanings who was a pacifist. He published tracts in line with his views supported by Buddhist references, was tried for treason and executed.[25] However, there is historically few if any large-scale political movements in protest led by Buddhist until the modern period elsewhere in Asia. Examples of protests may be under the influence of modernization and globalization as different ideas of the relationship between religion and political authority spread.

Today, there are still large- and small-scale festivals, ceremonies and celebrations across the Buddhist world. Many of these are open to the general public or to the public by permission (as they may include prerequisites). From traditional dances held in front of the Great Buddha in Nara, Japan to Vesak (commemoration of the birth, awakening, and death of Shakyamuni) in Sri Lanka people are called together in remembrance and offer respect, gathering as a community in celebration.

Personal and large-scale political protest also continues in our times. An example of a large-scale public expression of Buddhist disapproval was the Saffron Revolution in Myanmar (Burma) in 2007. A more personal protest is exemplified by self-immolation of Tibetan monks.

Chapter 9

In 2007, the government of Myanmar stopped the subsidy for fuel causing prices to skyrocket. This acted as the flash point for the long growing discontent on economic stagnation, low spending on education and inflation for basic commodities all due to government policies. There also was discontent in general as people wished for a less restrictive more representative government. People also noted the wealth of the military and the apparent corruption of top government officials. However, the government was also well known for sever reactions to any criticism or political protest.

Some brave individuals took to the streets calling for lower prices. They were arrested. The protest over prices grew quickly and the government response was more arrests and people beaten in the streets. Myanmar troops broke up a peaceful protest which included a few Buddhist monks. Fellow monks captured some government officials and demanded an apology from the government. The govern-ment's refusal put more protesting monks into the streets and the stoppage of religious services for government officials. Soon the whole of the country was in peaceful protest with monks playing a prominent role. This protest is called "saffron" because of the color of the monks' robes.

With peaceful street marches of up to fifty thousand people, including hundreds or even a thousand monks, the government was caught off guard at first. Monasteries were then raided, the monks as well as lay people beaten, people arrested. Military troops began shooting at protesters as a very forceful crackdown was launched after three months of protests. The number killed is widely disputed and tens of thousands were injured and arrested. These events garnered worldwide support for the monks and the protesters.

In 1959 the Chinese military launched a large-scale crackdown in Tibet leading the Dalai Lama, the heads of all four Tibetan Buddhist Schools, many of the greatest prelates, thousands of monks and nuns, government officials and 100,000 refugees to flee for India, Nepal and Bhutan. Since then, there have been political protests both large and small in Tibet supporting resistance against the communist government. These protests have taken different forms. Recently, self-immolation has been on the rise.

Readers may recall reading about a few Buddhist monks in Vietnam protesting the war by self-immolation. This practice in modern Vietnam actually started before the war with protests against the French colonial government. The first recorded incident of a Buddhist monk burning himself took place in the period of the fourth and fifth century in China, also in protest against an illegitimate ruler. Buddhism disavows suicide, the one major exception is out of compassion. In Buddhist terms this is seen as "self-sacrifice" and in English it has been called martyrdom. In the Tibet community, since 2009 there have been 148 confirmed cases of self-immolation with the first being a monk from Kirti Monastery. The self-sacrifice of the monks is in protest against Chinese occupation of Tibet and the Dalai Lama claims this is also in response to the cultural genocide of Tibetans.

Conclusion

The early Christian identity vis-a-vis political authority was forged by the preceding Jewish experience, particularly with Egypt but including other mid-Eastern powers, and by the Roman world that it was born into. This dynamic relationship was further heightened with the inclusion of the symbolic significance of Simon the Zealot and Matthew the tax collector being apostles and their relationship with authority. These diverse impetuses could allow a varied response to the ever-changing political

Chapter 9

reality in the early centuries, but historic events and dynastic orientations often predicted how these would unfold.

Jesus was understood as one upsetting the stability established by the cooperation between the Roman tetrarchy and the Jerusalem high priests who were given significant power and wealth along with the prestige of their office in the religious sphere. Both the religious institution and the political institution of the time did not what a disruption of the status quo. Jesus was crucified as a criminal along with two other criminals. This more than other impulses set the early Christians in opposition to the state. Christians questioned the legitimacy of Roman politico-religious institutions and customs and because of their refusal to participating in such (a rather treasonous act), were seen as suspicious. Sometimes excluded and sometimes persecuted the Christians passed the first few centuries understood as an obscure Jewish cult.

The Emperor Constantine undertook several activities that relieved the Christian community but would have long term effects with regard to the relationship between church and state. Not all of the claims regarding Constantine's advocacy are historically valid but both fact and myth would have far reaching significance. The fall or Rome was viewed by many as resting on the acceptance of Christianity and the forsaking of the Roman gods. In response to such sentiments, St. Augustine writings developed the idea of two separate spheres (of earth/man and of God) that intermingle but are in conflict. This universal conflict in short is between God and the Devil with people aligning with either side. *The City of God Against the Pagans* presents St. Augustine's thoughts on a host of topics, some of which have important political significance. This philosophical approach was incorporated in the Reformation with divine authority over the religious institutional authority and the political authority. This division between jurisdictions help lay part of the foundation of the Enlightenment.

Another key feature as we move into the Enlightenment period, was the development of universities. Beginning as religious schools studying theology and ecclesiastic law, University developed in such a manner that they could speak with the authority of knowledge and understanding about both the religious and the political spheres. Because of their importance, they were able to establish for themselves a status of independence from both religious and political authority allowing for more free thinking. The relationship between the independent secular authorities and the church in separation from universities was not always an accepting one. Over time, this relationship developed as a system of checks on each other.

The Catholic Church, after careful evaluation and understanding the multiple changes taking place in the mid-twentieth century, produced *Gaudium et Spes* providing for the modernization of the church. This included an impactful statement on the relationship of Christians on the public square. This promoted the idea the engagement in the political sphere in solidarity with the needy. This in turn provided a grounding for Liberation Theology to develop in Latin America. Both Protestant and Catholic theologians have identified various ways of being public for Christians. The spheres of Church, secular government and universities have interacted with each other for centuries, but the exact nature of this interaction is formulated with nationalistic characteristics. For example, the highest political authority in the United Kingdom, i.e., the King/Queen is also the head of the Church of England whereas in the United States, there is an official separation between church and state. Canada and many other countries fall somewhere in-between. Both the church and the state have as one of their goals the good of the citizens. As such, they often can and do cooperate for the betterment of

Chapter 9

humanity. There are, however, times when the two institutions are in a more contentious relation.

The relation between the public square and Buddhism offers an utterly different history than that of Christianity. The Buddha Shakyamuni, along with other wondering sages, was understood to be outside of the societal realm. Thus, the political authorities were extremely limited in their abilities to influence or control the Buddha and his establishments. Masters would be consulted on political, military, social, and spiritual matters by rulers but being beyond society allowed these masters to speak their minds freely. Shakyamuni advised both republics and monarchies while early Buddhist literature offered a negative critique of monarchial rule and denied the king's divine right to rule, it still maintained that people should pay their taxes and uphold conscription duties. Buddhism as an institution, developed along with and supported by the establishment of empire. Yet empires were always short in duration in India and the stable political unit was the kingdom. More local and often with unique cultural aspects, languages, and customs, Buddhism proved itself well able to adopt to each circumstance. This included local Buddhist public festivals, ceremonies, and public events both connected with local culture and history and maintaining participation in the pan Indic culture as monks and nuns frequently traveled for educational purposes or on pilgrimages. This was well in keeping with the Buddhist ideas of respecting tradition and maintaining long held customs.

As the centuries passed some monasteries evolved into large universities housing thousands of monks and the children of the elite. Multiple subjects were taught and not just Buddhist philosophy and monastic rule. Students from across the Buddhist world came to study at these institutions. Because the monastic establishment was perceived as outside of society, the universities were free from political authority to make inquires and develop

Christian-Buddhist Conversations

insights, of course this was within the confines of contemporaneous culture just as it is presently.

Buddhist festivals large and small pan-Indic or local dotted the calendar of ancient India. Whole communities turning out to presents gifts to the monks and nuns at the end of the rainy retreat or simply ceremonies in memory of a past great master held at his home monastery were anticipated and supported by the people. Large juggernauts with important icons being pulled through the city seem similar to processions of this or that saint in an Italian city like the celebration of St. Joseph on Father's Day and it procession in the cities of Palermo and Syracuse still today. These celebrations travelled along with Buddhism as it moved into different cultures and we see juggernauts in China or Buddha's birthday being celebrated.

Large scale public political protest led by Buddhist is an advent of the modern period in the wake of different ideas of the relationship between religions and political authority. The historic record is devoid of any such account from the ancient period but example from the modern period are significant. Perhaps the most famous Buddhist protest took place at the beginning of the twenty-first century in Myanmar called the Saffron Revolution. Thousands of monks participated in political protests against the government's policies. One also sees more personal protests with the example of Tibetan monk's self-immolation in protest to claimed occupation of their country and destruction of their culture.

Both Buddhist and Christians have been more or less active in the public square according to the contemporaneous circumstances. However, in both cases, these religious communities have helped safeguard the interests of the people, have helped political authorities both democratic and monarchial morally responsible, and have be a significantly contributing force in constantly reminding all that human life, in all its spheres of interest, is more than material existence.

---

[1] See Walter Brueggemann, *The Prophetic Imagination Second Edition* (Minneapolis: Fortress Press, 2009).

[2] Quoted in Richard A. Horsley, *Jesus and Empire: The Kingdom of God and the New World Order* (Minneapolis: Fortress Press, 2003), 15.

[3] Howard Clark Kee, *Who Are the People of God? Early Christian Models of Community* (New Haven: Yale University Press, 1995), 179–207.

[4] Jed W. Atkins, *Roman Political Thought* (Cambridge: Cambridge University Press, 2018), 136–165.

[5] Allen M. Ward, Fritz M. Heichelheim, Cedric A. Yeo, *A History of the Roman People Sixth Edition* (New York: Routledge, 2016), 420–431.

[6] Saint Augustine, *City of God* trans. Henry Bettenson (London: Penguin Classics, 2003).

[7] See Robert Kolb and Charles P. Arand, *The Genius of Luther's Theology* (Grand Rapids: Baker Academic, 2008), 21–101.

[8] See Ian P. Wei, *Intellectual Culture in Medieval Paris: Theologians and the University, c. 1100–1330* (Cambridge: Cambridge University Press, 2012).

[9] Ernst Troeltsch, *The Social Teaching of the Christian Churches Volume II* trans. Olive Wyon (Louisville: Westminster John Knox Press, 1992), 1009.

[10] Troeltsch, *The Social Teaching of the Christian Churches Volume II*, 470.

[11] The classic text on this is Max Weber, *The Protestant Ethic and the Spirit of Capitalism*, trans. Talcott Parsons (London: Unwin University Books, 1965).

[12] Immanuel Kant, "An Answer to the Question: What is Enlightenment?" *Practical Philosophy* trans. ed. Mary J. Gregor (Cambridge: Cambridge University Press, 1996), 17–22.

[13] This history in Latin America was instrumental in developing liberation theology. See Gustavo Gutiérrez, *A Theology of Liberation: History, Politics, and Salvation* trans. Sr. Caridad Inda and John Eagleson (Maryknoll: Orbis Books, 1999).

[14] David Tracy, *The Analogical Imagination: Christian Theology and the Culture of Pluralism* (New York: Crossroad Publishing, 1981).

[15] Hermann Kulke and Dietmar Rothermund, *A History of India* 6th ed. (London: Routledge, 2016), 33 *ff*.

[16] *Ibid*. 39 *ff*.

[17] T.W. Rhys Davids and C.A.F. Rhys Davids, *Dialogues of the Buddha* vol III (London: The Pali Text Society, 1977), 79 *ff*.

[18] T.W. Rhys Davids and C.A.F. Rhys Davids. *Dialogues of the Buddha*. (London: Oxford University Press, 1977), 87-88.

[19] A.K. Warder. *Indian Buddhism*. (Delhi: Motilal Banarsidass, 1980), 171 *ff*.

[20] *Ibid*. 466 *ff*.

[21] Kulke and Rothermund, *ibid.* 114.
[22] John S. Strong, *The Legend of King Aśoka A Study and Translation of the Aśokāvadāna* (Princeton: Princeton University Press, 1983), 44 *ff.*
[23] John K. Locke, *Karunamaya* (Kathmandu: Sahayogi Prakashan, 1980), 243 *ff*.
[24] Hsüan-chih Yang, *A Record of Buddhist Monasteries in Lo-Yang* trans. Yi-t'ung Wang,(Princeton: Princeton University Press, 1984), 126.
[25] Brian Daizen Victoria. *Zen at War.* (Lanham: Rowman and Littlefield Publishing, Inc. 2006), 38 *ff.*

Bibliography

Documents:

Pope Benedict XVI, *Caritas in Veritate*.

Pope Francis, *Evangelii Gaudium*

Pope Francis, *Laudato Si*

Pope John Paul II, *Ut Unum Sint*

Second Vatican Council, *Dignitatis Humanae*

Second Vatican Council, *Dei Verbum*

Second Vatican Council, *Lumen Gentium*

Second Vatican Council, *Nostra Aetate*

References:

The Compact Edition of the Oxford English Dictionary. Oxford: Oxford University Press, 1971.

General:

Atkins, Jed W. *Roman Political Thought*. Cambridge: Cambridge University Press, 2018.

Aulén, Gustav. *Christus Victor: An Historical Study of the Three Main Types of the Idea of the Atonement*. (A.G. Herbert trans.) London: SPCK Publishing, 1931.

Barber, A.W. *Sinicizing Buddhism Studies in Doctrine, Practice, Fine Arts, Performing Arts*. Calgary: Vogelstein Press, 2019.

Barber, A.W. (ed.) *The Tibetan Tripitaka: Taipei Edition*. Taipei: Southern Materials Center Ind., 1991.

Barber, Malcolm. *The Two Cities: Medieval Europe 1050–1320 Second Edition*. New York: Routledge, 2007.

Barad, Judith. *Aquinas on the Nature and Treatment of Animals*. Maryland: International Scholars Publications, 1995.

Bar-Efrat, Shimon. *Narrative Art in the Bible*. Sheffield: Sheffield Academic Press, 1997.

Basham, A.L. *The Wonder that was India*. Calcutta: Rupa and Company, 1991.

Bauckham, Richard. *The Theology of the Book of Revelation*. Cambridge: Cambridge University Press, 1993.

Beal, Samuel. *Si-Yu Ki Buddhist Records of the Western World*. Delhi: Motilal Banarsidass, 1981.

Bender, Kimlyn J. "Martin Luther and the Birth of the Protestant Ecclesial Vision," *Perspectives in Religious Studies* 41.3 (2014).

Benedict of Norcia. *The Rule of St. Benedict: In Latin and English with Notes* (Fry, Timothy, O.S.B. ed.). Collegeville: The Liturgical Press, 1981.

Briskin, Lawrence. "Tanakh Sources Of Judas Iscariot" *Jewish Biblical Quarterly* 32.3 (2004).

Bronkhorst, Johannes. "Did the Buddha Believe in Karma and Rebirth," in *Journal of the International Association of Buddhist Studies,* vol. 21, no. 1, 1998.

Brown, Raymond E. *An Introduction to the New Testament*. New York: Doubleday Publishing, 1997.

Brown, Raymond E. and Meier, John P. *Antioch and Rome: New Testament Cradles of Catholic Christianity*. New York: Paulist Press, 1983.

Brueggemann, Walter. *The Land: Place as Gift, Promise, and Challenge in Biblical Faith Second Edition*. Minneapolis: Fortress Press, 2002.

--- *The Prophetic Imagination*. Minneapolis: Fortress Press, 2001.

Buddhaghosa, Bhadantacariya. *The Path of Purification* (Nyanamoli, Bhikkhu. trans.). Colombo: A. Semage Publishing, 1964?

Calvin, John. *The Bondage and Liberation of the Will* (Davis, G.I. trans.). Grand Rapids: Baker Books, 2002.

--- *Institutes of the Christian Religion*, (McNeill, John T. trans.). Philadelphia: The Westminster Press, 1960.

Campbell, J. McLeod. *The Nature of the Atonement*. Edinburgh: The Handsel Press, 1996.

Carr, David M. and Conway, Colleen M. *An Introduction to the Bible: Sacred Texts and Imperial Contexts*. Malden, MA: Wiley-Blackwell, 2010.

Chang, Garma C.C. (ed.) *A Treasury of Mahayana Sutras*. University Park: The Pennsylvania State University Press, 1983.

Clough, David L. *On Animals Volume 1: Systematic Theology*. New York: T & T Clark, 2012.

--- *On Animals Volume 2: Theological Ethics*. New York: T & T Clark, 2018.

Conze, Edward. *The Short Prajñāpāramitā Texts*. London: Luzac and Co., 1973.

Costigan, Richard F.S.J. *Consensus of the Church and Papal Infallibility: A Study In the Background of Vatican I*. Washington DC: The Catholic University of America Press, 2005.

Cousar, Charles B. *The Letters of Paul*. Nashville: Abingdon Press, 1996.

Darwin, Charles. *On The Origin of Species* (New York: Bantam Classics, 2008.

Davidson, Ronald M. "An Introduction to the Standards of Scriptural Authenticity in Indian Buddhism," in Buswell, Robert E. *Chinese Buddhist Apocrypha*. Honolulu: University of Hawaii press, 1990.

Davies, Brian. and Evans G.R. (eds.), *Anselm of Canterbury: The Major Works*. Oxford: Oxford University Press, 1998.

Dayal, Har. *The Bodhisattva Doctrine in Buddhist Sanskrit Literature*. Delhi: Motilal Banarsidass, 1970.

Deane-Drummond, Celia. *The Wisdom of the Liminal: Evolution and Other Animals in Human Becoming*. Grand Rapids: William B Eerdmans Publishing, 2014.

De Las Casas, Bartolomé. *A Short Account of the Destruction of the Indies.* (Griffin, Nigel trans.) London: Penguin Books, 1992.

--- *In Defense of the Indians.* (Poole, Stafford, C.M. trans.). DeKalb: Northern Illinois University Press, 1993.

Donovan, J. (trans.) *Catechism of the Council of Trent*. Charlotte: Saint Benedict Press, 2006.

Duffy, Eamon. *Saints and Sinners: A History of the Popes* (3rd Edition). New Haven: Yale University Press, 2006.

Duggan, Michael. *The Consuming Fire: A Christian Guide to the Old Testament*. Huntington: Our Sunday Visitor Publishing, 2010.

Dunn, James D.G. *A New Perspective on Jesus: What the Quests for the Historical Jesus Missed*. Grand Rapids: Baker Academic, 2005.

Dupuis, S.J., Jacques. *Toward a Christian Theology of Religious Pluralism.* Maryknoll: Orbis Books, 2001.

Eckel, Malcolm David. "Perspectives on the Buddhist-Christian Dialogue," in Lopez, Jr. Donald S. and Rockefeller, Steven C. (eds.) *The Christ and the Bodhisattva* New York: SUNY Press, 1987.

Evans-Wentz, W. Y. *Tibet's Greatest Yogi Milarepa.* London: Oxford University Press, 1971.

Fahey, Michael A. "Church," *Systematic Theology: Roman Catholic Perspectives Second Edition* (Fiorenza, Francis Schüssler. and Galvin, John P. eds.). Minneapolis: Fortress Press, 2011.

Falk, Harvey. *Jesus the Pharisee.* New York: Paulist Press, 1985.

Foucaux, Edouard (trans. Bay, Gwendolyn) *The Voice of the Buddha: The Beauty of Compassion.* Berkeley: Dharma Publishing, 1983.

Frauwallner, E. *The Earliest Vinaya and the Beginnings of Buddhist Literature.* Roma: Istitute Italiano Per Il Medio Ed Estreme Oriente, 1956.

Fretheim, Terence E. *Deuteronomic History.* Nashville: Abingdon Press, 1983.

Gomez, Luis O. *The Land of Bliss The paradise of the Buddha of Measureless Light.* Honolulu: University of Hawai'i Press, 1996.

Goodman, Martin. "The Emergence of Christianity" in Hastings, Adrian (ed.). *A World History of Christianity.* Grand Rapids: Wm. B. Eerdmans, 1999.

Grumett, David and Muers, Rachel. *Theology On The Menu: Asceticism, Meat and Christian Diet*. New York: Routledge, 2010.

Gutiérrez, Gustavo. *Las Casas: In Search of the Poor of Jesus Christ*. Maryknoll: Orbis Books, 1995.

--- *A Theology of Liberation: History, Politics, and Salvation* (Inda SR. Caridad. and Eagleson, John. trans.). Maryknoll: Orbis Books, 1999.

Hasler, August Bernhard. *How the Pope Became Infallible: Pius IX and the Politics of Persuasion*. New York: Doubleday, 1981.

Hazony, Yoram. *The Philosophy of Hebrew Scripture*. Cambridge University Press, 2012.

Hirakawa, Akira. *A History of Indian Buddhism From Sakyamuni to Early Mahayana* (Groner, Paul. trans.). Delhi: Motilal Banarsidass, 1993.

Holmqvist, W. (ed.). "Excavations at Helgö, I, report for 1954-56," Stockholm, in: www.asianart.com/forum/takaki/dozen/Dozenns.htm

Horner, I.B. (ed.). *The Minor Anthologies of the Pali Canon, Vol. III: Buddhavaṁsa (Chronicle of Buddhas) and Cariyāpiṭaka (Basket of Conduct)*. London: Pali Text Society, 1975.

Horsley, Richard A. *Jesus and Empire: The Kingdom of God and the New World Disorder*. Minneapolis: Fortress Press, 2003.

Ikeda, Daisaku. (trans. Watson, Burton) *The Flower of Chinese Buddhism*. Santa Monica: Middleway Press, 2009.

Ishigami, Zenno. *Disciples of the Buddha*. Tokyo: Kosai Publishing Co. 1989.

Jeremias, Joachim. *Jesus and the Message of the New Testament* (Hanson, K.C. ed.). Minneapolis: Fortress Press, 2002.

Johnson, Elizabeth. *Ask The Beasts: Darwin and the God of Love*. London: Bloomsbury Publishing, 2014.

Josephus, Flavius. *Antiquities of the Jews*. (Whiston, Wm. trans.) *The Complete Works of Josephus*. Grand Rapids: Kregel Publications, 1981.

Judge, E.A. "Rank and Status in the World of the Caesars and St Paul," *Social Distinctives of the Christians in the First Century: Pivotal Essays by E.A. Judge* (Scholer, David M. ed.). Peabody: Hendrickson Publishers, 2008.

Kant, Immanuel. "An Answer to the Question: What is Enlightenment?" *Practical Philosophy* (Mary J. Gregor, Mary J. trans., ed.). Cambridge: Cambridge University Press, 1996.

Kee, Howard Clark. *Who Are the People of God? Early Christian Models of Community*. New Haven: Yale University Press, 1995.

Kim, Andrew. *An Introduction to Catholic Ethics Since Vatican II*. Cambridge: Cambridge University Press, 2015

Knitter, Paul F. *Without Buddha I Could Not Be A Christian*. London: Oneworld Academic, 2009.

Kogen, Mizuno. *The Beginning of Buddhism*. Tokyo: Kosei Publishing Co. 1987.

--- *Essentials of Buddhism*. Tokyo: Kosei Publishing Co. 1996.

Kolb, Robert. and Arand, Charles P. *The Genius of Luther's Theology*. Grand Rapids: Baker Academic, 2008.

Kulke, Hermann and Rothermund, Dietmar. *A History of India* (6th ed.). London: Routledge, 2016.

Küng, Hans. *On Being a Christian* (Quinn, Edward trans.). New York: Doubleday Books, 1976.

Latourelle, René, S.J., *Theology of Revelation*. New York: Alba House, 1966.

Lavin, Margaret. *Vatican II: Fifty Years of Evolution and Revolution in the Catholic Church*. Toronto: Novalis Press, 2012.

Lawhead, William F. *The Voyage of Discovery: A History of Western Philosophy*. Belmont: Wadsworth Publishing Company, 1996.

Lay, U Ko. *Guide to Tipitaka*. Selangor: Selangori Buddhist Vipassana Meditation Society, 2000.

Legge, James. *A Record of Buddhist Kingdoms*. New York: Paragon Book Reprint Corp and Dover Publications, Inc. n.d.

Locke, John K. *Karunamaya*. Kathmandu: Sahayogi Prakashan, 1980.

Lubac, Henri de. *Catholicisme: Les aspects sociaux du dogme*. Paris: Les *Éditions du Cerf*, 2009.

Mack, Burton L. *The Lost Gospel: The Book of Q and Christian Origins*. San Francisco: Harper Collins, 1993.

Makransky, John J. *Buddhahood Embodied*. Albany: State University of New York Press, 1997.

Marenhon, John. *Medieval Philosophy: An Historical and Philosophical Introduction*. New York: Routledge, 2007.

McFarland, Ian A. *In Adam's Fall: A Meditation on the Christian Doctrine of Original Sin*. Oxford: Wiley Blackwell, 2010.

Merrick, J. and Garrett, Stephen M. (eds). *Five Views On Biblical Inerrancy*. Grand Rapids: Zondervan Academic, 2013.

Merton, Thomas. *Mystics and Zen Masters*. New York: Farrar, Straus, and Giroux, 1967.

--- *New Seeds of Contemplation*. New York: New Directions Books, 1972.

Meyers, Carol. *Discovering Eve: Ancient Israelite Women in Context*. New York: Oxford University Press, 1988.

Moltmann, Jürgen. *The Crucified God* (Wilson, R.A. and Bowden, John. trans.). Minneapolis: Fortress Press, 1993.

--- *The Way of Jesus Christ: Christology in Messianic Dimensions* (Kohl, Margaret. trans.). London: SCM Press, 1990.

Nelson, Richard D. *The Historical Books*. Nashville: Abingdon Press, 1998.

Newman, John Henry Cardinal. *The Letters and Diaries of John Henry Newman* (Dessain, C.S. and Gornall, T. ed.). Vol. XXIX, Oxford: Clarendon Press, 1973.

O'Malley, John W., S.J. *A History of the Popes: From Peter to the Present*. Plymouth: Sheed and Ward, 2010.

--- *Trent And All That: Renaming Catholicism in the Early Modern Era*. Cambridge: Harvard University Press, 2002.

--- *What Happened at Vatican II*. Cambridge: The Belknap Press of Harvard University Press, 2008.

Outram, Dorinda. *The Enlightenment Second Edition*. New York: Cambridge University Press, 2005.

Pelikan, Jaroslav. *The Christian Tradition Volume 1: The Emergence of the Catholic Tradition (100–600)*. Chicago: The University of Chicago Press, 1971.

Perrin, Norman. *What is Redaction Criticism?* Philadelphia: Fortress Press, 1969.

Pope John Paul II, *Crossing the Threshold of Hope*. New York: Knopf Doubleday Publishing, 1995.

Poussin, Louis De la Vallèe. *Abhidharma Kośa Bhāṣyam* (Pruden, Leo M. trans.) Berkeley: Asian Humanities Press, 1988.

Prebish, Charles S. *A Survey of Vinaya Literature*. Taipei: Jin Luen Publishing House, 1994.

Rahner, Karl. "Christology Within an Evolutionary View of the World" in *Theological Investigations Volume 5* (Kruger, Karl H. trans.). Baltimore: Helicon Press, 1966.

--- "Experience of the Spirit and Existential Commitment," in *Theological Investigations Volume 16* (Morland, David. O.S.B.). London: Darton, Longman & Todd, 1979.

--- *Foundations of Christian Faith: An Introduction to The Idea of Christianity* (Dych, William V. trans.). New York: The Seabury Press, 1978.

--- "Personal and Sacramental Piety," in *Theological Investigations Volume 2* (Kruger, Karl H. trans.). New York: The Seabury Press, 1975.

Ratzinger, Joseph Cardinal. *In the Beginning: A Catholic Understanding of the Story of Creation and the Fall*.

(Ramsey, Boniface O.P.trans.). Grand Rapids: Wm B Eerdmans, 1995.

--- *Introduction to Christianity*. San Francisco: Ignatius Press, 2004.

Rhys Davids, Caroline A.F. *A Buddhist Manual of Psychological Ethics*. London: The Pali Text Society, 1974.

Rhys Davids, T.W. *Dialogues of the Buddha (the Brahma-Gāla Suttanta)*. London: The Pali Text Society, 1977.

--- *The Questions of King Milinda*. New York: Dover Publications, Inc. 1963.

--- *Sacred Books of the Buddhist*. London: The Pali Text Society, 1977.

Richardson, Christopher A. *Pioneer and Perfecter of Faith: Jesus' Faith as the Climax of Israel's History in the Epistle to the Hebrews.* Tübingen: Mohr Siebeck, 2012.

Roberts, Alan. *The Karandavyuha Sutra.* http://www.pacificbuddha.org/wp-content/uploads/2014/02/Karandavyuha-Sutra.pdf

Robinson, Richard H. and Johnson, Willard L. *The Buddhist Religion A Historical Introduction.* (4th ed.) Belmont: Wadsworth Publishing Company, 1997.

Sadakata, Akira. *Buddhist Cosmology Philosophy and Origins*. Tokyo: Kosei Publishing Co. 1999.

Saint Athanasius. *On the Incarnation*. New York: St. Vladamir's Seminary Press, 1998.

--- *The Life of St. Antony*. New York: Newman Press, 1950.

Saint Augustine. *City of God* (Bettenson, Henry. trans.). London: Penguin Classics, 2003.

--- *The Confessions* (Maria Boulding, O.S.B. trans.). New York: Vintage Books, 1997.

--- *The Literal Meaning of Genesis vol. 1*. (Taylor, John Hammond S.J. trans.). New York: Newman Press, 1982.

Saint Thomas Aquinas. O*n Evil* (Richard, Regan. trans.). New York: Oxford University Press, 2003.

--- *Summa Theologiae*.

Samtani, N.H. "Buddha: the Teacher Extra-Ordinary," in Narain, A.K. *Studies in Pali and Buddhism*. Delhi: B.R. Publishing Corporation, 1979.

Schatz, Klaus. *Der Päpstliche Primat: Seine Geschichte von den Ursprüngen bis zur Gegenwart*. Würzburg: Echter Verlag GmbH, 1990.

Schleiermacher, Friedrich. *The Christian Faith* (Mackintosh H.R. and Stewart, J.S. eds.). Edinburgh: T & T Clark, 1999.

Schopen, Gregory. *Bones, Stones, and Buddhist Monks*. Honolulu: University of Hawai'i Press, 1997.

Snellgrove, David. *Indo-Tibetan Buddhism Indian Buddhist and their Tibetan Successors*. Boston: Shambhala, 1987.

Southgate, Christopher. *The Groaning of Creation: God, Evolution, and the Problem of Evil*. Louisville: Westminster John Knox Press, 2008.

Speiser, E.A. *Genesis*. New York: Doubleday & Company, Inc., 2007.

Stein, Aurel (Sir). *On Ancient Central-Asian Tracks*. Taipei: Southern Materials Center, Inc., 1982.

Strong, John. S. *The Experience of Buddhism Sources and Interpretations.* (3rd ed.) Belmont: Thomson Wadsworth, 2008.

--- *The Legend of King Aśoka A Study and Translation of the Aśokāvadāna.* Princeton: Princeton University Press, 1983.

te Velde, Rudi A. "Evil, Sin, and Death: Thomas Aquinas on Original Sin" in Van Nieuwenhove, Rik and Wawrykow, Joseph. *The Theology of Thomas Aquinas.* Notre Dame: University of Notre Dame Press, 2005.

Thera, Narada. *The Dhammapada Pali Text and Translation with Stories in Brief and Notes.* Taipei: The Corporate Body of the Buddha Educational Foundation, 1993.

Tracy, David. *The Analogical Imagination: Christian Theology and the Culture of Pluralism.* New York: Crossroad Publishing, 1981.

Troeltsch, Ernst. *The Social Teaching of the Christian Churches Volume II* (Wyon, Olive. trans.). Louisville: Westminster John Knox Press, 1992.

Vasubandhu. *Karmasiddhiprakarana The Treatise on Action by Vasubandhu* (Lamotte, Étienne Fr. trans./ Pruden, Leo M. Eng. trans.). Berkeley: Asian Humanities Press, 1988.

Victoria, Brian Daizen. *Zen at War.* Lanham: Rowman and Littlefield Publishing, Inc. 2006.

von Balthasar, Han Urs. *Dare We Hope "That All Men Be Saved"?* (Kipp, David. and Krauth, Lothar. trans.) San Francisco: Ignatius Press, 1988.

--- *The Office of Peter and the Structure of the Church.* San Francisco: Ignatius Press, 1986.

--- *Truth is Symphonic: Aspects of Christian Pluralism* (Harrison, Graham trans.). San Francisco: Ignatius Press, 1987.

Wader, A.K. *Indian Buddhism.* Delhi: Motilal Banarsidass, 1980.

Walker, Williston., Norris, Richard A., Lotz, David W., Handy, Robert T. *A History of the Christian Church Fourth Edition.* New York: Scribner, 1985.

Ward, Allen M., Heichelheim, Fritz M., Yeo, Cedric A. *A History of the Roman People Sixth Edition.* New York: Routledge, 2016.

Warder, A.K. *Indian Buddhism.* Delhi: Motilal Banarsidass, 1980.

Weber, Max. *The Protestant Ethic and the Spirit of Capitalism* (Parsons, Talcott. trans.). London: Unwin University Books, 1965.

Wei, Ian P. *Intellectual Culture in Medieval Paris: Theologians and the University, c. 1100–1330.* Cambridge: Cambridge University Press, 2012.

Westberg, Daniel. "The Relation Between Positive and Natural Law in Aquinas," in *Journal of Law and Religion* 11.1 (1994–1995).

Westermann, Claus. *Genesis 1–11: A Continental Commentary* John J. Scullion S.J. trans. Minneapolis: Fortress Press, 1994.

Wolterstorff, Nicholas. *Divine Discourse: Philosophical Reflections on the Claim that God Speaks.* Cambridge: Cambridge University Press, 1995.

Wright, N.T. J*esus and the Victory of God*. Minneapolis: Fortress Press, 1996.

--- *What Saint Paul Really Said: Was Paul of Tarsus the Real Founder of Christianity*. Grand Rapids: Wm. B. Eerdmans, 1997.

Yamauchi, Edwin M. *Persia and the Bible*. Grand Rapids: Baker Books, 1996.

Yang, Hsüan-chih. *A Record of Buddhist Monasteries in Lo-Yang* (Wang, Yi-t'ung trans.). Princeton: Princeton University Press, 1984.

Zizioulas, John D. *Being As Communion: Studies in Personhood and the Church*. New York: St. Vladamir's Seminary Press, 2002.

Index

A

Aaron, 244
Abhidharma, 91, 92, 94, 96, 97, 155, 229, 232, 235
absolute, 35, 39, 42, 149, 151, 163
Aesop's Fables, 182
Ajatashatru, 255, 256, 257
Akshobhya, 154
Alara Kalama, 203
Alexander the Great, 8, 27
Alexandria, 9, 27, 195, 256
Alta Khan, 66
American, 4, 253
Amitabha, 40, 152, 153, 157
Angulimala, 129, 130
animals, 109, 124, 127, 140, 144, 180, 199, 211, 218, 219, 224, 227, 228, 230, 233, 234, 235, 237
Antioch, 50
apostles, 48, 49, 50, 194, 215, 266
Aquinas, Thomas, 111, 114, 140, 172, 173, 220, 224, 251
Arabian Sea, 10
Aramaic, 21
Arhat
 Worthy, 9, 29, 129
Aristotle, 219
Aryans, 6, 7, 27, 202
asceticism, 8, 195, 196, 197, 203, 215
Ashoka, 8, 10, 11, 32, 256, 261
Asian, 6, 10, 11, 13, 14, 64, 98, 99, 154, 155, 213, 231
Assyria, 102, 244
Assyrian Empire, 78
Athanasius, 3, 25, 196
Athens, 7, 30, 57, 206
atman, 34, 231
Auditors, 9, 10, 11, 12
Augustinan, 200
Augustine, 83, 110, 111, 113, 218, 219, 247, 267
Aulén, Gustav, 139
Avalokiteshvara, 66, 154, 187, 188, 190
Averroes, 220
Avicenna, 220
awakening, 8, 9, 28, 29, 30, 32, 33, 34, 35, 37, 38, 39, 40, 87, 92, 93, 122, 129, 156, 157, 160, 163, 182, 184, 186, 187, 188, 202, 203, 205, 233, 262, 264
awards, 68
Axis mundi, 28

B

Babylon, 49, 244
Babylonian Empire, 78
Bactria, 11
Barth, Karl, 145
Basilians, 200
Basket's Display, The, 187
Benedict, 52, 198, 225, 251
Bernard, 200
Bible, 75, 79, 81, 82, 83, 84, 85, 86, 91, 102, 103, 104, 162
Bihar, 261
Bimbisara, 88, 255, 256, 262
Bodhi Tree, 34
Bodhisattva, 28, 29, 39, 63, 71, 148, 154, 164, 187, 188, 190, 211, 232, 234, 263
Bodhisattva code, 34, 62, 63, 65, 66, 71, 148, 154, 187, 190, 212, 213, 263
Bologna, 248
Brueggemann, Walter, 78

Buddha Dharma, 8, 32
Buddha Nature, 38
Buddhist Manual of Psychological Ethics, The, 229
Bultmann, Rudolph, 22

C

Calvin, John, 114, 115, 174
Calvinist, 249
Canadian, 14, 15
Canticle of the Creatures (Francis), 199
Cassius, 21
caste, 30, 37, 41, 120, 259, 261, 262
Cathars, 200
cenobitic, 198
Central Asia, 11, 13, 64, 71, 98, 99, 202
Chalcedon, 23
Chandragupta, 256
Chicago, 85
China, 11, 12, 13, 40, 61, 62, 63, 64, 67, 70, 72, 91, 96, 98, 99, 100, 152, 154, 209, 211, 212, 213, 261, 264, 266, 270
Chinese, 10, 11, 12, 13, 14, 39, 40, 58, 63, 67, 68, 71, 72, 90, 91, 97, 98, 99, 100, 104, 153, 177, 187, 209, 210, 212, 214, 231, 263, 265, 266
christology, 18, 22, 23, 24, 25, 26
Cistercians, 200
City of God Against the Pagans, The (Augustine), 267
Clement, 49, 50
Clough, David, 224, 225
Colossians, 80, 144, 194
Commandments, 234
Compendium of Phenomena/ *Dhamma Sangaṇi*, 229
Complete Perfect Buddha, 28, 31, 33, 38
Concentration of Extinction, 235, 237
Confucians, 12

Constantine, 3, 54, 193, 194, 215, 246, 267
Copernicus, Nicolaus, 222
Corinth, 49, 137, 140
Corinthians, 80, 144, 193
council, 1, 3, 53, 55, 89, 104, 200, 252, 255, 257
Council of Nicaea, 2, 23
crucifixion, 21, 24, 43, 48, 137, 139, 141, 142, 161, 162, 224, 245
Cunctos populous, 246
Cupid, 28
Cur Deus Homo, 25, 138, 161

D

Dalai Lama, 13, 56, 66, 67, 68, 70, 71, 265, 266
Damian, 197
Daniel, 78, 82
Darwin, 222, 223, 232
Davidic, 18
Dead Sea Scrolls, 19, 100
Deborah, 17
Decius, 194
Deuteronomy, 76, 77, 168
Dhammapada, 175
Dharma, 32, 33, 44, 146, 149, 150, 151, 157, 163, 181, 261
Diamond Sutra, The, 154, 183
Didache, 84
Diocletian, 194
Dominant Reciprocalities, 236, 237
Dominicans, 199, 200
Domitian, 82
Dunhuang, 99

E

Ecclesiastes, 78
ecclesiology, 51
Ecumenical Councils, 55
Egypt, 10, 76, 77, 102, 167, 169, 193, 195, 243, 253, 266
elders, 10, 60
Elohist, 76, 167

Index

Emerson, Ralph Waldo, 14
Emperor, 8, 11, 32, 35, 54, 61, 97, 102, 194, 211, 212, 215, 245, 246, 267
Enlightenment, 4, 223, 238, 248, 250, 268
Ephesians, 80
epikeia, 173
eremitic, 197, 198
Essenes, 19, 20
Esther, 78, 82
Europe, 4, 6, 13, 14, 15, 63, 64, 152, 224, 239, 249
European Enlightenment, 4, 142, 239, 250
Evangelicals, 86
Evangelii Gaudium, 56
Exalted Dwellings, 235, 237
Exalted Stations, 180, 187
excommunication, 57
Ezra, 78

F

First Vatican Council, 52, 53
Flavius Josephus, 19
France, 55
Franciscans, 199, 200
free will, 115, 120, 125
French Revolution, 250

G

Galatians, 80
Galilee, 2, 26, 245
Galileo Galilei, 222, 238
Gallicanism, 54, 55, 70
Ganges, 88, 256
Gaudium et Spes, 252, 253, 268
Gelugpa, 64, 66, 71
Genesis, 75, 107, 109, 217, 218, 226, 243
Geza, 22
ghosts, 127, 209, 227, 228, 233, 234
gospels, 18, 20, 21, 22, 48, 69, 80, 81, 174, 196

Great Vehicle, 91, 95, 96, 97, 99, 100, 101, 104, 159, 164, 182, 184, 185, 186, 187, 188, 190, 211, 212, 214
Mahayana, 9, 10, 11, 12, 40
Greek, 2, 10, 17, 19, 21, 22, 27, 75, 82, 102, 108, 137, 167, 202, 228, 238
Gregory, 47, 53, 140, 141, 144, 145, 162, 248
guru, 63, 71

H

Hawaii, 14
Heart of Wisdom, 188
Hebrew, 17, 19, 22, 25, 75, 79, 82, 83, 101, 102, 113, 117, 137, 171, 217, 218, 219, 227, 238
Hebrews, 81, 83, 84
hell, 28, 33, 119, 125, 127, 129, 131, 143, 145, 157, 158, 164, 176, 179, 233, 234, 236
Hellenistic, 18, 22, 102
Himalayas, 13, 88
Hindu, 8, 33, 59, 123, 262, 263
homoousion, 3
Hosea, 78, 169
human, 1, 2, 4, 5, 9, 15, 23, 24, 25, 27, 28, 29, 30, 35, 36, 39, 43, 47, 68, 78, 84, 85, 103, 107, 108, 109, 110, 111, 112, 113, 114, 115, 119, 126, 128, 137, 138, 140, 141, 142, 143, 144, 145, 148, 158, 161, 162, 163, 171, 175, 177, 182, 183, 189, 217, 219, 220, 224, 225, 228, 231, 232, 233, 234, 235, 237, 238, 239, 247, 250, 254, 271

I

Ignatius, 50, 200
India, 6, 7, 8, 9, 10, 11, 12, 13, 27, 29, 32, 35, 36, 37, 38, 43, 57, 58, 59, 60, 61, 62, 63, 64, 67, 70, 71, 72, 90, 91, 94, 95, 96, 98, 99, 100, 101, 102, 119, 124, 146, 147, 149,

152, 154, 164, 202, 203, 205, 206, 207, 208, 209, 211, 213, 215, 230, 254, 256, 260, 261, 262, 263, 266, 269, 270
Individual Buddha, 28, 31, 37
Indo-Europeans, 6, 27
Innocent, 84, 200, 248
Inquisition, 222
intention, 128, 173
Isaiah, 78, 170
Israel, 17, 18, 22, 23, 76, 77, 78, 79, 81, 87, 167, 168, 169, 172, 243, 244
Israelite, 17, 76
Italy, 198, 206, 222, 223, 250

J

Jacob, 243
Jainism, 7, 203, 227
Japan, 11, 12, 14, 62, 71, 88, 96, 99, 152, 153, 154, 159, 212, 256, 264
Jataka, 182, 232
Jeremiah, 78, 82
Jeroboam, 169
Jerusalem, 19, 21, 244, 267
Jesuits, 200
Jews, 2, 102, 103, 189, 225
John, 5, 23, 36, 42, 47, 48, 53, 81, 103, 140, 144, 145, 167, 172, 174
John the Baptizer, 23
Johnson, Elizabeth, 171
Joseph, 243, 270
Josiah, 76, 170
Jubilee, 169, 170, 174
Judah, 169
Judas Iscariot, 20, 145
Jude, 81, 83
Judges, 17, 77
Judith, 82
Juggernaut, 262
Jupiter, 6, 30, 88, 148, 222
justice, 111, 117, 118, 138, 161, 173, 202, 247, 251, 253, 254

K

Kalinga, 256
Kama, 28
Kanishka, 11
Kant, Immanuel, 4, 250
Kargyupa, 64, 65, 66
karma, 30, 33, 34, 38, 42, 68, 96, 119, 120, 121, 122, 124, 125, 127, 128, 129, 130, 157, 178, 229, 234, 257
Karthikeya, 28
Kashmir, 13
Kathmandu, 60, 187
kenosis, 170
King Pasenadi, 124
Kisa Gotami, 37
Knitter, Paul, 5
Korea, 11, 12, 96, 99, 212
Korean, 12, 68, 97, 214
Koshala, 124
Kublai Khan, 66
Kukai, 213
Kumarajiva, 99
Kumari, 263
Küng, Hans, 1
Kushana, 11
Kyoto, 212

L

Lalitpur, 263
lama, 63, 64, 66, 71
Lamentations, 78
Latin Vulgate, 83
Laudato Si, 217, 225
Lazarus, 36
Leo, 5, 251
Leviticus, 75, 168, 169
liberated, 39, 127, 130, 150, 151, 157, 187, 229, 253
liberation, 76, 117, 122, 127, 128, 146, 147, 148, 149, 151, 152, 155, 156, 157, 158, 159, 160, 163, 164, 171, 177, 181, 191, 203, 205, 211, 229, 233, 243, 253
Long Discourses, 92, 97

Index

Los Angeles, 14, 214
Luke, 20, 21, 22, 80, 170, 189
Lumbini grove, 148
Lumen Gentium, 53, 55
Luther, Martin, 4, 51, 83, 85, 139, 247

M

Madonna, 150, 154
Magadha, 255, 256
Mahamaya, 7
Mahasanghika, 60, 93
Maitreya, 39, 154, 176, 233
Manjushri, 154, 188
Mara, 30
Mark, 22, 80, 103, 140, 171, 238
Marpa, 64
Mars, 28, 247
martyrs, 194, 195, 196, 215
Matthew, 22, 48, 81, 140, 195, 197, 245, 266
McFarland, Ian, 107
Medellín, 253
medieval, 3, 4, 51, 58, 167, 173, 199, 219, 220, 222, 248
Mediterranean Sea, 10
Melanchthon, Philip, 139
Menander I, 11, 27
mendicant, 199, 203, 260
merit, 30, 35, 39, 101, 114, 117, 120, 121, 122, 123, 124, 125, 126, 127, 128, 129, 130, 132, 152, 158, 181, 182, 183, 185, 188, 208, 210, 229, 231, 233, 234, 237, 239, 258
Merton, Thomas, 5, 200, 201
Mesopotamia, 218
Mesopotamian, 244
Milan, 194, 246
Milarepa, 151
millennial movements, 40, 264
Minerva, 28
Ming, 97
Moltmann, Jürgen, 22, 145, 172
Mongolia, 13, 14, 64, 66, 96
Mongolian, 13, 64, 66

monks, 8, 9, 12, 13, 37, 57, 58, 59, 61, 62, 63, 65, 66, 70, 71, 88, 89, 93, 94, 95, 97, 130, 154, 155, 177, 185, 186, 197, 198, 203, 204, 205, 207, 208, 210, 211, 212, 213, 214, 215, 255, 258, 259, 260, 261, 262, 263, 264, 265, 266, 269, 270
Monte Cassino, 198
Moses, 19, 76, 116, 167, 244
Mt. Meru, 6
Mt. Olympus, 6
muni, 31
Murano, 238
Myanmar, 63, 264, 265, 270

N

Nalanda, 261
Namo Amito Fo/ Jp. *Namu Amida Butsu*, 152
Nara, 154, 212, 264
Nazareth, 2, 17, 18, 20, 21, 22, 24, 26, 41, 79, 137, 170, 189, 245
Nehemiah, 78
Nepal, 7, 13, 63, 67, 90, 96, 149, 185, 263, 266
Nero, 82, 194
New Testament, 18, 20, 22, 48, 49, 75, 79, 80, 81, 82, 83, 86, 102, 103, 108, 141, 167, 193
New York, 14
Newman, John Henry Cardinal, 1, 55, 223, 249, 251, 252, 253
Nicaea, 197
nirvana, 33, 38, 39, 89, 101, 104, 122, 126, 127, 130, 147, 150, 159, 160, 163, 164, 181, 184, 189, 190, 227, 229, 232, 233, 235, 236, 237, 239, 255, 259
  complete nirvana / *parinirvana*, 29, 34, 59, 60, 89, 147, 149, 156, 163, 164, 236
North America, 14, 63
nuns, 8, 37, 57, 58, 61, 62, 63, 70, 88, 89, 93, 94, 95, 97, 154, 155, 185, 203, 204, 205, 207, 208, 209, 210,

211, 214, 215, 258, 259, 260, 262, 263, 266, 269, 270
Nyingmapa, 64, 66

O

Olcott, Henry Steel, 14
Old Testament, 75, 102, 103
OM MANI PADME HUM, 187
On Evil (Aquinas), 114
Origen, 145
Original sin, 107
Orthodox, 82

P

Palermo, 270
Palestine, 2, 3, 19, 21, 83, 244
Palestinian, 2, 21, 22
parable, 42
Parens Scientarum, 248
Paris, 68, 248
Parthia, 11
Pastor Aeternus, 53, 69
Path, 159, 164, 177, 182, 190
Paul, 50, 53, 79, 80, 108, 137, 140, 144, 145, 162, 170, 172, 174, 193, 223
Pentateuch, 75, 218
People's Republic of China, 67
Pepin, 54
Perfections, 183
Persian Empire, 14, 78
Peter, 47, 48, 49, 50, 51, 53, 55, 69, 81, 84, 141, 197
Pharisees, 19, 20, 22
Philemon, 80
Philip, 248
Philippians, 80, 171, 172
Piprahwa, 29
Pius IX, 53, 250, 253
Pope, 4, 5, 47, 48, 51, 52, 54, 55, 56, 68, 69, 72, 84, 145, 174, 200, 217, 223, 225, 248, 250, 251, 252
Pope Benedict XIV, 52
Pope Francis, 56, 217, 225

Pope Leo XIII, 5, 251
Pope Pius IX, 4, 52, 54, 223, 250
Pope Saint John XXIII, 5
Predestination, 249
Priestly, 76, 77, 107, 109
Prophets, 75, 77, 78
Protestant, 4, 5, 22, 40, 51, 52, 82, 85, 107, 112, 114, 115, 139, 141, 142, 145, 152, 153, 172, 174, 200, 224, 248, 249, 250, 268
Psalm, 18
Puebla, 253
Pure Land, 40, 62, 152, 153, 187
Puri, 262
Puritan, 249

Q

Q hypothesis, 81
Qumran, 19, 20

R

Rabbi Hillel, 20
rebirth, 28, 29, 30, 33, 34, 35, 39, 41, 121, 123, 126, 127, 130, 131, 146, 151, 152, 156, 157, 158, 159, 160, 163, 164, 176, 179, 181, 189, 203, 227, 229, 233, 234, 235, 236, 239
Reciprocalities, 236, 237
Red Sea, 10
redemption, 107, 108, 109, 247
Reformation, 4, 51, 52, 83, 200, 247, 267
refuge, 157, 163, 215
Rehoboam, 77, 169
Renaissance, 238, 239
renunciation, 9, 30, 31, 211
republic, 7, 57, 206, 256
Rerum Novarum, 251
res publica, 243, 246, 251
resurrection, 19, 24, 25, 26, 36, 43, 79, 137, 139, 140, 141, 142, 143, 144, 146, 162, 193, 197
Revelation, 81, 83, 84

Index

Revolutions of the Heavenly Bodies, The (Copernicus), 222
Roman, 2, 19, 21, 47, 48, 50, 79, 80, 81, 82, 86, 102, 113, 117, 140, 145, 193, 194, 195, 202, 228, 233, 243, 244, 245, 246, 247, 266, 267
Roman Catholic Church, 1, 4, 47, 48, 52, 82, 83, 86, 93, 113, 114, 115, 117, 145, 214, 215, 222, 223, 248, 250, 251, 268
Romans, 10, 21, 27, 28, 80, 142, 144
Rome, 3, 7, 10, 20, 21, 27, 30, 47, 48, 49, 50, 51, 53, 54, 55, 57, 68, 69, 102, 108, 198, 244, 246, 247, 267
Russia, 13
Ruth, 78

S

Sadducees, 19
Saicho, 212
Saint Anselm, 25, 138, 161
Saint Anthony, 195
Saint Athanasius, 2, 23, 24, 195
Saint Augustine, 25, 110, 247, 267
Saint Benedict, 198
Saint Francis, 199
Saint Simeon, 197
Sakya Pandita, 64
Sakyapa, 64
salvation, 24, 39, 41, 51, 107, 115, 117, 122, 137, 139, 140, 141, 142, 143, 144, 146, 152, 153, 161, 163, 223
Samson, 17
San Diego, 14
sangha, 57
Sanskrit, 34, 90, 97, 100, 102, 119, 120, 176, 261
Sarasvati, 28
Satan, 31, 139, 162, 196
savior, 39, 122, 132, 146, 157, 163
Schleiermacher, Friedrich, 112
scientific knowledge, 217, 224
scripture, 51, 52, 83, 84, 85, 86, 103, 143, 170, 201, 219

Sea of Galilee, 21
Second Vatican Council, 1, 5, 53, 54, 55, 86, 251
self, 2, 4, 32, 34, 41, 43, 48, 58, 70, 75, 78, 103, 118, 121, 126, 127, 129, 130, 157, 160, 164, 170, 171, 175, 177, 179, 181, 183, 184, 185, 190, 195, 197, 202, 209, 215, 243, 250, 257, 264, 266, 270
Sepphoris, 21
Septuagint, 82, 83, 101
Shakya, 7, 124, 146, 148
Shammai, 20
Shepherd of Hermas, 84
Shotoku, 12
shramana, 31
Shuddhodana, 7
Siddhartha Gautama Shakya, 7, 28, 29, 34, 146, 148, 164
Silk Route, 11, 13, 63, 97
Simon the Zealot, 20, 245, 266
sin, 24, 25, 43, 107, 108, 109, 110, 111, 112, 113, 114, 115, 116, 117, 118, 121, 137, 138, 139, 141, 142, 145, 146, 161, 162, 163, 223, 224
Sirach, 82
Six Perfections, 190
Sogdiana, 11
Sol Invictus, 247
sola gratia, 85
sola scriptura, 83, 85
Solomon, 77, 82, 169
soteriology, 25, 39, 51, 107, 146, 163
Sri Lanka, 9, 10, 14, 32, 59, 63, 91, 93, 104, 159, 177, 211, 214, 256, 264
Stein, Aurel, 99
Sthaviravada, 60
stupa, 101
Summa Theologiae, 114
sutra, 92, 94, 96, 98, 101, 183, 184, 187, 188, 230, 236
Sweden, 27
Syllabus of Errors, 4, 250
Syracuse, 270

T

Tacitus, 244
Tang Zhongzong, 61
Tantras, 62, 71, 91, 100
tantric code, 62
Tarjan, 102
Ten Commandments, 116
Tenzin Gyatso, 66
Thailand, 59, 63, 88, 159, 177, 211
theocratic state, 13
Theodosius, 3, 193, 246
Theravada, 10, 59, 63, 93, 159, 164, 177, 179, 181, 182, 183, 190, 211, 212
Thessalonians, 80
Thoreau, Henry David, 14
Three Jewels, 154, 155, 157, 163
Tibet, 11, 13, 56, 63, 64, 65, 66, 67, 70, 71, 96, 100, 151, 159, 213, 261, 264, 265, 266
Timothy, 80
Titus, 80
Tobit, 82
Todai ji Temple, 154
Torah, 19, 75, 77, 79
Toronto, 14
Tracy, David, 253
Trajan, 50
Trent, 52, 83, 104
Trinity, 3, 23, 25, 137, 138, 140, 161, 162, 163
Troeltsch, Ernst, 249

U

Ubi Primum, 52
Uchiyama Gudo, 264
Uddaka Ramaputta, 203
Ultramontanism, 54, 55

V

Vairocana, 154
Vancouver, 14
Vasubandhu, 232, 233, 235

Vatican, 1, 5, 15, 52, 54, 55, 69, 86, 223, 251
Vedas, 207, 227
Vedic, 6, 7, 27, 36, 43, 202
vegetarianism, 230, 231
Venice, 68, 238
Vermes, 22
Victoria, 14
Vietnam, 11, 12, 63, 96, 212, 266
Vinaya, 91, 93, 94, 96, 97, 155, 204, 205, 206, 207, 211, 212, 213, 214, 230
Virgin Mary, 54
Virudhaka, 124
Vishnu, 43
Visigoth, 247
von Balthasar, Hans Urs, 53, 145
Vriji, 256, 257
Vulture Peak, 255, 257

W

Waldensians, 200
Wesleyan, 86, 103
White Lotus of Compassion, 187
Wider die Mordischen und Reubischen Rotten der Bawren Against the Murderous Thieving Hordes of Peasants, 249
Wright, N.T., 22
Wu, 211

Y

Yahweh, 18, 168
Yahwist, 76, 107, 109, 217
yogic, 7, 8, 36, 37, 203

Z

Zealots, 20
Zen, 62, 157, 160, 231, 264
Zephaniah, 78, 170
Zwingli, Ulrich, 139

www.ingramcontent.com/pod-product-compliance
Lightning Source LLC
Chambersburg PA
CBHW022051160426
43198CB00008B/196